BURNS-LORE OF DUMFRIES AND GALLOWAY

James A. Mackay

Alloway Publishing
AYR

© JAMES A. MACKAY

First Published in 1988
by
Alloway Publishing Ltd.,
Ayr.

Printed in Scotland
by
Walker & Connell Ltd.,
Hastings Square, Darvel,
Ayrshire.

ISBN 0-907526-36-5

Also in this series:—

"Burns-Lore of Ayrshire" by Andrew Boyle

CONTENTS

Front Cover photographs show Burns House, Ellisland Farm, St. Michael's Church, Burn's Statue, Theatre Royal and Burns Mausoleum.

4

INTRODUCTION

It was on 11th June 1788 that Robert Burns, Scotland's national Bard, took up the lease of a farm at Ellisland in Nithsdale. Thus began the close association between Burns and Dumfriesshire which lasted until his death on 21st July 1796. Of course, the poet had previously visited the area in June 1787 at the end of his Border Tour, and it was then that he received the highest honour which Dumfries could bestow; he was made a freeman and honorary burgess of the town. Little did he realise then, that within a few short years he would actually take up residence in the town itself.

This book, therefore, deals with the last eight years of Burns's life. In many respects this was the most crowded part of his all too short life. In addition to working his farm Burns entered the Excise service in September 1789 and from then until July 1790 was engaged on survey duties which involved 200 miles hard riding every week in all weathers, covering the ten parishes of Upper Nithsdale. Things became a little easier after his transfer to the Dumfries Third Division, but it was not until the end of 1791 that he managed to extricate himself from farming and could move his family into Dumfries.

On 11th November 1791 the Burns family settled in an upstairs flat in the Wee Vennel (now Bank Street). Promotion to the more lucrative Dumfries Port Division in February 1792 enabled him to move to a larger house in Millbrae Vennel (now Burns Street) in May 1793. In addition to Ellisland and the two Dumfries houses, Burns also resided temporarily with David and Agnes Cullie and then occupied David Newall's house at Isle. In the last month of his life he stayed at Brow on the Solway. Furthermore he was closely associated with such inns as the Globe in Dumfries, which he described as his 'favourite howff', and the hostelries run by the Whighams in Sanquhar and the Bacons at Brownhill. He took a leading part in the promotion of the libraries in Dunscore and Dumfries, and was also closely associated with the establishment of the Theatre Royal, now the oldest provincial theatre extant in Scotland. Dumfries has the honour of containing, in St Michael's churchyard, the mortal remains of the poet and his family.

These locations, of course, are familiar to anyone with no more than a passing knowledge of Burns, his life and works; but throughout the length and breadth of Dumfries and Galloway Region there are many other places which have their Burns associations: places which he actually visited, as, for example, during his two tours of Galloway with John Syme (in 1793 and 1794); places whither his Excise duties took him, from Penpont, Dunscore and Thornhill in the northwest to Annan, Ecclefechan and Sarkfoot in the southeast. There were the mansions of the country gentry, such as the Riddells of Friars' Carse and Woodley Park, who befriended him, no less than the farms of William Lorimer at Craigieburn or Kemys Hall, or the homes of the McMurdo family at Drumlanrig or the Stewarts of Closeburn, where he was always welcome.

But there were also countless places where the association was not so obvious. I have endeavoured to pinpoint all the sites and locations in the region that have a connection with Burns, however slight. I have attempted, for example, to identify the estates and farms of the gentlemen of Annandale, Nithsdale, the Stewartry and Galloway whom Burns mentioned in his election ballads and epigrams. So far as possible I have identified the places associated with everyone mentioned in the poems, including the reworking of traditional ballads, as well as identified everyone referred to in the poet's voluminous correspondence. References to the appropriate poem or letter are indicated in brackets, the abbreviations C.L. and C.W. (followed by page numbers) denoting *The Complete Letters*(1987) and *The Complete Works* (1986), published by Alloway Publishing and the Burns Federation.

The entries in this book have been arranged in alphabetical order by place. Because of its size and importance in Burns's last years, Dumfries has had to be sub-divided. I felt that it was logical to include all streets and buildings which were within the burgh in Burns's time under that heading, although they, too, have been treated alphabetically.

Also biographical notes on individuals, not otherwise discussed under the name of their homes, are given in alphabetical sequence at the end of the Dumfries section of the book. For greater convenience, however, cross-references to place-names in the text are rendered in bold lettering, and there is an index of people's names at the end of the volume.   To assist the reader to locate country places associated with Burns a six-figure map reference is included in each heading as far as possible. These map references are preceded by the two-letter reference to the 100-kilometre squares. The majority of places in Dumfries and Galloway are covered by the NX square, but parts of Annandale to the east will be found on square NY, while a few places in the northwest or northeast of the region will be found on squares NS and NT. I have avoided using the numbers of the sheets themselves, because of the renumbering of maps by the Ordnance Survey in the changeover from the old one-inch scale to the metric system. The individual map references are identical in both systems.

I must stress that the use of the words 'Burns-Lore' in the title is deliberate; for it is difficult at this remove in time to distinguish between hard fact and the myths and legends which have developed and which have been transmitted orally from one generation to the next. As far as possible, however, I have tried to substantiate facts, by relevant quotations from Burns's letters, or advertisements in the local newspaper. It should be noted, however, that the newspaper during Burns's period in the region was the *Dumfries Weekly Journal*— a paper singularly devoid of real local news. Thus the move from Ellisland into Dumfries by the Burns family in November 1791 passed without comment. It is difficult to assess what impact Burns made on Dumfries. The only complete set of this paper (now preserved in the Ewart Library) lacks all references to Burns himself. Some years ago the Burns references were cut out of the file copies of the paper and mounted in a scrap-book which was lodged in the burgh museum for safe-keeping. Sad to relate, this scrap-book has apparently vanished without trace. I therefore take this opportunity to appeal for information regarding its whereabouts, in the hope that it may be returned to its rightful place in the Ewart Library. The entire volume of 1796, which contained Maria Riddell's memoir of Burns and the account of his death and funeral, has likewise disappeared.

Many of the stories concerning Burns in Dumfries and Galloway first saw the light of day (in guid black prent) in the writings of 'Honest Allan' Cunningham (1834), a biographer who has since been roundly condemned for outright fabrication as well as the distortion of facts to which most of the poet's early biographers were prone. In addition, I have combed all of the parochial histories published in the late 19th and early 20th centuries and extracted anything of Burns relevance from them. Articles and letters published in the *Dumfries and Galloway Standard* in more recent years, particularly the writings of the late William McVittie, have yielded a few snippets.

I should like to take this opportunity to thank the many people whose interest and labours have made this book possible. Thanks are due first to Andrew Boyle, whose own book on Ayrshire Burns-Lore has served as a model and, indeed, as an inspiration. It was the publication of this book in 1985 which encouraged Donald Urquhart of the Southern Scottish Counties Burns Association. With a view to producing a companion volume on Dumfries and Galloway, Donald circularised all of the Burns Clubs and kindred societies in the region with extensive questionnaires, seeking details of any Burns connections in their localities. I am sorry to say, however, that the response was very poor. Donald did get replies from Ronald Crichton, J.I. Hawkins, Mrs E. Kirkland, John Lauder, H. George McKerrow, R. McDonald, Joseph Jordan, J. Dodds, R. Raphael, G. Smith, W. Jones, W.J. McCulloch of Ardwall, Gordon D. Niven, Mrs May Roberts of Lochmaben and Norman Shearer of Gretna, as well as his uncle, James Urquhart of Dumfries, to whom I also extend my thanks.

Donald himself has put a tremendous amount of effort into checking through stent rolls, old maps and other burgh records, as well as helping in countless other ways which have made my task a great deal lighter.

I must also express my gratitude to Alistair Cowper and the staff of the reference department of the Ewart Library, to David Lockwood of the burgh museum and William Sinclair of Burns House, and the staff of the Robert Burns Centre. Last, but by no means least, I have to thank my old friend and neighbour, Noel Dinwiddie, for help, advice and the loan of material used in this book.

James A. Mackay   11 Newall Terrace, Dumfries, DG1 1LN

CHRONOLOGY OF BURNS IN DUMFRIES AND GALLOWAY

1787

2nd June (?). Burns crosses the Sark from England at the end of his Border Tour and passes through Annan.

4th June. Made an honorary burgess of Dumfries.

1788

27th February (?). Visits Ellisland with John Tennant of Glenconner as his adviser.

18th March. Signs the lease of Ellisland.

20th March. Leaves Edinburgh and makes preparations to settle down at Ellisland.

April-May. Receiving a six-week course of Excise instruction at Mauchline and Tarbolton.

11th June. Moves to Nithsdale to begin work at Ellisland. Lodges with David and Agnes Cullie, the outgoing tenants.

14th July. Excise comission issued to Burns.

5th August. Marriage to Jean Armour formally recognised by Mauchline Kirk Session.

August. Friendship established between Burns and the Riddells of Friars' Carse.

September-October. Burns commuting between Ellisland and Mauchline.

14th October. Burns and Alexander Crombie cross the Nith and go to watch the first steamboat trial on Dalswinton Loch.

26th November. In Sanquhar on his way to Mauchline to collect Jean and his son Robert.

4th December (?). The Burns family move into temporary accommodation in David Newall's house at Isle.

1789

February-June. Work still progressing slowly on the farmhouse at Ellisland.

March-April. The library of the Monkland Friendly Society established at Dunscore.

May. Reading Adam Smith's *Wealth of Nations* and hoping for an Excise appointment.

June. Burns family finally move into their new farmhouse at Ellisland.

June-July. Burns meets Francis Grose at Friars' Carse.

18th August. Francis Wallace Burns born.

1st September. Commences work as an Excise officer, at a salary of £50 per annum.

Late September. Meets Willie Nicol and Allan Masterton at Moffat: 'Willie Brew'd a Peck o Maut' composed.

October. Parliamentary election for the constituency of the Dumfries burghs: 'Five Carlins' composed.

16th October. Contest for the Whistle at Friars' Carse. Second contest at Sanquhar a few days later.

November. Ill with 'malignant squinancy and low fever'.

23rd December. Influenced by reading Shakespeare, plans 'some thoughts of the Drama'. *Rob Mcquechan's Elshon* outlined, but plans never materialise.

1790

January. Burns riding up to 200 miles a week on Excise duties and attempting to run a farm, but complains of 'An incessant headache, depression of spirits, and all the truly miserable consequences of a deranged nervous system...'

27th January. Placed on list of those eligible for promotion to Examiner or Supervisor of Excise.

18th February. Inaugural meeting of subscribers to the Theatre Royal.

Spring. James Halliday completes work on the drains at Ellisland.

June. Jean Armour visits Mauchline. Burns has a brief affair with Helen Anne Park of the Globe Inn.
July. Transferred to the Dumfries Third Division of Excise, 'a vacant foot-walk in Dumfries'.
1st November. Sends off list of subscribers to *The Bee*.
November. Composes 'Tam o Shanter'; manuscript sent to Grose on 1st December

1791

January. Crippled by a fall 'not from my horse, but with my horse.'
31st March. Helen Anne Park gives birth to a daughter at Leith and allegedly dies soon after. The baby raised as Elizabeth Burns.
9th April. William Nicol Burns born.
April. 'Tam o Shanter' published in the second volume of Grose's *Antiquities of Scotland*.
27th April. Glenriddell Manuscript collection formed.
11th June. Burns intervenes on behalf of James Clarke of Moffat.
17th June. The Earl of Buchan invites Burns to the coronation of Thomson's bust.
19th-22nd June. Burns in Ayrshire, attending brother Gilbert's wedding.
25th August. Roup of crops at Ellisland.
August-September. Account of the Monkland Friendly Society Library sent to Sir John Sinclair.
10th September. Formal renunciation of Ellisland lease.
11th November. Burns family move into the three-room flat in the Wee Vennel, above Syme's stamp office.
29th November. Burns goes to Edinburgh.
11th December. Returns to Dumfries.

1792

23rd January. Visits the mines at Wanlockhead with Maria and Walter Riddell.
February. Writes to William Corbet, Supervisor General of Excise. Is subsequently promoted to Dumfries Port Division, with an income of almost £90 per annum.
29th February. Capture of the brig *Rosamond* at Sarkfoot.
16th April. Offers Creech 'about fifty pages of new material' for a fresh edition of his *Poems*.
19th April. Roup of the *Rosamond*. Burns sends four carronades to the French revolutionaries, but gift stopped by the Customs at Dover.
August. Fourth volume of *Scots Musical Museum* published, including 60 songs contributed by Burns.
29th September. Theatre Royal opens in Dumfries.
October. Begins work on fifth volume of *Scots Musical Museum*.
13th November. Subscribes to the Edinburgh *Gazetteer*.
21st November. Elizabeth Riddell Burns born.
December. Four-day visit to Dunlop House with Dr Adair. Much political unrest in Dumfries.
31st December. John Mitchell, Collector of Excise, ordered by his Board to investigate Burns's political conduct 'as a person disaffected to Government'.

1793

5th January. Burns defends himself to Robert Graham of Fintry, Excise Commissioner.
January (?). Suggests improvements in the local ale tax to Provost Staig. Recommendations implemented soon afterwards, to great benefit of the revenue.
18th February. Second Edinburgh edition of *Poems* published by Creech.
28th February. Writes to Creech for twenty complimentary copies.
March. Petition to Provost and Council for burgess privileges for his children. Free education granted.
19th May. Burns family move into Millbrae Vennel (now Burns Street).

May. First set of Thomson's *Select Collections* published. Over twenty letters, many accompanied by songs, sent to Thomson in the ensuing seven months alone.

30th July — 2nd August. First tour of Galloway with Syme. They travel via Barncailzie, Parton and New Galloway, thence to Laurieston and over the moorland road to Gatehouse, then Kirkcudbright, St Mary's Isle and back to Dumfries via Dalbeattie.

1st August. Meets Pietro Urbani at St Mary's Isle, home of the Earl of Selkirk.

December. Lends his collection of bawdy ballads to John McMurdo.

Late December. 'Rape of the Sabines' incident at Friars' Carse. Breach between Burns and the Riddells.

1794

7th January. Proposes re-organization of the Dumfries Excise service.

12th January. Maria Riddell breaks with Burns.

20th April. Robert Riddell dies.

June. Friars' Carse put up for sale.

25th-28th June. Second Galloway Tour with Syme.

12th August. James Glencairn Burns born.

22nd December. Promoted to Acting Supervisor of Excise, Dumfries. Correspondence with Maria Riddell resumed.

1795

January. Working harder than ever on Excise duties, but income much reduced. Drastic curb on imports arising from the French Revolutionary War reduces Burns's income by a third.

12th January. Burns writes the letter which estranges Mrs Dunlop.

31st January. Burns a founder member of the Royal Dumfries Volunteers.

5th February 1795. Stranded at Ecclefechan by a severe snow storm.

February-March. Burns and Maria Riddell fully reconciled.

March. First of the Heron Election Ballads composed.

April. Alexander Reid paints a miniature portrait of Burns. Alexander Findlater resumes his duties as Excise Supervisor at Dumfries.

18th May. Complaint (probably drafted by Burns) by Volunteers against proposal to raise funds by public subscription.

September. Death of Elizabeth Riddell Burns.

December. Burns very ill with 'a most severe Rheumatic fever'.

1796

31st January. Making a slow recovery and 'beginning to crawl across my room'.

January-March. Famine in Dumfries. 'Many days my family, and hundreds of other families, are absolutely without one grain of meal; as money cannot purchase it.'

12th-14th March. Meal riots in Dumfries. Maxwell Hyslop injured by rioters.

1st June (?). Last letter to James Johnson.

3rd-16th July. Burns at Brow, sea-bathing in a vain attempt to regain his health.

12th July. Burns, fearing legal action for debt, writes a despairing letter to George Thomson.

16th July. Clark of Locharwoods lends his spring-cart to convey Burns back to Dumfries where he is confined to bed.

18th July. Burns writes his last letter: to his father-in-law, James Armour.

21st July. Burns dies.

25th July. Funeral of Burns, and birth of his posthumous son Maxwell.

BURNS-LORE OF DUMFRIES AND GALLOWAY

AIRDS OF KELLS   NX 677 705

A farm in the parish of Kells, in the Stewartry. It is located on the west side of Loch Ken, about half a mile from the Viaduct and a mile east of Mossdale. On 30th July 1793, during the Galloway Tour, Burns and John Syme, in the company of Gordon of Kenmure, visited the tenant of Airds, John Lowe, tutor to the McGhies of Airds and author of 'Mary's Dream' whose melody Burns used for 'Thou Lingering Star' (C.W. p.372). Lowe, a student of divinity and a minor poet, emigrated to America where he died in 1798.

The farm was then part of the estate of John Livingston who had been a draper in his early career but then inherited a farm from his father and subsequently added to his lands. Cunningham, in his Diary, has left a most unflattering picture of him: 'Livingstone's whole conduct and character by general report shows him to be still the low bred, designing packman, void of honour, troublesome and assuming in his neighbourhood. He has a vote upon Airds for Member of Parliament, but which it is reported must be bought before any candidate upon a competition gets it.' The estate was sold to the Heuchan family in 1804. The present Airds House, on the east side of Loch Ken, was not erected till the early 1800s but Airds of Kells farmhouse is still extant.

ANNAN   NY 188 662

A royal and parliamentary burgh situated on the east bank and two miles from the mouth of the River Annan. Annan Hill was a signal station in Roman times and the burgh itself is of great antiquity, having been a seat of the Bruce family and a regal mint from 1249. It was destroyed by the English in 1298 but its castle was restored two years later by Robert Bruce, later King of Scots. In 1332 Edward Baliol, after his coronation at Scone, summoned the Border nobility to do homage to him, and provoked the attack by Archibald Douglas which forced him to flee to Carlisle. Annan was reduced after siege in 1547 and destroyed by Lord Wharton. Subsequently it was raided by the English on many occasions until 1550 when it was garrisoned by French troops. The castle was destroyed by the Earl of Sussex in 1570, later rebuilt, but demolished in 1609 to provide stone for the parish church. Annan suffered grievously during the Civil War but its fortunes recovered at the Restoration when it was granted the privilege of collecting customs. The retreating army of Prince Charles Edward bivouacked here in December 1745. A charter was granted by King James V in 1538 and renewed by King James VI in 1612. The oldest buildings date from the late 18th century. The town made Dorothy Wordsworth 'think of France and Germany, many of the houses large and gloomy, their size outrunning their comforts'.

Burns paid his first visit to Annan in June 1787, while travelling from Carlisle to Dumfries at the conclusion of his Border Tour. In February 1792 Burns was promoted to the Dumfries Port Division of the Excise and as this included the 26-mile stretch of coast from Dumfries to the River Sark at Gretna, his duties frequently necessitated an overnight stay in Annan. Burns habitually resided at a house in the High Street (now occupied by the Cafe Royal). Burns's bedroom was on an upper floor and its window commanded a fine view of the High Street. The 17th century brick house was the home of the merchant Thomas Williamson (1752-1840) who was Provost of the burgh in 1831-3. Miss Harkness, the Provost's great- granddaughter, recalled that some of the window-panes in that bedroom bore the marks of the poet's diamond. One evening Burns suddenly left a large company which had asssembled in the house, remarking that he would come back shortly and read something new. He walked to Annan Bridge, evidently working out his ideas; and on his return to the house wrote down 'The Deil's awa wi th' Exciseman' (C.W. p. 467) and read it amid loud applause. Thomas Williamson, who was present on that occasion, often described in later years the sensation made by the poet's recital. A stone tablet in the wall looking towards the

Town Hall records that literary event. The actual building was demolished in 1831 and the present building was erected at the beginning of this century. Lockhart, however, claimed that Burns composed these verses extempore while waiting for his colleague John Lewars to bring up reinforcements before seizing the brig *Rosamond* at **Sarkfoot** on 28th February 1792. The composition at Annan seems much more probable, as Burns first sang it at an Excise dinner in Dumfries the following month.

Annan was the birthplace of Dr Thomas Blacklock on 10th November 1721, the bricklayer's son who lost his sight as a result of smallpox before he was a year old. His father John Blacklock spent a great deal of time with him, reading to and conversing with him and he owed what education he had, as well as a love of learning, to his father. John Blacklock, however, was killed in an accident when Thomas was eighteen, but Dr Stevenson, an Edinburgh physician who had been impressed with young Blacklock's poetry, invited him to Edinburgh and at considerable expense had him educated for the ministry. He was ordained minister of Kirkcudbright in 1762 — the first blind man ever ordained — but his parishioners complained that his handicap prevented him carrying out his parochial duties. He retired to Edinburgh in 1765 on a small annuity. A minor poet and the friend of both Samuel Johnson and Benjamin Franklin, Blacklock took a keen interest in struggling young writers. He received a copy of the Kilmarnock Poems from the Rev. George Lawrie of Loudoun and wrote, via Lawrie, a letter of encouragement to Burns who abandoned his plans to emigrate to Jamaica and turned seriously towards a literary career.

In the old Academy (which was located on Port Street) Thomas Carlyle led 'a doleful and hateful life' under Old Adam Hope, and was for a time the mathematics master there. William Nicol, born at **Dumbretton** in Annan parish, was also educated at the Academy. 'Kind honest hearted Willie' accompanied Burns on his Highland Tour of 1787 and was the recipient of the only extant letter by Burns written in the vernacular.

Annan was one of the five Dumfriesshire burghs which returned one member to Parliament and, as such, was satirised by Burns in 'The Five Carlins' (C.W. pp. 364-6) as Blinkin Bess of Annandale.

ANNAN WATERFOOT   NY 190 646

Modern maps locate Waterfoot on the west bank of the Annan but in the 1790s it was sited on the opposite bank. Road access to Annan at that period indicated the east bank. This side is part of the Annan Common Good and Waterfoot Road extends from the Port Street area. While small vessels could go upstream to within half a mile of the town, larger ships had to load and unload at two wooden jetties at the river's mouth. Ships plied regularly between Waterfoot and Liverpool, the passage generally accomplished within twelve hours, that is, in one tide only from harbour to harbour. Rum from Antigua was one of the more lucrative cargoes discharged at Waterfoot, hence the need for constant vigilance by Excise officers. It was from 'this wild place of the world' that Burns wrote to Mrs Dunlop on 22nd August 1792, saying that he had convoyed Lesley Baillie and her family from Dumfries on their way to England 'fourteen or fifteen miles' & dined & spent the day with them. — 'Twas about nine, I think, when I left them; & riding home I composed the following ballad...' This was the song 'Saw ye bonie Lesley' (C.W. p.435).

ARBIGLAND   NX 989 575

An estate on the Solway, with a handsome mansion and finely planted grounds, in Kirkbean parish, on the west side of the Nith estuary. It is approached by the minor road running two miles south of **Kirkbean Church**. The Earl of Southesk sold the estate in 1722 to the grandfather of William Craik, a noted agricultural improver. His son became Chief of the American Medical Service during the War of Independence and was personal physician to George Washington. Craik's daughter Helen (1750-1825) was a friend of Burns and a poetess of some merit and composed the lines, inscribed in her handwriting, on the title page of the Glenriddell Manuscript of Burns's poems. She published five novels between 1796 and 1805. Burns is thought to have been introduced to her by either Robert Riddell of Glenriddell or Captain John Hamilton of Allershaw, early in 1790. James Johnson published Riddell's collection of strathspeys about 1785 and six years later Burns ordered two copies which were to be sent by the Dumfries carrier 'directed to Captain Craik of Arbigland, care of Captain Hamilton'.

Two letters from Burns to Helen Craik have survived. The first, from **Ellisland** on 9th August 1790, refers to the pleasure Burns had received 'in perusing a certain manuscript volume of Poems, in the possession of Captain Riddel' — presumably a collection of Miss Craik's own compositions and not the Glenriddell Manuscript, which Burns did not complete till April 1791. This letter also refers to Burns having been prevented from paying a second visit to Arbigland, thereby implying that his first visit had taken place not very long before. A second letter was written from Dumfries on 12th January 1792. 'Now that I have, by my removal to town, got time & opportunity, I shall often intrude on you...' he wrote. There are no other extant letters. This may be explained by the tragic events that led to Helen leaving Arbigland soon afterwards.

It was at Arbigland that Burns met Anna Dorothea Benson (1773-1856), the daughter of a York wine-merchant and, in later life, a close confidante of Jane and Thomas Carlyle. During this visit, when the gentlemen rejoined the ladies in the drawing-room after the port had gone the rounds, Burns admired Miss Benson's embroidery and asked 'Can a tipsy man thread a needle?' — and then did so. When Allan Cunningham ascribed to her a statement that Burns drank 'as other men drank', she wrote to Jane Welsh on 25th February 1834: 'Burns was incapable of rudeness or vulgarity... well bred and gentlemanly in all the courtesies of life', adding that even during the meeting of the Caledonian Hunt she never saw Burns once intoxicated, though the worthy Member for Dumfries, and the good Laird of Arbigland, and twenty more... were brought home in a state of glorious insensibility.' Incidentally Cunningham, a stonemason before he embraced a literary career, carved the ornamental gateposts at the entrance to Arbigland estate. John Paul Jones was the son of the gardener to the Craiks and was born in a cottage on the estate in 1747; a plaque now marks the spot.

ARBIGLAND

Anne Craik, Helen's elder sister, married Captain John Hamilton of Allershaw, Burns's landlord in **Bank Street** and **Burns Street**, Dumfries. This marriage took place in 1758 and their son, Douglas Hamilton was born four years later. He took the surname Craik on being served heir male to Arbigland. Relations between Helen and her nephew were never good; but at the age of 41 she had an affair with her father's groom named Dunn, who was shot soon afterwards. The murderer was never brought to book, and it was even rumoured that Dunn had committed suicide. Suspicion has since fallen on Douglas Hamilton Craik. Helen herself was ostracised by Dumfries society as a result. Of all her former friends the only one who remained loyal to her was Jessie Staig, to whom Helen addressed a very poignant verse epistle. At the end of February 1792 Helen left Arbigland and went into self-imposed exile at Flimby Lodge, Cumbria where she died in June 1825.

ARDWALL   NX 581 548
An estate and mansion, in Anwoth parish, Stewartry, at the head of Skyreburn Bay, east of the A75, two miles west of **Gatehouse**. It has been in the possession of the McCulloch family for centuries, although the oldest charter extant dates only from 1536. Megalithic earthworks have been discovered to the east of the mansion. David McCulloch (1769-1825), fourth son of David McCulloch II, went to France as a young man to learn the language and was an eye-witness of some of the most dramatic events of the French Revolution. He returned home in 1793, some months before his father's death and, in the absence of his elder brothers abroad, took charge of the funeral arangements and the management of the estate. A rather high-flown testimonial to his filial piety was published at this time, somewhat negated by the minutes of Anwoth Kirk Session which record a charge of fornication made against him and Peggy Bailey, a serving maid at Ardwall.

David McCulloch met Burns through membership of St Andrew's Lodge at Dumfries where both were ardent freemasons. Lockhart recounts, in his biography of Sir Walter Scott, how Burns was ostracised by polite society in Dumfries early in 1794 (possibly as a result of the 'Rape of the Sabines' incident) and was snubbed by the ladies and gentlemen coming into Dumfries for a county ball. McCulloch immediately dismounted and crossed the street to join Burns who greeted him warmly, took him home and entertained him very agreeably until the hour of the ball arrived. Shortly after this incident, Burns wrote to McCulloch on 21st June, inviting him to meet him and Syme during their forthcoming Galloway tour, at **Kerroughtree.**

David McCulloch was an exceptionally fine singer, on whom Burns tested many of his songs before sending them to George Thomson for publication. Chambers confirmed that he himself heard Burns state on more than one occasion that he never fully knew the beauty of his songs until he heard them sung by David McCulloch.

AUCHLEAND   NX 415 588
A farmhouse about half a mile west of the A714, three miles north of Wigtown. According to Currie's List of Letters which were in Burns's possession at his death, Luke Mullar (*sic*) an Irishman, sent a 'Poetical Address to the Bard' from this address in February 1794 but no letters from Burns to Mullar are extant.

AULDGIRTH   NX 912 865
A place in the southern angle of Closeburn parish, seven miles north of Dumfries, on the east bank of the river **Nith.** It owed its importance to the fine stone bridge over the Nith, built in 1782. Allan Cunningham and the father of Thomas Carlyle were both employed in its construction. Burns would have crossed this bridge on his travels between Dumfries and Upper Nithsdale, en route to Ayrshire and would have broken his journey at the 18th century inn nearby. A famous landmark in the poet's time was a three- trunked tree, known as the Three Brethren, but it was destroyed in the 19th century. The old bridge still stands, although it has been bypassed by the A76 road bridge in recent years.

AULDGIRTH INN

BALMAGHIE   NX 718 632

An estate in the parish of the same name, half a mile south of the B795, two miles west of Townhead of Greenlaw, and three miles north of Bridge of Dee. This parish in the centre of the Stewartry takes its name (meaning in Gaelic the town of Macghie) from an Irish chieftain called McGhie whose descendants obtained a charter from King James IV. Three quarters of the parish are hilly wasteland of boulder-strewn heath and moss which played a notable part in the Killing Times of the 1680s. The best-known Covenanters were the two David Hallidays, shot by Government troops in 1685 and interred in Crossmichael kirkyard. The description of the Hallidays' martyrdom in the chapter on Balmaghie parish, published in the *Statistical Account* (1794), inspired Burns's quatrain on the Solemn League and Covenant (C.W. p.560) which he wrote in the margin of the appropriate page. Balmaghie's reputation for radical Presbyterianism was maintained by its parish minister, John MacMillan (1669-1753) who founded the Reformed Presbyterian Church, and from whom a section of the Cameronians were sometimes known as MacMillanites.

The estate of Balmaghie was purchased by Thomas Gordon of Campbeltown in November 1785. He stood as Tory candidate in the Election for the Stewartry in February 1795, in opposition to Patrick Heron. Gordon owed much of his support to his uncle, Murray of Broughton, Peeblesshire, one of the wealthiest landowners in southern Scotland. Burns alluded to this in the first of the Heron Election Ballads (C.W. p.544):

> A beardless boy comes o'er the hills
> Wi's uncle's purse and a' that;

In the Second Ballad (C.W. p.545) the opening stanza includes the lines:

> And there will be Murray commander,
> An Gordon the battle to win:
> Like brothers, they'll stan' by each other,
> Sae knit in alliance and kin.

In the Third Ballad (C.W. p.548) a quatrain satirised the Tory candidate:

> And there was Balmaghie, I ween -
> In front rank he wad shine;
> But Balmaghie had better been
> Drinkin Madeira wine.

The last line was a side-swipe at the fact that Gordon owned a holiday home on the island of Madeira. In the Fourth Ballad, sub-titled 'The Trogger' (C.W. p.549) the pedlar recites his wares:

> Here's the worth o Broughton in a needle's e'e;
> Here's a reputation tint by Balmaghie.   lost

With or without the poet's intervention, Gordon lost the Election.

Burns visited the parish during his Galloway Tour of 1794 and sailed down Loch Ken in the company of the parish minister, whom he had to help disembark.

Balmaghie was the birthplace (on 10th May 1779) of William McQuhae who is said to have shared a room with Burns during his sojourn in Edinburgh and then painted the poet's portrait which he took with him to America in 1805. As McQuhae would have been eight or nine years old during Burns's Edinburgh period the notion that this portrait is authentic is ludicrous — yet this story has apparently been accepted without question and recounted in several books and periodicals.

BARNCAILZIE   NX 805 709

An estate and mansion in the Stewartry, half a mile northwest of the A75, two miles west of Crocketford and half a mile north of Springholm, on the east bank of Brooklands Burn. John Syme was born here in 1755 and followed his father into the legal profession after a period of service as an ensign in the 72nd Regiment. He retired to his father's estate where he conducted experiments in agricultural improvements. Syme senior, however, lost a great deal of money in the aftermath of the collapse of the Douglas, Heron & Company Bank and Barncailzie had to be sold. Syme turned to law, and became a Writer to the Signet. In 1791 he became Distributor of Stamps for Dumfries and had his office on the ground floor of the house in **Bank Street** where the Burns family took up residence about the same time. Syme purchased a small estate at **Ryedale.**

BARNCLEUGH   NX 902 761

A small estate lying to the south of the Terregles-Shawhead road in the parish of Kirkpatrick-Irongray, about two miles east of Shawhead. Formerly in the possession of the powerful Irving family, it passed to the Maxwells in 1665 when their head married a daughter of John Irving. In 1776 Wellwood Johnstone, a cadet of the **Westerhall** family, inherited Barncleugh and took the surname of Maxwell on the death of James Maxwell of Barncleugh, son of Wellwood's grandfather by his first marriage. He then strengthened his connection with the parent stem of the Dumfries and Galloway Maxwells by marrying Katherine, daughter of **Terraughty.** Wellwood Maxwell (1747-1833) was described on his tombstone in **St Michael's** as 'pious without ostentation, religious without intolerance, he sought to do his duty to God without offending men'. He later acquired The Grove, an estate to the northeast of Barncleugh, and this passed to his son Wellwood Maxwell (1786-1867). Wellwood Maxwell was first lieutenant in the Dumfries Volunteers. In the Second Heron Election Ballad (C.W. p.546) he is referred to as 'Wattie that girns for the fishes an loaves!' although the significance of the allusion is unknown.

BARNCROSH   NX 709 593

A farm in Tongland parish, in the Stewartry, half a mile north of the A75 road just west of the junction with the A711 and two miles west of the village of Bridge of Dee. In Burns's time it was the property of John Dalzell (or Dalyell) a noted stock-breeder. Dalzell met Burns and Syme in Kirkcudbright and dined with them before they went on to **St Mary's Isle** to meet the Earl of Selkirk on 1st August 1793.

BARNHILL   **NY 089 030**

A farm situated on the west bank of the River Annan, on the north side of the Beattock-Holmend minor road, in the parish of Kirkpatrick-Juxta, Annandale. Barnhill was farmed in the early 1790s by a ne'er-do-well named Whelpdale whom Jean Lorimer — the 'Chloris' of Burns's poems — met while visiting family friends at **Dumcrieff** nearby. With his devil-may-care charm Whelpdale soon swept Jean off her feet and in March 1793 eloped with her to Gretna Green. There is no note of the marriage in any of the surviving registers, but this is not significant as the records are far from complete. Mr and Mrs Whelpdale returned to Barnhill but after only a few weeks of marriage he abandoned his bride and ran off to escape from his creditors. Whelpdale is said to have been a spendthrift who went through four fortunes. The unfortunate Jean returned to her father at **Kemys Hall** and reverted to her maiden surname.

BARR   **NS 766 094**

A farm just off the Euchan Valley road, about a mile southwest of **Sanquhar** and lying north of the Barr Burn. In the late 18th century it was farmed by Robert Williamson, the local giant — seven feet tall and weighing 25 stone. He played the violin and was much in demand at the parties held by Burns at Bailie Whigham's Queensberry Inn in Sanquhar. Burns jocularly referred to him as the Big Fiddler. Williamson served as an ensign in the Royal Dumfries Volunteers.

BARR, SANQUHAR

BENNAN HILL   **NX 648 725**

A hill (845 feet above sea level) on the east side of Cairn Edward Forest, above the western shore of Loch Ken. The summit is approachable by footpaths from the A762 about a mile north of Mossdale, or along a path by the Lowra Burn from Lochside, two miles north of Mossdale. Several chalybeate wells are located in the woods to the northwest. Burns and Syme climbed this hill in the course of their Galloway Tour, before heading for **Laurieston**.

BONSHAW   NY 242 720

The ancestral home of the Irvings, in the extreme northeast of Annan parish, 3.75 miles southeast of **Ecclefechan**. Bonshaw Tower dates from the Middle Ages, with 18th and 19th century additions. A marshy tract, called Bonshaw Flow, extends to the southwest. A cave cut into the cliff-face above the Kirtle Water on the estate is alleged to have been the abode of Bruce and the Spider, but in fact it is man-made and of much later vintage, being part of mine-workings in the area. Bonshaw is mentioned by Burns in 'The Trogger' (C.W. p.604), the song composed as a result of a wager with John Lewars who bet that Burns 'could not get a word to clink (rhyme) with Ecclefechan'.

BROWNHILL INN   NX 902 911

A former hostelry on the west side of A76 about a mile south of Closeburn in Nithsdale. It was a coaching inn of some importance on the Dumfries-Ayr route. The stables were on the west side of the road, opposite the inn. Dorothy and William Wordsworth, accompanied by Coleridge, spent a night at the inn during their Scottish tour. In the late 18th century the landlord was John Bacon, with whom Burns spent many a merry night while engaged on Excise duties. Burns is reputed to have given Bacon a 'cloot' — a snuff-box made from a sheep's cloven hoof mounted with silver. At the sale of Bacon's personal effects after his death in 1825 the 'cloot', inscribed 'Robert Burns Officer of the Excise' fetched £5.

One day, when Burns was at Brownhill, a friend read some verses composed after the manner of Pope's 'Song by a Person of Quality' and implied that poetry of this standard was beyond Burns, adding 'The muse of Kyle cannot match the muse of London City'. The poet took the paper, hummed the verses over, and then recited extempore 'Delia — An Ode' (C.W. p.358) which was subsequently published by Peter Stuart in the London *Star* of 18th May 1789.

On another summer evening Burns was at Brownhill with Dr Purdie of **Sanquhar** and another friend, when a poor wayworn soldier passed the window. Burns asked the soldier to recount his adventures and 'The Soldier's Return' (C.W. p.487) was composed as a result — or so the story goes, because this song, set to 'The Mill, Mill, O' was actually a reworking of 'Beneath a Green Shade', which Ramsay had refined from a piece of ancient bawdry in 1733.

One day an English commercial traveller named Ladyman arrived at the Inn and was informed by Bacon that he would be dining with Robert Burns and his friends. The landlord himself presided over the dinner, whose menu included a dish of bacon. Some of the party, including Burns, would rather have dispensed with the landlord's presence and when he had withdrawn from the room for a few minutes Ladyman, not absolutely convinced that he was indeed dining with the celebrated poet, put him to the test by asking him to produce some verses extempore. After a moment's cogitation Burns produced the following punning epigram (C.W. p.522):

> At Brownhill we always get dainty good cheer
> And plenty of bacon each day in the year;
> We've a' thing that's nice, and mostly in season,
> But why always bacon — come, tell me the reason?

Bacon's wife Catherine was the sister of William Stewart, the factor of **Closeburn** estate. In a verse epistle to William Stewart (C.W. p.350), written from Brownhill on a Monday evening probably early in 1789, Burns begins 'In honest Bacon's ingle-neuk'. During a drinking bout Catherine Bacon refused her husband and the poet more liquor, provoking Burns to write the lines entitled 'The Henpecked Husband' (C.W. p.610). Bacon purchased from Gilbert Burns the bed in which the poet was born, and charged visitors to see it. Subsequently it was broken up and the wood used to make snuff boxes bearing a commemorative inscription.

BROW WELL
NY 083 675

A chalybeate spring which enjoyed a certain reputation in the 18th century as a watering-place, both for the spring and for sea-bathing. The well is situated on the east side of the Raffles Burn not far from the point at which it debouches into the estuary of the Lochar Water on the Solway Firth in the parish of Ruthwell. On the advice of his physician, Dr William Maxwell, Burns spent three of the last weeks of his life in the decayed hamlet of Brow, drinking the chalybeate waters from an iron cup affixed to the side of the well. Part of the treatment recommended by Maxwell consisted of wading up to the armpits into the icy waters of the Solway — a treatment that was singularly inappropriate for a man in the last stages of emaciation and debility and in the grip of the incurable heart disease endocarditis.

Burns arrived about the beginning of July 1796 and put up at a nearby house, owned by James Morpeth. Burns lodged in 'the chaumer'en', but this house was demolished in 1863 during road-widening on the B725. Maria Riddell, who had come thither for her own health's sake, invited Burns to dine with her on 5th July and sent her carriage to fetch him to her lodgings. Soon afterwards she recorded her impressions of this poignant meeting: 'I was struck with his appearance on entering the room. The stamp of death was imprinted on his features. He seemed already touching the brink of eternity. His first salutation was: "Well, madam, have you any commands for the other world?" I replied, that it seemed a doubtful case which of us should be the soonest, and that I hoped he would yet live to write my epitaph. He looked at my face with an air of great kindliness, and expressed his concern at seeing me look so ill... We parted about sunset on the evening of that day. The next day I saw him again, and we parted to meet no more!' Burns subsequently wrote to John Clark of **Locharwoods** (C.L. p.706) for the use of his gig to convey him back to Dumfries.

Little now remains of the old hamlet of Brow which had served the cattle-drovers on their way from Dumfries to Carlisle. An ancient tradition maintains that Agricola's Roman legions landed here. The first pigs in Scotland were raised at Brow, and inspired great terror in their beholders. Dr Burnside, in the account of Ruthwell parish in the *First Statistical Account* (1794), states that there were few or no hogs in 1760, but that they were very common by 1790.

BUCHAN HA' see NEW CAMPLE

BUITTLE OLD PARISH CHURCH

BUITTLE   **NX 807 599**

The coastal parish in the Stewartry lying between **Castle Douglas** and Dalbeattie. The present church, south of the A745, was built in 1819 and seats 400. Nearby stand the ivy-clad ruins of the original First Pointed church, held anciently of Sweetheart Abbey. In Burns's day the minister, nicknamed the Buittle Apostle, was the Rev. George Maxwell (1762-1807). In the Second Heron Election Ballad (C.W. p.546) Maxwell was described as being 'mair o the black than the blue' — i.e. his extreme Presbyterianism outweighed his Tory politics. Burns returned to this theme in the third Ballad (C.W. p.548):

> And Buittle was na slack,
> Whase haly priesthood nane could stain,
> For wha could dye the black?

In the fourth Ballad, sub-titled 'The Trogger' (C.W. p.549), the sixth couplet enumerates;

> Here's a little wadset, Buittle's scrap of truth,
> Pawn'd in a gin-shop, quenching holy drouth.

CAERLAVEROCK   **NY 026 656**

A coastal parish of Nithsdale which derives its name from the ancient castle near the mouth of the Nith, seven miles southeast of Dumfries. The name is a corruption of *Caer Lewarch Og* — the fortress of Lewarch the younger — who, according to ancient but unsubstantiated tradition, erected it about two thousand years ago. Although both Caledonian and Roman remains have been discovered in the vicinity the castle dates only from 1220, frequently destroyed and rebuilt until the present structure was completed about 1420. The castle belonged to the Earls of Nithsdale, but gradually fell into disrepair from the 1660s when they transferred their residence to a square tower near the parish church. The church (026 692) is situated near the west bank of the Lochar Water about half a mile north of Bankend. It was erected in 1781 and contains 470 sittings. In its kirkyard is the grave of Robert Paterson (died 1801), the 'Old Mortality' of Sir Walter Scott whose publisher, Messrs Black of Edinburgh, erected the fine memorial to the old stone-carver in 1869. The minister of Caerlaverock from 1784 until his death in 1832 was the Rev. William McMorine (Moderator of the General Assembly in 1812). McMorine baptised Elizabeth Riddell Burns (born 21st November 1792) at Burns's house in Bank Street, Dumfries on 3rd January 1793. Little more than three years later he also officiated at the poet's funeral, on 25th July 1796.

CAIRN WATER

A small river of the Stewartry and Nithsdale, formed in **Glencairn** parish by the confluence of the Castlefern, the **Craigdarroch** and Dalwhat burns, a little below the village of Moniaive. It then runs in a southeasterly direction for a total of 23 miles before entering the **Nith** a mile north of Dumfries. About seven miles west of its junction with the Nith it is joined by the **Cluden**, whose name it assumes in the lower reaches. The Cairn is noted for its finely wooded scenery. In 'The Whistle' (C.W. p.369) Burns mentions Sir Robert Laurie of **Maxwelton** as 'the lord of the Cairn and the Scaur'. In the 'Ode to Willie Nicol's Mare' (C.W. p.380)Burns laments the loss of Peg Nicholson:

> But now she's floating down the Nith,
> And past the mouth o Cairn.

The mouth of the Cairn is about four miles south of **Ellisland**.

CAIRNMILL   **NX 843 943**

A farm on the north bank of the **Scaur Water,** about half a mile southwest of **Penpont,** Nithsdale. The tenant in 1791 was one Lorimer whose 'dark manoeuvres of a smuggler' got Burns into trouble in June of that year. The poet, in his capacity as Excise officer, had surveyed Lorimer's stock prior to the latter going to Edinburgh. 'The surveys made in Lorimer's absence might as well have been marked'' key absent'' as I never found any body but the lady, who I know is not mistress of keys, &c. to know any thing of it, and one of the times it would have rejoiced all Hell to have seen her so drunk.' Burns was subsequently accused of making errors in his assessment of Lorimer's stock. 'I know the gentleman's ways are, like the grace of God, past all comprehension; but I shall give the house a severe scrutiny tomorrow morning, & send you in the naked facts'.

Previous editors have fallen into the trap of supposing this Lorimer to have been William Lorimer, the father of 'Chloris', but the *Annals of Glencairn* (p. 127) positively identify Cairnmill, and not **Kemys Hall**. Based on this false premise is the canard that Jean Lorimer's mother was a drunkard, like the Mrs Lorimer referred to by Burns in the letter to Alexander Findlater (C.L. p.540) quoted above. Had the parents of 'Chloris' been the smuggler and drunkard of this letter it is extremely doubtful whether Burns would have been on such intimate terms with that family.

CALLY HOUSE   NX 599 549

Now a hotel, it was formerly a mansion in the estate of the same name, in Girthon parish, Kirkcudbrightshire, a mile south of **Gatehouse**. It was built in 1763, wholly of granite, from a design by Robert Milne. It was noted for its pleasure gardens and deer park (no longer extant) which Robert Heron, Burns's first biographer, described in 1792: 'Every deformity within these grounds is concealed or converted into beauty by wood'. The house was greatly improved and extended about 1835 and was noted for its magnificent collection of paintings and sculpture. The mansion which replaced Old House of Cally (now an ivy-clad ruin to the north) was built for James Murray of Broughton (1727-99). Murray was MP for Wigtownshire in the 1790s and supported the Tory candidature of his nephew Gordon of **Balmaghie** in the election for the Stewartry in February 1795. Murray had left his wife (his first cousin, Lady Catherine Stewart, daughter of the sixth Earl of Galloway) and eloped with his niece Grace Johnston. His immense wealth and power enabled him to do this with relative impunity, and his actions in no way affected his political association with his wife's family, one of whose close relations he was supporting in the election. In his Second Heron Election Ballad (C.W. p.545) Burns satirises Murray's familial and political connections:

> Fy, let us a' to Kirkcudbright,
>   For there will be bickerin there;
> For Murray's light horse are to muster
>   An O, how the heroes will swear!
> And there will be Murray commander,
>   An Gordon the battle to win:
> Like brothers, they'll stan' by each other,
>   Sae knit in alliance and kin.

In the last years of his life Murray made a great show of religiosity and endowed a number of churches and chapels, including an Episcopal chapel at Cally, thus inspiring Burns's jibe in the closing lines of the Second Ballad:

> An hey for the sanctified Murray
>   Our land wha wi chapels has stor'd;
> He founder'd his horse among harlots,
>   But gie'd the auld naig to the Lord!

The Third Ballad, subtitled 'John Bushby's Lamentation' (C.W. p.547), states:

> Then Murray on the auld grey yaud,
>   Wi winged spurs did ride;

a reference to the motif on the armorial bearings of the Johnstone family whose daughter Grace he had debauched. Grace Johnstone had been governess to Murray's legitimate daughter, before bearing him two sons out of wedlock.

In the Fourth Ballad (C.W. p.549) there is a couplet which refers to the fact that Sir William Douglas stood as godfather to Murray's illegitimate son:

> Here's the font where Douglas stane and mortar names,
> Lately used at Cally christening Murray's crimes.

Murray was an absentee laird who paid his gardener at Cally no wages. In lieu of a salary, however, the gardener was allowed to sell the produce, and this apparently yielded £70 in 1786 alone — a considerable sum for that period.

CALLY HOUSE

CARDONESS CASTLE   NX 591 553

Situated on the Water of Fleet, a mile southwest of **Gatehouse**, it was a stronghold of the McCulloch family. The last resident was Sir Godfrey McCulloch who was beheaded in 1697 at Edinburgh for the murder of William Gordon at Bush o' Bield. The roofless tower was in a ruinous condition in Burns's day, but has been partially restored in more recent times and is a tourist attraction, noted for its curious two-tier toilet known as the 'Lang Dreep'. The castle is referred to in the Third Heron Election Ballad (C.W. p.548):

> Sae in the tower o Cardoness
> A howlet sits at noon.

CARDONESS HOUSE   NX 565 535

A mansion-house and estate in Anwoth parish, in the southwest of the Stewartry. The mansion stands amid fine grounds on the western side of Fleet Bay, three miles west of **Gatehouse** at the western end of the A75 bypass. David Maxwell of Cardoness featured in the Second Heron Election Ballad (C.W. p.545):

> An there'll be Cardoness, Esquire,
> Sae mighty in Cardoness' eyes:
> A wight that will weather damnation,
> For the Devil the prey would despise.

In the fourth Ballad (C.W. p.549) Burns refers to Cardoness's head as 'Fine for a soger, a' the wale o lead'. Cardoness supported the Tory candidate, Gordon of **Balmaghie,** but he had previously earned Burns's contempt. In a letter of June 1793 to Mrs Dunlop he wrote: 'The following is an epigram which I made the other day on a stupid, money-loving dunderpate of a Galloway laird — Maxwell of Cardoness —' and then inscribed the eight lines beginning 'Bless Jesus Christ, O Cardoness' (C.W. p.491), later published under the title of 'Epigram on a Country Laird not quite so wise as Solomon'. Burns composed a second epigram on this subject, during the first Galloway Tour with Syme in July-August 1793. Syme records the poet's splenetic mood on this tour, especially whenever he beheld the fine mansions of the gentry. He must have been in a particularly sour frame of mind when he wrote 'On being shown a Beautiful Country Seat' (C.W. p.492):

> We grant they're thine, those beauties all,
> So lovely in our eye:
> Keep them, thou eunuch, Cardoness,
> For others to enjoy.

Both epigrams on Cardoness were sent by Burns to Peter Hill on 30th May 1795. David Maxwell was created a baronet in 1804 and died in 1825.

CARLINWARK — see CASTLE DOUGLAS

CARRUCHAN   NX 949 738
An estate with a mansion, in Troqueer parish, two miles southwest of Dumfries. In the time of Burns the proprietor was George Maxwell, one of the Justices of the Peace who attested Burns on 27th October 1789 at the Quarter Sessions where he was inducted as an Excise officer. He appears as 'Staunch Geordie' in the Second Heron Election Ballad (C.W. p.546).

CARSE MILL   NX 936 834
A grain mill on the bank of the Laggan Burn near its confluence with the Nith, between **Ellisland** and **Isle.** The miller in 1788 was John Currie who also kept a public-house in the vicinity. On 22nd December 1788 Burns wrote to his old friend John Tennant Junior (C.L. p.73), complimenting him on the strength and quality of the whisky which he had distilled. Currie, a man who was good for a £500 bargain, sold a great deal of foreign spirits (brandy) but considered the local brands of whisky so rascally that it would have degraded his house. Burns let Mr and Mrs Currie try some of Tennant's whisky and subsequently he reported: 'They were perfectly astonished at my whisky, both for its taste & strength'. Burns was writing on their behalf in the hope that Tennant would be able to supply them with liquor of an equal quality.

CARSETHORN   NX 993 599
A coastal hamlet of Kirkbean parish to the south of the entrance to Carse Bay and a mile northeast of **Kirkbean** village. Although nowadays mainly given over to holiday homes, it was an important seaport in the 18th century. Timber ships from the Baltic, of too great a draught to navigate the **Nith,** discharged their cargoes at Carsethorn, the mooring posts being maintained by the Town Council. As an outpost of Dumfries it had a Coastguard barracks and was frequently visited by Burns on Excise duties.

CASSENCARRY   NX 475 576
A mansion in Kirkmabreck parish, half a mile south of Creetown. An old building with a tower, it stands finely in a level holm with the **Cree** estuary in front and Larg Hill (969 feet) at the rear. It is situated near the A75 and is now a caravan park. The old building was burned out but has been partly restored and now contains a hostelry. Colonel Mackenzie was apostrophized in the Second Heron Election Ballad (C.W. p.546) — 'An there'll be gay Cassencarry'.

CASTLE DOUGLAS   NX 76 62

A town in the north of Kelton parish in the Stewartry, it was a mere hamlet, known as Causewayend, until 1765. The exploitation of the marl-pits of Carlinwark Loch nearby led to the rapid development of the village, which was renamed after the loch. In 1792, however, Carlinwark became the property of Sir William Douglas of Gelston who renamed it in his own honour as Castle Douglas and had it erected into a burgh of barony. Some years earlier (in 1778) Douglas had purchased the estate of Castle Stewart in Wigtownshire and changed its name to Newton Douglas, but the name never caught on and the village soon reverted to its original title of **Newton Stewart.** With Castle Douglas, however, he had more success and it rapidly grew into a market town of considerable importance. Burns poked mild fun at Sir William and his brother James in the Second Heron Election Ballad (C.W. p.545):

> An there'll be Douglasses doughty,
> New christening towns far and near.

Burns was a frequent visitor to the town and two letters written at Carlinwark Inn are extant. On 25th June 1794 he wrote to Mrs Dunlop (C.L. p.210): 'Here in a solitary inn, in a solitary village' and probably on the same day he penned the very last letter to Agnes McLehose (C.L. p.411), with those poignant lines: 'Ah! my ever dearest Clarinda! — Clarinda? — What a host of Memory's tenderest offspring crowd on my fancy at that sound! — But I must not indulge that subject. — you have forbid it. —' Later in the letter he made a wry comment about his present situation: 'Here am I set, a solitary hermit, in the solitary room, of a solitary inn, with a solitary bottle of wine by me...'

CAVENS   NX 977 585

An estate, with a mansion, in Kirkbean parish, 13 miles south of Dumfries, and lying just off the A710, about half a mile south of **Kirkbean** village.

The Regent Morton had a castle here which King James VI visited as a boy. In the 18th century the estate belonged to the Oswald family, later better known on account of their Ayrshire estate of Auchencruive, which Richard Oswald purchased from Lord Cathcart in 1764. Richard Oswald started out as the penniless youngest son of the Rev. George Oswald, minister of Dunnet and a cadet of the Oswald family. Later in life he inherited Cavens and went on to amass a huge fortune in London as a merchant and contractor during the Seven Years War (1756-63). Through his wife, Mary Ramsay, he acquired estates in America and the West Indies. On her husband's death, Mrs Oswald settled in London where she herself died in 1788. It was her funeral cortege which stopped at **Sanquhar** on its way to Ayrshire and so incommoded Burns that he was inspired to compose a bitter ode sacred to her memory (C.W. p.342).

Richard Oswald (1771-1841) inherited Cavens as well as the other estates, and although he lived mainly in London and Ayrshire he played a prominent part in Stewartry affairs. It was in this context that he was mentioned in the Second Heron Election Ballad (C.W. p.546):

> An there'll be wealthy young Richard,
> Dame Fortune should hang by the neck:
> But for prodigal thriftless bestowing,
> His merit had won him respect.

It is not known whether these were the lines referred to by Burns in his letter to Oswald, written from Dumfries on 23rd April 1795, beginning 'You see the danger of patronising the rhyming tribe: you flatter the poet's vanity — a most potent ingredient in the composition of a son of rhyme — by a little notice; and he, in return persecutes your good nature with his acquaintance...' (C.L. p.717).

That Burns had modified the hostile opinions expressed about the Oswalds in 1789 was evident in a letter to John Syme from Dumfries in May 1794 (C.L. p.708), saying: '...did you ever... meet with a man who owed more to the Divine Giver of all good things than Mr Oswald? A fine fortune; a pleasing, engaging exterior, self-evident amiable dispositions, with an ingenuous, upright mind,

& that too informed much beyond the usual run of young fellows of his rank & fortune: & add to all this, such a Woman!' The woman was Lucy, daughter of Wayne Johnstone of Hilton-on-Merse, whom Oswald had married in 1793. She was a famous beauty who inspired Burns to modify 'O Wat Ye Wha's in Yon Town' (C.W. p.541), which had originally been written for Jean Lorimer. He substituted 'Lucy' for 'Jean' and sent it to her in May 1795. Writing to George Thomson the previous February, Burns had commented on this song 'I have a fair Dame in my eye to whom I would consecrate it'. Burns met the Oswalds while they resided at Cavens, and it was probably there that Lucy gave the poet her own composition, the air entitled 'Captain Cook's Death' which he used as the melody for 'Thou Lingering Star' (C.W. p.372) before settling upon 'Mary's Dream'.

CAVENS

CHAPEL   NX 834 846
A farm in Glenesslin, Dunscore parish, Nithsdale, lying to the north of the minor road between Dunscore village and Loch Urr and about two miles west of the former. It was the estate of Major James Dodd (or Dods), the Army officer to whom Burns apparently gave offence at a private gathering in Dumfries in July 1794. Burns had been asked to propose a toast, and his response was the ambivalent words 'May our success in the present war be equal to the justice of our cause'. The gallant major made a retort whose words 'were such as generally, I believe, end in a brace of pistols...' as Burns wrote to his friend Samuel Clark, Jr. the following day (C.L. p.702). Burns sought Clark's intervention in the matter before it got out of hand and came to the attention of his superiors in the Excise. He concluded: 'I am truly sorry that a man who stood so high in my estimation as Mr Dods, should use me in the manner in which I conceive he has done.'

CLACKLEITH   NS 829 170
A farm in Sanquhar parish lying between Upper Nithsdale Forest and Wanlock Water, half a mile south of the B740 at Spango Bridge. It was the property of William Johnston (1733-1820)

who held office as Provost of **Sanquhar** in 1790-3. Burns made his acquaintance while engaged on Excise riding work in Upper Nithsdale. Johnston shared Burns's interest in traditional ballads and folk-songs and collected a number of old airs and fragments for Burns to mend and adapt. He is referred to in one of the presentation stanzas of 'The Kirk's Alarm' (C.W. p.361) which Burns sent to certain favoured correspondents 'To that trusty auld worthy, Clackleith'. His daughter Susan died on 29th October 1881 at the ripe old age of 101. She often reminisced about the poet's visits to Clackleith when she was a little girl.

CLARENCEFIELD   NY 092 685

A village in Ruthwell parish, Nithsdale along the B724 about 9 miles east of Dumfries. The fifth house on the left, going into the village from the west, was run as a shop and hotel by John Burney in 1796, when Burns was at **Brow**, a mile south of the village. Burns was in straitened circumstances and could afford little more than porridge for sustenance. It is alleged, however, that Dr Maxwell had prescribed port wine as a tonic and when Burns exhausted the supply he had with him he tried to obtain some more. His landlord at Brow, Davidson, did not deal in wines, so Burns had to go to Clarencefield to see if Burney (Davidson's son-in-law) could supply him. Placing an empty bottle on the counter, Burns asked for a bottle of port; and when that was handed to him he whispered to Burney that 'the muckle deil had got into his pouch and was its only occupant', but taking out his seal (bearing his armorial device) he tendered it to the innkeeper as security. The landlady, who was standing by, observing that Burns was about to unfasten the seal, stamped indignantly with her foot by way of protest, while her husband,in the same generous mind as herself, pushed the poet gently to the door, making him welcome to the wine without money and without pledge.

CLARENCEFIELD – SHOWING JOHN BURNEY'S HOUSE

This story came to McDowall from Scott, the Clarencefield schoolmaster, who got it from Mrs Burney about 1840. Mrs Burney gave Scott the Bible used by Burns when lodging at Brow saying that 'it was much used by him when there'. A similar version of this story was communicated by R.P. Drummond of Perth to a newspaper about 1876. Some doubt has been expressed, however, on the grounds that Burns could easily have obtained medicinal port from friends such as Maria Riddell or James Gracie.

CLOSEBURN   NX 896 923

A village and parish of Upper Nithsdale, it takes its name from the 12th century Kylosbern ('church of St Osbern'). It is situated on the A76 about 12 miles north of Dumfries and 2.75 miles southeast of **Thornhill**. Closeburn was the birthplace (in 1761) of James Clarke, the schoolmaster at Moffat Grammar School, whom Burns helped, by lending him money and writing letters on his behalf, when Clarke was the victim of a conspiracy between some of his pupils' parents and the Earl of Hopetoun to have him dismissed. Burns wrote two letters to Clarke in January-February 1792 (C.L. p.595), first offering his help and then congratulating him on the successful outcome of the affair. Clarke was still paying off the debt by instalments at the time of the poet's death. Burns's last letter to Clarke, less than a month before he died, acknowledged one of these repayments and appealed in desperation for another by return of post.

Kirsty Kirkpatrick, who resided at a cottage in Closeburn, frequently played hostess to Burns on his visits to the village. She had a beautiful voice and sang many of the traditional airs which Burns used for his songs. As she sang, Burns sat back in the large armchair by the fireside and listened carefully for any grating word or phrase. Then the urchins, gathered round the door, to the sneck of which the poet's horse was tied, would hear: 'No, Kirsty, that sounds ill. I maun change that word. Try this now! Ah! that's better.' Thus they went through stanza after stanza until the song was completed, and every harsh word or phrase had been removed. Kirsty lived till 1838, to boast of the part she had played in perfecting some of Burns's best-loved songs. After her marriage to William Flint she moved to **Dinning** where the friendship with the Burns family was strengthened.

CLOSEBURN CASTLE   NX 907 921

A quadrangular tower consisting of a ground floor and three vaulted apartments. Hill Burton described it as a featureless Scotch peel, which never seems to have possessed the Norman archway depicted in Grose's *Antiquities*, but according to the local historian, Dr Ramage, the Norman mouldings were plastered over in the 19th century. The barony of Kylosbern belonged to the crown in the reign of King David I (1123-54). His grandson, Alexander II, confirmed its possession (1232) to Ivan de Kirkpatrick, ancestor of that Roger de Kirkpatrick who in 1305 made siccar of the Red Comyn at Dumfries. The estate was sold in 1783 to the Rev. Dr. James Stuart-Menteath, Rector of Barrowby in Lincolnshire. William Stewart, born in 1750 to the couple who kept the ale-house at Closeburn Kirk Brig, moved to Lincolnshire as a young man and worked there as a draper's packman. In the course of his work he got to know the Rector of Barrowby who asked him if he knew Closeburn, then up for sale. On learning that it was Stewart's birthplace, and being impressed with the intelligent nature of his answers, the Rector asked Stewart to accompany him on an inspection, which he did, and the purchase having been effected, he was installed as factor.

Probably through the Bacons of **Brownhill** Burns made William Stewart's acquaintance and was a frequent visitor at Closeburn Castle. Burns found in Stewart a very congenial spirit, hence the lines 'You're Welcome, Willie Stewart' (C.W. p.522) which Burns inscribed on a crystal tumbler at the inn of Closeburn Kirk Brig. The landlady, Stewart's mother, took umbrage at this vandalism, but was appeased when a gentleman present on that occasion paid a shilling for the tumbler and took it away as a memento. Lockhart, however, attributes this story to Mrs Bacon at Brownhill (Stewart's sister). Be that as it may, the engraved tumbler was later acquired by Sir Walter Scott and is now on display at Abbotsford House.

Mrs Agnes Lawson (née Yorstoun) of Nithbank, Dumfries was a niece of the minister of Closeburn and on one occasion visited Closeburn Castle when Burns was also present. She was asked to sing Mrs Grant of Carron's song of 'Roy's Wife of Aldivaloch' which closed with the wistful lines:

> Her face sae fair, her een sae clear,
> Her wee bit mou' sae sweet and bonnie,
> To me she ever will be dear,
> Though she's for ever left her Johnnie.

At the end, Burns exclaimed, 'Oh! Miss Yorstoun, dinna leave him lamenting that way; let him console himself thus' and extempore he recited the lines

> Roy's age is three times mine,
> I'm sure his years can not be mony,
> An when that he is dead an gane
> She may repent, an tak her Johnnie.

According to Dr Ramage, Mrs Lawson invariably added this verse whenever she sang the song, although later scholars have been inclined to dismiss the story as apocryphal. Significantly, Burns himself never used these lines, even though he used the melody 'Roy's Wife' for 'Canst Thou Leave Me Thus, My Katie?' (C.W. p.530) which he composed on the night of 19th November 1794.

William Stewart's daughter Mary, familiarly known as Polly (1775-1847), was the subject of Burns's song 'Lovely Polly Stewart' (CW p.523). Polly married her cousin, Ishmael Stewart, by whom she had three sons. He got into trouble, fled the country and died abroad. In 1801, when Ishmael was probably still alive, she contracted a quasi-matrimonial alliance — very much against her better judgment by all accounts — with George Welsh, farmer in Morton Mains and grand-uncle of Jane Welsh Carlyle. Polly was too frivolous and light-headed for the sober, respectable George. They quarrelled and eventually separated, and Polly went to **Maxwelltown** to live with her father in 1806. Subsequently she took up with a Swiss mercenary named Fleitz who had been serving in the French Army and had been sent as a prisoner of war to the Dumfries area. When Fleitz was repatriated Polly went with him, first to France and later to Switzerland where they settled in Lauffenburg near Basle, and where she died in her 72nd year. A number of pathetic letters from her, addressed to Mr Pagan of the King's Arms, Dumfries, are recorded, mainly enquiring after her sons by her first marriage.

When **Friars' Carse** was up for sale in 1794 Burns wrote to John McLeod of Colbecks (C.L. p.710), a prospective purchaser of the estate, saying that the trustees for the late Captain Riddell of Glenriddell had appointed William Stewart to estimate the value of the estate. 'Stewart is my most intimate friend; and has promised me a copy of his estimate — but please let this be a dead secret...' Despite this advantage, however, McLeod failed in his bid. On 15th January 1795 Burns wrote a 'painful, disagreeable letter' to Stewart from Dumfries, asking for 'three or four guineas' because his Excise emoluments had been drastically reduced 'in these accursed times, by stopping up Importation...' Stewart endorsed this letter on 16th January 'This day forwarded and enclosed in a letter to Mr Burns £3 3s str. and for which I hold no security in writing.' Earlier letters from Burns to Stewart (C.L. pp.444-5), were written in a happier vein, and indicate that Stewart shared the poet's interest in bawdry.

CLUDEN WATER

A small river formed by the confluence of the **Cairn** and the Old Water of Cluden, close to the beautiful Routing Bridge on the boundary of the parishes of Kirkpatrick-Irongray and Holywood. Thence it winds about seven miles in a generally southeasterly direction and empties into the **Nith** at **Lincluden** north of Dumfries. The Cluden figures in the second version of 'Ca' the Yowes' (C.W. p.519).

COLLIESTON   NX 811 824

This name is borne by a moor, a hill and a burn south of Glenesslin in Dunscore parish, Nithsdale. On the banks of the Collieston Burn are the remains of a mansion which was the home of John Welsh (1570-1623), the illustrious ancestor of Jane Welsh, wife of Thomas Carlyle. In the 18th century, however, the estate passed into the hands of William Copland, an advocate who apparently hailed from Kirkcudbrightshire. Copland of Collieston was referred to in the Second Heron Election Ballad (C.W. p.546):

> An there'll be Collieston's whiskers.

In an age when men, for the most part, were clean-shaven, such a feature would have been sufficiently unusual to occasion comment. In the final stanza of the third Ballad (C.W. p.548) William Copland was lampooned:

> And last cam creepin Collieston,
>   Was mair in fear than wrath;
> Ae knave was constant in his mind -
>   To keep that knave frae scaith.

In the fourth Ballad (C.W. p.549) we find among the 'braw troggin':

> Here's the worth and wisdom Collieston can boast:
> By a thievish midge they had been nearly lost.

William Copland is also considered to be the subject of the Dumfries epigram (C.W. p.532):

> C------d faithful likeness, friend Painter,
>   would'st seize?
> Keep out Worth, Wit and Wisdom: Put in what
>   you please.

COLVEND   NX 862 542

A hamlet and parish, five miles southeast of Dalbeattie in the Stewartry and 14 miles southwest of Dumfries. Southwick church, which fell into disuse about 1743, was either Norman or First pointed in origin. Colvend church was itself rebuilt in 1791, the year in which the Rev. James Little, minister of Colvend and Southwick, wrote to Burns (8th July) saying that he would be glad to see him any time and that his company would be 'a great treat'. No letters from Burns to Little, however, are extant.

CORBIETON   NX 796 658

An estate and mansion-house south of Urr Water, a mile west of Haugh of Urr, midway between the Old Military Road and the A75. The proprietor in the late 18th century was Captain William Roddick, a 'noted coxcomb' whose vanity was satirised by Burns in a mock epitaph (C.W. p.505). It is thought that Captain Roddick may also have been the butt of the epigrams 'on an old acquaintance who seemed to pass the Bard without notice' (C.W. p.533), although William Graham of **Mossknowe** is another possible contender.

COURANCE HOUSE   NY 054 902

Mansion in Kirkmichael parish, Nithsdale, 9 miles northwest of Lockerbie, lying between the A701 and Kinnel Water. It was the property of Francis Shortt (1754-1839), for many years Town Clerk of Dumfries before he retired thither. During his Dumfries period he owned a fine Georgian house on Castle Street. Shortt is, however, best remembered as the Secretary of the right-wing political club known as the Loyal Natives which he helped to found on 18th January 1793 for 'supporting the Laws and Constitution of the Country'. Shortt is suspected of being the author of the attack on Burns and his friends in some scurrilous verses 'more distinguished for drunken loyalty, than either for respectability or poetical talent':

> Ye sons of Sedition, give ear to my song,
>   Let Syme, Burns and Maxwell persuade every throng,
> With Cracken, the attorney, and Mundell the quack,
>   Send Willie, the monger, to hell with a smack.

Burns was thus linked with John Syme, Dr William Maxwell, William McCraken and Dr James Mundell. 'Willie the monger' was, of course, the Prime Minister, William Pitt. Burns retaliated with at least two epigrams, of which the following is the better known:

Ye true 'Loyal Natives' attend to my song:
In uproar and riot rejoice the night long!
From Envy and Hatred your core is exempt,
But where is your shield from the darts of Contempt?

Francis Shortt, however, deserved the poet's gratitude the previous year when he defended John Lewars against charges of drunkenness, disorderly conduct, assault and breach of the peace, following an incident during the night of 17th-18th May 1792. Burns himself was with Lewars when these 'crimes of a heinous nature and severely punishable' took place and it was entirely to the poet's credit that he succeeded in restraining his drunken friend and dragging him away, after Lewars had attacked two young women, servants of Wellwood Maxwell. The case dragged on from 18th till 29th May, when David Newall and Robert Jackson resolved the matter: 'The pror. fiscal, on account of several favourable circumstances to the def. which have come to his knowledge since raising this summons deserts this process pro loco et tempore'. Shortt is believed to have made a powerful plea of mitigation, pointing out how Lewars was a diligent Exciseman and had provided a home for his sister Jessie. Powerful friends, such as David Newall, David Staig and Captain Riddell, contrived to keep Burns himself out of the case, even though he was named in Lewars' deposition.

CRAIGDARROCH   NX 741 909

An estate and mansion in Glencairn parish, Nithsdale, just south of the B729 two miles west of Moniaive. It was the home of Alexander Fergusson (1746-96), a lawyer in Dumfries and eldest son of Annie Laurie. In his capacity as a Justice of the Peace for Dumfriesshire, he was approached by Burns who wrote to him about October 1789 (C.L. p.538), interceding 'for poor Robie Gordon' whom he had been forced to prosecute for an Excise offence but for whom he showed characteristic compassion.

Fergusson married Deborah, daughter of Robert Cutlar of Arroland in the Stewartry. The laird of Craigdarroch was a prominent Freemason and was present on that memorable occasion in Edinburgh (13th January 1787) when Burns was hailed as Caledonia's Bard. Fergusson was noted for his prowess as a hard drinker, winning the contest immortalised by Burns in 'The Whistle' (C.W. p.368). On that occasion Fergusson downed 'upwards of five bottles of claret'. This epic drinking bout took place at **Friars' Carse** on 16th October 1789 and involved Sir Robert Laurie of Maxwelton and Robert Riddell of Glenriddell as well as Fergusson who drank his companions under the table and went on to blow the winning blast on the little ebony whistle which had been the prize in previous drinking contests as far back as the reign of King James IV. John McMurdo of Drumlanrig judged the contest at which Burns himself was present, but only as an observer. William Hunter, one of the servants, later testified that 'when the gentlemen were put to bed, Burns walked home, without any assistance, not being the worse for drink'.

The quatrain 'Answer to an Invitation' (C.W. p.370) was preserved at Craigdarroch. The lines were allegedly written extempore by Burns in answer to an invitation to the contest over the whistle, but doubts as to their authenticity have been cast, because they were written on a page torn fron an Excise book before the poet had begun his active career in that service. On the other hand, Burns's Excise commission dated from 1st September that year and one cannot rule out the possibility that he had Excise stationery in his possession shortly thereafter.

In 'Sketch for an Elegy' (C.W. p.337) Burns writes of 'Craigdarroch, fam'd for speaking art'. In the 'Election Ballad' of 1790 (C.W. p.404):

Craigdarroch led a light-arm'd core:
Tropes, metaphors, and figures pour,
Like Hecla streaming thunder.

He was a man well-known for the powers of his oratory, hence the poetic allusions above.

Burns also composed 'A Mother's Lament' (C.W. p.344) for Mrs Fergusson of Craigdarroch, whose son died on 5th November 1787. He made it serve double duty, however, by transcribing it for the Afton Lodge collection in 1791, wherein it was annotated as commemorating Alexander Gordon Stewart of Afton who had died at Strasbourg military academy on 5th December 1787.

It has been alleged that Burns's 'Address to the Deil' (C.W. p.161) was derived from an account published at Glasgow in 1772 by John Stevenson, a farm-labourer of Craigdarroch, who claimed to have had a personal confrontation with Satan in the Craigdarroch woods.

CRAIGDARROCH

CRAIGENGILLAN   NX 637 948

A farm in Carsphairn parish in the north of the Stewartry, on the west bank of the Water of Ken about a mile north of its junction with the Craigengillan Burn. Craigengillan is approached along an unfenced minor road running due north from the B729, two miles east of the junction with the B7000 at High Bridge of Ken. The farm belonged to John McAdam, a wealthy landowner and agricultural improver whose other estates included Barbeth, Straiton and Dunaskin in Ayrshire. McAdam was the recipient of a verse epistle from Burns (C.W. p.274) 'In answer to an obliging letter he sent in the commencement of my poetic career'. It has been assumed from this sub-title, that the poem beginning 'Sir, o'er a gill I gat your card' was composed in 1786, but McAdam and his family appear only in the addenda and not the main subscription list in the Edinburgh Edition. This would date composition to about March 1787, rather than late 1786 as implied in Burns's annotation in the Glenriddell MS which, long after the event, may have been due to faulty memory. John's son, Colonel Quinton McAdam (who committed suicide in 1805) was referred to in the closing stanza as 'young Dunaskin's laird'. In the Second Heron Election Ballad (C.W. p.546) occurs the line 'An Quinton — o lads no the warst!'

Writing to Dr Mackenzie from Edinburgh on 11th January 1787 (C.L. p.114) Burns mentions Sir John Whitefoord's son John who had 'had the good luck to pre-engage the hand of the beauty-famed and wealth-celebrated Miss McAdam, our Country-woman. — Between friends, John is desperately in for it there; and I am afraid will be desperate indeed.' The lady in question was the elder of John McAdam's two daughters whom Burns, in his verse epistle, describes as

... bonnie lasses baith

(I'm tauld they're loosome kimmers!)   lovable wenches

McAdam, with William Chalmers, was the recipient of a command (C.L. p.218) 'In the name of the NINE. Amen', from Mauchline on 20th November 1786, wherein Chalmers and McAdam were described as 'Students and Practitioners in the ancient and mysterious Science of Confounding Right and Wrong'. From the contents of this humorous mock-mandate it is clear that John McAdam was another of the poet's friends who shared his love of bawdy ballads.

CRAIGIEBURN   NT 116 055

An estate and mansion in Moffat parish, on the right bank of Moffat Water, 275 miles east of the town of **Moffat**. The house lies at the foot of Hunterheck Hill, on the northwest side of the A708. The lease of the farm was granted in 1755 to James Lorimer whose son William eventually took it over. On 1st November 1790 William Lorimer moved to **Kemys** Hall but retained the lease of Craigieburn until the following year. The plantation of trees to the north of Craigieburn, bounded by the main road and Craigie Burn, was settled in the mid-18th century and well-established by 1789 when Craigieburn Wood became one of Burns's favourite haunts, immortalised in his song of that name (C.W. p.436), his first contribution to the *Scots Musical Museum*, volume IV. The subject of the song was Jean Lorimer, William's daughter, who was born at Craigieburn in 1775. The song contains the verse:

I see thee gracefu, straight, and tall,
I see thee sweet and bonie;
But O, what will my torment be,
If thou refuse thy Johnie!

'Johnie' in this context was the poet's Excise colleague, John Gillespie, for whom Burns wrote several poems to assist in the courtship of Jean. Despite these ardent effusions, however, Jean eloped with the worthless Whelpdale. She later became Burns's Chloris, for whom he wrote at least two dozen songs, including some of his very best. James Hogg, the Ettrick Shepherd and an early editor of Burns's works, averred that Burns himself had an ongoing affair with Jean and stayed with her at Craigieburn every time his Excise business took him to Moffat. A second version of 'Craigieburn Wood' was composed in the winter of 1794-5 and sent to George Thomson on 15th January 1795. Much has been made of the lines:

But secret love will break my heart,
If I conceal it langer.

An ale-house known as **Willie's Mill**, at the edge of the woods on the Moffat Water side of the road is claimed as the meeting place of Allan Masterton, Willie Nicol and Burns, immortalised in the carousing ballad 'Willie Brew'd a Peck o Maut' (C.W. p.364) in the autumn of 1789 when Nicol was on holiday at Moffat. Masterton, who was the writing-master at Edinburgh High School, composed the music to which this bacchanal was set.

CRAIGMUIE   NX 736 866

An estate and mansion in the northeast of the Stewartry, on the borders with Nithsdale, half a mile southeast of the A702, four miles southwest of Moniaive and ten miles northeast of New Galloway. It was the seat of the Goldie family who played a prominent part in Dumfries politics in the 18th century. John Goldie of Craigmuie (1712-76) was for many years Commissary of Dumfries and Sheriff-Depute of the County, and was responsible for the defence of Nithsdale from the Jacobite troops during the Rebellion of 1745. By his wife, Jean Corrie of Speddoch, he had a large family. His fifth son, Thomas Goldie (1748-1823) succeeded him as Commissary and was, after Provost David Staig, one of the most influential men in Dumfries at the end of the 18th century. He married Helen, daughter of Hugh Lawson of **Girthead.** Thomas Goldie had five daughters, one of whom, Jane Goldie, endowed Goldie Park in Maxwelltown.

Thomas Goldie and Burns were politically poles apart, the Commissary being a high Tory and President of the Loyal Natives following the outbreak of war with France in 1793. He was the subject of one of the Dumfries epigrams (C.W. p.533) 'Immediate extempore on being told by W.L. of the Customs Dublin that Com. Goldie did not seem disposed to push the bottle.' according to Syme's annotation.

CRAIGS   NX 994 746

Formerly an estate and house, about a mile southeast of Dumfries on the Infirmary road, but now swallowed up by the Georgetown housing development. It was the property of James McNeil (1765-1832) whose father of the same name was the oldest man in Dumfries (1735-1836). James Junior was born at Royal Oak, a cottage on the edge of Lochar Moss which took its name from the large oak-tree that formerly stood in its garden. The suburb of Gasstown developed around this once solitary house. James Junior was regarded as one of the more entrepreneurial spirits in the town at the turn of the century. Possessed of uncommon energy and enterprise, he carried on business as a baker, brewer and banker simultaneously and for a long period with great success. When he purchased Craigs he developed a quarry there. A block of buildings that stood in Dumfries High Street, known as the Turnpike, was constructed of stone from Craigs quarry, but was demolished about 1830. Like Craigs itself, the Turnpike had belonged to Sir Robert Grierson of Lag, the notorious persecutor of the Covenanters. In his declining years Old Lag had become so gross that when he died, in 1736, the bedroom window had to be knocked out so that his corpse could be lowered to the ground. McNeil not only lived in the Turnpike but actually occupied the room which had been Lag's — a matter of awe to the superstitious citizenry. McNeil's banking enterprise, however, collapsed spectacularly, his loss amounting to about £20,000. His unmarried sister kept house for him and used to recall that her brother was a close friend of Burns. 'She aye kend richt weel when her brother had been spending his nichts wi the poet.'

CRAWICK FORGE   NS 775 109

A smithy in the hamlet of Crawick, beside the B740 near its junction with the A76 a mile northwest of **Sanquhar.** In the 1780s the blacksmith was John Rigg (1750-1833), a native of Dalston in Cumbria, whose main employment came from the manufacture of machinery for the mines at **Wanlockhead.** He was also a close friend of Burns and furnished the necessary 'graith' (tools) for **Ellisland** when the poet took up farming there in 1788.

CREE   NX 41 65

A river of Galloway, issuing from Loch Moan 675 feet above sea level on the boundary between Ayrshire and Kirkcudbrightshire. Thence it winds 11 miles southwest along that boundary, then flows southeast for 21 miles along the boundary between Kirkcudbrightshire and Wigtownshire, till at Creetown it falls into the head of Wigtown Bay. Through most of its lower courses it flows through flat, flowery meadows, its banks being only occasionally adorned with heathery knolls and fern-clad rocks. The 'crystal Cree' inspired Lady Elizabeth Heron (1745-1811) to compose the beautiful melody entitled 'The Banks of Cree' which she sent to Burns. He wrote the song 'Here is the Glen' (C.W. p.513) which he sent to Lady Heron from Dumfries on 3rd April 1794, saying 'The inclosed, I am afraid, will not be found in any degree worthy of the charming melody'. A month later he sent the song to George Thomson, saying how he had 'got an air, pretty enough' from Lady Heron. 'Cree is a beautiful romantic stream; and as her Ladyship is a particular friend of mine, I have written the following song to it.' Unfortunately, he also added 'The air I fear is not worth your while, else I would send it you'. Thomson did not like 'Banks of Cree' and published 'Here is the Glen' in 1798, two years after the poet's death, to the tune 'Flowers of Edinburgh'.

RIVER CREE, NEWTON STEWART

CREEHEAD   NX 343 859

A cottage in Glentrool Forest on the western side of Loch Moan, where the River Cree has its beginning, about 19 miles west of New Galloway. It was here, in 1764, that Robert Heron, Burns's first biographer was born, the son of a handloom weaver. After studying at Edinburgh University he obtained his theological licence in 1789, but was never ordained. Instead, he became a professional journalist and all-round hack. Later he was to record his impressions of the reception accorded to the Kilmarnock Edition when it was published in July 1786: 'Old and young, high and low, grave and gay, learned or ignorant, all were alike delighted, agitated, transported. I was at that time resident in New Galloway, contiguous to Ayrshire.' From this it is evident that, by 'New Galloway', Heron meant not the present village, but that extensive upland portion of the Stewartry to the northwest. He remembered 'how that even plough-boys and maid-servants would have gladly bestowed the wages which they earned the most hardly, and which they wanted to purchase necessary clothing, if they might but procure the works of Burns.'

Heron first met the poet at the house of Dr Blacklock in Edinburgh, when Heron was working as assistant to Hugh Blair. In the autumn of 1789 Heron called on Burns at **Ellisland,** while on his way to or from New Galloway. Burns gave him a letter to deliver to Blacklock but Heron forgot about it — a mistake which Burns referred to in his verse epistle to Dr Blacklock, sent on 21st October that year (C.W. pp. 370-2):

> The Ill-Thief blaw the Heron south,
> And never drink be near his drouth!
> He tauld mysel by word o mouth
>   He'd tak my letter;

I lippen'd to the chiel in trowth,
          And bade nae better.
But aiblins, honest Master Heron
Had, at the time, some dainty fair one
To ware his theologic care on.
          And holy study,
And, tired o sauls to waste his lear on,
          E'en tried the body.

This was a sly dig at Heron's theological ambitions, flawed by his falling for the temptations of the flesh. Heron himself frankly admitted as much in the *Journal of My Conduct*, which he kept between 1789 and 1798. The entry for 6th August 1791 reads: 'Mr Grierson dined with me and drank tea. He, Mr Bradefute and Mr Burns supped. Left me at eleven.' Unfortunately, as William Grierson did not begin his own famous diary till 1794, we do not have his version of the meeting.

Heron's *Memoir of the Life of the Late Robert Burns* was first serialised in *The Monthly Magazine* in 1796 and republished as a separate book the following year. Although it contained some shrewd comments on the poet's achievements its chief aim appears to have been the none too subtle assassination of Burns's character. Of Burns's Edinburgh sojourn, for example, he wrote: 'Too many of his hours were now spent at the tables of persons who delighted to urge conviviality to drunkenness, in the tavern, in the brothel, on the lap of the woman of pleasure...' and much, much more in similar vein. It is now suspected that Heron was in the pay of Henry Dundas, then Home Secretary in the Pitt administration and for thirty years the most powerful man in Scotland. Dundas was impeached for misappropriation of public funds when the Whigs briefly came to power (1806). Heron, the sanctimonious humbug, died the following year, a drunkard and a bankrupt, having been removed from Newgate Jail merely to die in St Pancras Hospital, London. Ironically he would now be completely forgotten but for his sinister role in Burns biography.

CRIFFEL   NX 957 629

A conical hill (1868 feet) two miles south of New Abbey, Nithsdale, on the west side of the **Nith** estuary. The summit may be approached by footpaths from Lochhill and Roadside on the A710 about half a mile and two miles respectively south of the village. From 'huge Criffel's hoary top', as Wordsworth described it, one commands a splendid view of the Solway basin, the mountains of Cumbria and even glimpses of Arran, Ireland and the Isle of Man on a clear day. Thomas the Rhymer prophesied that 'in the evil day coming safety shall nowhere be found except atweeen Criffel and the sea'. Perhaps Burns was mindful of this when he wrote his patriotic song 'Does Haughty Gaul Invasion Threat?' (C.W. p.537) about March 1795 when it was rumoured that Napoleon was planning to invade Britain:

          The Nith shall run to Corsincon,
             And Criffel sink in Solway,
          Ere we permit a foreign foe
             On British ground to rally!

Corsincon is a similarly conical hill in New Cumnock parish, Ayrshire and for the River Nith to run to it would have meant a reversal of the current.

CROSSFORD   NX 833 889

A farm in Glencairn parish, Nithsdale, north of the B729 on the east bank of the Cairn Water, about a mile and a half southeast of Kirkland. **Maxwelton** lies a mile to the northwest. According to *The Annals of Glencairn*, Burns frequently visited this farm on Excise duty.

## DALGARNOCK	NX 876 953

A hamlet on the east bank of the **Nith,** where **Thornhill** now stands. It was the site of a cattle market from medieval times, and is referred to in 'The Braw Wooer' (C.W. p.555). The town of Thornhill was originally known as New Dalgarno.

## DALGONAR	NX 863 849

A farm in Dunscore parish, half a mile northwest of the village of Dunscore on the north side of the B729. It was the home of James Grierson, whom Burns knew when he lived at **Ellisland.** Grierson, a descendant of the infamous Sir Robert Grierson of Lag, persecutor of the Covenanters during the Killing Times of the late 17th century, was one of the earliest collectors of Burnsiana, a hobby which he is said to have commenced about 1805. In fact, Grierson had been an avid collector of Burns material during the poet's lifetime and many of the snippets of information concerning Burns originated with him. It is to Grierson, for example, that we are indebted for the statement that James Smith, the poet's friend, had emigrated to St Lucia in the West Indies and died there. Grierson is also the source of the so-called 'Selkirk Grace' (C.W. p.408) which he claimed to have taken down verbatim at the dinner given by the Earl of Selkirk at **St Mary's Isle,** when Burns and Syme paid a visit there late in July 1793.

Grierson's version of the grace was written down in Standard English, which is presumably how Burns rendered it extempore on that occasion. The vernacular version, which is so widely used nowadays, did not appear in print until almost a century after Burns's death. Even Grierson's provenance for the grace has been questioned by many scholars, which explains why the words — in English or Lallans — are so often omitted from editions of the poet's works.

## DALSWINTON	NX 943 843

An estate in Kirkmahoe parish, Nithsdale, about seven miles northwest of Dumfries and about a mile southeast of the village of the same name. The estate lies between the Dalswinton-Kirkton road and the east bank of the River Nith opposite **Ellisland** which originally formed part of the estate. This elegant and commodious mansion was erected by Patrick Miller (1731-1815) on the site of an ancient castle of the Comyn family. Miller was the son of William Miller of Glenlee and brother of Sir Thomas Miller, President of the Court of Session. He went to sea as a boy and from this acquired a lifelong interest in all things maritime. He entered the world of commerce and in 1767 was made a director of the Bank of Scotland. In 1785 he purchased Dalswinton and left an interesting account of this, which he wrote in 1812: 'When I purchased this estate... I had not seen it. It was in the most miserable state of exhaustion and all the tenants in poverty. When I went to view my purchase, I was so much disgusted for eight to ten days that I never meant to return to this county.'

Miller, however, was an agricultural improver, inventing a drill plough and a threshing machine of improved pattern, as well as making several innovations in the rearing and feeding of cattle. It is as a pioneer of steam navigation, however, that he is best remembered. His first essay in this medium was a catamaran powered by hand-cranked paddles, but later he went on to devise the world's first practical steamboat, a twin-hulled vessel whose steam engine was built by William Symington, then a mining engineer at **Wanlockhead.** The maiden voyage took place on 14th October 1788 on Dalswinton Loch and 'afforded great pleasure to the spectators'. Popular tradition maintains that Burns himself was on the deck during that historic first voyage, but unfortunately this is not supported by the facts.

Burns first made Miller's acquaintance in Edinburgh in December 1786. Miller was an admirer of the Kilmarnock Edition, and left ten guineas for the poet at Sibbald's bookshop. Burns was invited to Miller's town house on 12th December and drank a glass of claret with him, as he recounted in a letter to John Ballantine the following day (C.L. p.99). On 14th January 1787 he wrote to the same correspondent about his generous friend, Mr Peter *(sic)* Miller who had 'been talking with me about the lease of some farm or other in an estate called Dasswinton *(sic)* which he has lately bought near Dumfries.' Even at that early stage Burns had certain misgivings about returning to the farming life. 'Mr Miller is no Judge of land; and though I dare say he means to favour me, yet he may give me, in his opinion, an advantageous bargain that may ruin me.'

DALSWINTON HOUSE

In September 1787 Burns took Miller up on his offer, and the following month wrote again on the subject. It was not until the spring of 1788 that he was able to inspect the farm, in the company of John Tennant of Glenconner who advised him to accept it. Burns took possession on 25th May 1788 but the erection of the farmhouse took about a year and caused Burns many a headache. The buildings were put up by Alexander Crombie, a stone-mason who resided in the hamlet which was developed into Dalswinton village by Patrick Miller in 1790. Doubtless Crombie played a prominent part in the erection of the cottages. The work of building Ellisland was supervised by Thomas Boyd, with whom Burns settled accounts in June 1791 by getting Boyd to take a bill of Crombie's to Burns for £20. 'Mr Crombie cannot take it amiss that I endeavour to get myself clear of his bill in this manner, as you owe him and I owe you'. By accommodating Crombie, however, Burns had run into financial embarrassment with James Gracie of the Dumfries Commercial Bank, the subject of a letter written by Burns to his banker about April 1791 (C.L. p.582).

Regarding Burns's involvement in the Dalswinton steamboat experiment it is highly significant that he mentioned it neither in any letter nor in any poem. An eye-witness of the occasion was Hugh Paisley, interviewed in 1854 when he was aged 76. Paisley deponed that a great number of people gathered on the shores of the loch to watch the fun and mentioned that Burns was there with Sandy Crombie. It seems plausible that Burns would take an hour from his harvesting and Crombie from his building and that the pair of them should go together to see an event which must have been the talk of that quiet countryside.

James Cleland (1825) published a list of these actually aboard the vessel and stated that they consisted of Mr and Mrs Miller, the Rev. Archibald and Mrs Lawson, Captain Grose and Robert Riddell of Glenriddell. William Aitken (1851) published a list which stated that Miller was accompanied by Henry Cockburn (later Lord Brougham), Robert Burns and Alexander Nasmyth the artist. As Aitken had had access to the Miller family papers his statement was accepted without question; but in 1865 Lord Brougham categorically denied that he had been with Burns at Dalswinton on that day. He was only nine or ten years old at the time, and never visited Dalswinton until ten or eleven years later, and after the death of Burns. Despite this, the *canard* of Burns and Lord Brougham being present has continued to be widely accepted to this day. Burns's presence on board was first seriously questioned in 1876 by Dr Crauford Tait Ramage who challenged a recent statement to that effect by Sir James Picton. Picton's only defence was to say that he had read it in Samuel Smiles's *Lives of Boulton and Watt* (1865), adding lamely 'Mr Smiles is usually so accurate in the information he furnishes that there can be no doubt he has had sufficient ground for the statement.'

The story was further confused by James Nasmyth, the engineer and son of Alexander Nasmyth, who published his *Autobiography* in 1883. James Nasmyth stated therein that the persons on board had been Patrick Miller, William Symington, Sir William Monteith, Robert Burns, William Taylor and Alexander Nasmyth, adding that Henry Brougham, then on a visit to Dalswinton, was on the edge of the loch. Thus the Brougham story was repeated eighteen years after Brougham had repudiated it. The list contained several obvious errors. 'Sir William Monteith' was an error for Charles G. Stuart Monteath of **Closeburn Castle** who wrote in 1834 that he was old enough to have seen the first steamboat, but would surely have mentioned the fact had he been a passenger. Alexander Nasmyth, best remembered for his portrait of Burns, also stated in 1834 that he had witnessed steamboat trials on the Firth of Forth 'about the year 1787' (which is patently untrue), but of the Dalswinton experiment he merely commented that it had succeeded to Mr Miller's wish. Significantly, for a man who was never slow to publicise himself, he makes no mention of having been at Dalswinton on that historic occasion, far less been on board the vessel. Equally inconclusive is the drawing of the loch and steamboat, alleged to have been made by Nasmyth at or soon after the event, subsequently engraved and much published ever since. The figures shown on the deck are too small and indistinct for positive identification to be made. As Elizabeth Ewing has said *(Burns Chronicle, 1941)* 'No clear evidence has been produced to show that Burns was on board the boat; and there is much to suggest, by implication or omission, that he was not.'

For many years it was not known whether Burns was even in Dumfriesshire on that fateful day, but in 1921 a letter from Burns to Jean Armour was discovered. This letter (C.L. p.478) was written at **Ellisland** on 14th October 1788 — the very day of the steamboat trial. The letter itself is disappointing, insofar as it was confined to purely domestic matters and made no mention of the event that heralded in the Age of Steam.

The laird of Dalswinton's heir, Patrick Miller Jr. (1769-1845) retired from the Army in 1790 with the rank of captain and entered politics. With the aid of the Duke of Queensberry he was elected to Parliament as Member for the Dumfriesshire Burghs — the Five Carlins of Burns's poem (C.W. p.364) in which young Miller was described:

> Then neist came in a sodger-boy,
> Wha spak wi modest grace,
> And he wad gae to Lon'on town,
> If sae their pleasure was.

In the 'Election Ballad' composed at the close of that election and addressed to Robert Graham of Fintry (C.W. pp.402-6) the winning candidate is referred to in the lines:

> Miller brought up th'artillery ranks,
> The many-pounders of the Banks,
> Resistless desolation!

A punning reference to Captain Miller's brief military career and his father's connections with the Bank of Scotland.

Writing to Graham of Fintry on 9th December 1789 (C.L. pp.431-3) Burns described Captain Miller as 'a youth by no means above mediocrity in his abilities; and is said to have a huckster-lust for shillings, pence & farthings. — This is the more remarkable as his father's abilities & benevolence are so justly celebrated.' A lengthy description of the actual election proceedings was given in a letter to Mrs Dunlop (C.L. p.189) on 9th July 1790. In fairness to Captain Miller, it should be added that it was through his intercession that Perry of the *London Morning Chronicle* offered Burns a position on the paper's staff in 1794. Burns wrote to Miller in March 1794 declining the offer (C.L. p.699) on the grounds that he had family responsibilities and dared not place his Excise commission in jeopardy by making his political sentiments public, although he did submit several of his works, including 'Scots Wha Hae' to Miller with a view to having them published anonymously.

Burns also wrote a letter to Mrs Patrick Miller on 2nd November 1789 (C.L. p.245) enclosing verses on Captain Grose (C.W. p.373) and a political ballad (C.W. p.367) about Sir James Johnstone but really attacking the Duke of Queensberry. Sir James was the candidate who lost to Captain Miller. Janet Miller, eldest daughter and third child of Patrick Miller, was also the recipient of a letter from Burns on 9th September 1793 (C.L. p.245) enclosing the song 'Where Are the Joys?' (C.W. p.504) and saying that he had taken the liberty of making her the heroine. Major William Miller, second son of Patrick Miller, settled in Dumfriesshire after serving in the Royal Horse Guards, and married Jessie Staig, daughter of the Provost of Dumfries. 'The Keekin Glass' (C.W. p.362) is said to have been written on the back of a letter at Dalswinton about 1789, on hearing that a drunken judge on the Dumfries bench had pointed to one of Patrick Miller's beautiful daughters and — his vision 'much affected' — asked, 'Wha's yon howlet-faced thing in the corner?'

DALVEEN PASS   NS 90 07
A wild pass (1200 feet) through the Lowther Hills from the headstream of Powtrail Water in Crawford parish, Lanarkshire, to those of Carron Water in Durisdeer parish, Upper Nithsdale. The pass extends about four miles between steep hills, the modern A702 adhering fairly closely to the line of the original toll road. Known locally as 'the lang glen' it appears thus in the opening line of 'The Braw Wooer' (C.W. p.555), which Burns sent to George Thomson on 3rd July 1795.

DINNING   NX 893 899
A farm in Closeburn parish, Nithsdale, two miles south of **Closeburn** on a minor road between the River Nith and the A76. A medieval motte and bailey lie to the north of the farmhouse. Dinning lies about five miles north of **Ellisland**. In 1791 Gilbert Burns, brother of the poet, married Jean Breckenridge of Kilmarnock and removed from Mossgiel to Dinning in 1798 where he spent two years. On getting a better offer from Captain Dunlop (son of Mrs Frances Dunlop of Dunlop) in 1800 he moved to Morham West Mains, near Haddington, East Lothian, as farm-manager. As the lease on Dinning had not expired, it was transferred to John Begg, husband of Isabella Burns, the poet's sister. During his tenancy of Dinning, Gilbert Burns introduced the Ayrshire system of dairy-farming, making excellent cheese. The poet's widowed mother lived at Dinning with Gilbert until the move to Morham. Kirsty and William Flint had a house at Dinning after moving from **Closeburn** on their marriage.

DRUMLANRIG   NX 852 993
A seat of the Duke of Buccleuch and Queensberry in Durisdeer parish, Nithsdale, 17 miles northwest of Dumfries, on the right bank of the Nith about half a mile west of the A76 just north of the village of Carronbridge. The castle was built in 1679-89 by William, first Duke of Queensberry who spent a fortune on its construction, yet only spent one night in it and left in disgust when

he could not get medical attention for a temporary ailment. Afterwards he endorsed the bills for the castle's erection with the words 'The Deil pike out his een wha looks herein!' The fourth Duke was William, third Earl of March (1724-1810), who succeeded in 1786 on the death of his cousin. A notorious hell-rake, gambler and patron of the turf, he was familiarly though unfavourably known in contemporary memoirs and gossip columns as 'Old Q'. He was Lord of the Bedchamber to King George III from 1760 till 1789, but was dismissed for backing the Prince of Wales in the Regency controversy. He died unmarried in 1810, despite a numerous illegitimate progeny and his titles were then dispersed. The dukedom, together with Drumlanrig, passed to the third Duke of Buccleuch.

DRUMLANRIG CASTLE

Burns wrote a very fulsome letter to the Duke from **Ellisland** on 24th September 1791 (C.L. p.589). A copy of it appears in the Glenriddell MS with the annotation: 'This was written shortly after I had the honor of being introduced to the Duke, at which introduction I spent the evening with him, when he treated me with the most distinguished politeness, & marked attention. — Though I am afraid his Grace's character as a Man of worth is very equivocal, yet he certainly is a Nobleman of the first taste, & a Gentleman of the first manners.'

The poet expressed much stronger feelings against 'Drumlanrig's haughty Grace' when he lampooned him in the 'Election Ballad' at the close of the contest for representing the Dumfries Burghs in 1790 (C.W. pp.4026). Burns alludes to the Duke deserting the King in favour of the Prince of Wales. Thus, in 'Election Ballad for Westerha' (C.W. p.367) he wrote:

> The Laddies by the banks o Nith
> Wad trust his Grace wi a', Jamie;
> But he'll sair them, as he sair'd the King   serve
> Turn tail and rin awa, Jamie.

Burns wrote to Graham of Fintry on 9th December 1789 (C.W. pp.431-3) at great length concerning the forthcoming election. The Duke was contemptuously dismissed with the lines: 'The Great Man here, like all Renegadoes, is a flaming Zealot. — Kicked out before the astonished indignation of his deserted Master, and despised I suppose by the Party who took him in to be a mustering faggot at the mysterious orgies of their midnight iniquities, and a useful drudge in the dirty work of their Country Elections, he would fain persuade this part of the world that he is turned Patriot... Were you to know his sins, as well of Omission as Commission to this outraged land, you would club your curse with the execrating voice of the Country.'

Having squandered his patrimony, the Duke felled the woodlands around Drumlanrig and Neidpath (his Peeblesshire estate) to raise money as a dowry for Maria Fagniani (whom he believed to be his daughter) to provide a dowry when she married the Earl of Yarmouth. George Selwyn also left this lady a fortune in the belief that she was *his* daughter! The wholesale despoliation of the castle policies in such a dubious cause incurred the anger of Burns. There persists a local tradition that Burns inscribed some verses on the destruction of the woods on the back of a window-shutter in an inn or toll-house in the vicinity, ending:

> The worm that gnawed my bonny trees,
> That reptile wears a ducal crown.

But J.C. Ewing *(Burns Chronicle,* 1919) showed that the verses had been composed by Henry Mackenzie as a Burnsian pastiche. He confessed in a letter to Dr James Currie in 1802 that he had invented the tale of the inscription on the window shutter. William Wordsworth visited the denuded policies of Drumlanrig in 1803 and lamented their destruction at greater poetic length.

The fourth Duke of Queensberry seldom stayed at Drumlanrig and after his chamberlain, John McMurdo, retired in 1797 the castle was unoccupied and in an increasingly dilapidated condition until 1827 when the fifth Duke began its restoration on the attainment of his majority. John McMurdo (1743-1803) succeeded his father as chamberlain in 1780 and lived with his large family in the castle itself. Burns first met McMurdo in the summer of 1788, when he was settling in at **Ellisland.** Between November of that year and 1793 McMurdo was the recipient of at least eight letters from the poet (C.L. pp.492-5), the most important being the fourth, written from Dumfries about February 1792 to accompany Burns's collection of bawdy ballads. Burns also transcribed a number of his poems for McMurdo. He married Jane Blair (1749-1836), daughter of the Provost of Dumfries. The couple were mentioned in the 'Election Ballad' of 1790 (C.W. p.404):

> M'Murdo and his lovely spouse
> (Th'enamour'd laurels kiss her brows!)
> Led on the Loves and Graces:
> She won each gaping burgess' heart,
> While he, sub rosa, played his part
> Among their wives and lasses.

Mrs McMurdo received a letter from Burns on 2nd May 1789 (C.L. p.529) thanking her for her hospitality and enclosing a poem, probably 'To John McMurdo, Esq., of Drumlanrig' (C.W. p.356). Burns composed 'To the Woodlark' (C.W. p.550) at her request. Her sister Rebecca was the wife of Colonel De Peyster, commandant of the Dumfries Volunteers. The McMurdos had seven sons and seven daughters, and one of his grandsons was Vice Admiral Archibald McMurdo of Cargenholm, near Dumfries, after whom McMurdo Sound in Antarctica was named. Burns inscribed the following lines on a window-pane in the chamberlain's quarters at Drumlanrig (C.W. p.356):

> Blest be McMurdo to his latest day!
> No envious cloud o'ercast his evening ray -
> No wrinkle furrow'd by the hand of care,
> Nor ever sorrow add one silver hair.
> O may no son the father's honour stain,
> Nor ever daughter give the mother pain.

The poet's fervent hopes seem to have been abundantly fulfilled. John McMurdo was also the recipient of a brief verse epistle (C.W. p.356) beginning 'O, could I give thee India's wealth'.

The eldest daughter Jean (1777-1839) and her sister Philadelphia (1779-1825) were taught to play the piano by Burns's friend Stephen Clarke, whom he persuaded to come down from Edinburgh. Jean Armour sang an old song which Clarke transcribed and taught to the McMurdo girls, and as a compliment to Miss McMurdo — and possibly also his own wife — Burns composed the lyrics of 'Bonie Jean' (C.W. p.493) Burns sent part of the song, together with Clarke's manuscript of the music, to Thomson in April 1793 giving the background circumstances to both words and music (C.L. p.631). Thomson, however, rejected Clarke's 'beautiful little air' which has sadly been lost to posterity. A copy of the song was sent to Jean McMurdo with a letter in July 1793 (C.L. p.693).

Philadelphia, more familiarly known as Phillis, was a noted beauty and inspired several of Burns's songs: 'Phillis the Fair' (C.W. p.495), 'Philly and Willy' 'C.W.p.529' and 'Adown Winding Nith' (C.W. p.497):

> Adown winding Nith I did wander,
> Of Phillis to muse and to sing.

In 1793 John McMurdo purchased **Hardriggs** near **Annan** as an investment, but also had a town house in Dumfries where he took a keen interest in municipal politics and was Provost the following year, although he did not actually retire from his position as chamberlain at Drumlanrig until 1797. The McMurdos were an old Nithsdale family, well-connected by marriage with many county families, such as Charteris of Amisfield, the Sharpes of **Hoddam** and the Duncans of Torthorwald and **Lochrutton**. Through the last-named, therefore, they were related to both the Rev. Dr Henry Duncan, minister of **Ruthwell** and Dr James Currie, the poet's editor and biographer. Towards the end of his life John McMurdo moved to **Mavis Grove** on the western outskirts of Dumfries.

DRUNGANS LODGE   NX 952 749

A lodge situated on the northeast south side of the minor road, known as Garroch Loaning, linking the A711 at Cargenbridge with the A75 main road west of Dumfries in Troqueer parish. It was the home of Robert McMurdo, father of John McMurdo of **Drumlanrig**. Deborah Duff Davies, the petite beauty related to the Riddell family, was residing at Drungans Lodge in 1791 when Burns first wrote to her (C.L. p.590) saying that Robert Riddell 'my very worthy neighbour' had told her that Burns had made her the subject of some verses. Miss Davies replied from Drungans on 10th October 1791 saying that she was 'vain of the poem addressed' to her, but going on to speak of its 'Jacobite sentiments'. This would suggest that either 'Lovely Davies' (C.W. p.422) was not the poem enclosed, or that her comment dealt with another poem. Miss Davies was one of those heroines whom Burns placed on a very high pedestal and, for the most part, the three extant letters written to her are in his most artificial and high-flown style. On 6th April 1793 he wrote to her, enclosing 'Wee Thing' (C.W. p.446), one of his most pompous letters (C.L. pp.591-2). A brief letter, written two months later to accompany 'Blythe hae I been on yon hill' (C.W. p.490) was more revealing: 'By the bye, I am a great deal luckier than most poets. When I sing Miss Davies or Miss Lesley Baillie, I have only to feign the passion — the charms are real.'

Writing to Mrs Dunlop in June 1793 (C.L. p.205), Burns enclosed his extempore lines 'on being asked why God had made Miss Davies so little, and Mrs S--- so big' (C.W. p.491):

> Ask why God made the gem so small,
> And why so huge the granite?
> Because God meant mankind should set
> That higher value on it.

He added, by way of explanation, Miss D--- you must know, is positively the least creature ever I saw, to be at the same time unexceptionably, & indeed uncommonly, handsome & beautiful; & besides has the facility to be a peculiar favorite of mine. — On the contrary, Mrs S--- is a huge, bony, masculine, cowp-carl, horse-godmother, he-termagent of a six-foot figure, who might have been bride to Og, king of Bashan or Goliath of Gath.'

Mercifully, the identity of 'Mrs S' has never been revealed.

DRUNGANS LODGE

DUMBRETTON   NY 216 714

A farm in **Annan** parish, along an unclassified road a few hundred metres west of the B722, about 2 miles north of Annan, and a mile and a half southwest of Kirtlebridge. It was here, in 1744, that William Nicol was born, the son of a tailor of **Ecclefechan**. His father died when he was a child and he received most of his education from an itinerant teacher named John Orr.

While a teenager, Nicol opened a school in his mother's house, although later he rounded off his own education at Annan Academy and Edinburgh University. At Edinburgh he switched courses, from divinity to medicine, but in the end became classics master at Edinburgh High School (1774). He remained there until 1795 when he quarrelled with the Rector, Dr Alexander Adam, and left to found a school of his own, which he conducted till his death two years later. An irascible man, and something of a classroom tyrant, Nicol nevertheless had his more amiable moments.

It is not known when or where Burns first encountered him; Nicol was hardly the convivial, social being which one tends to associate with Burns. Yet they were on sufficiently intimate terms for Nicol to be the recipient of a letter written by Burns during his Border Tour (C.L. pp.342-3), addressed to 'Kind, honest-hearted Willie'. This letter, written at Carlisle on 1st June 1787 — 'or I believe the 39th o' May rather', is the only prose epistle by Burns in the vernacular. Nicol accompanied Burns on his Highland Tour in August-September 1787, but their friendship was sorely strained by Nicol's tiresome and unreasonable behaviour. Burns bore Nicol's tantrums with considerable equanimity, even though he was acutely embarrassed at times. Some laconic entries in the journal of the Highland Tour, and the apologetic letter to James Hoy (C.L. p.361) give some idea of the strain on the relationship. Nevertheless, Burns and Nicol remained on fairly good terms, to judge by the sporadic correspondence which continued until 1793, if not later. The poet named his second surviving son William Nicol in 1791, telling George Thomson in May 1795 (C.L. p.674) of 'that propensity to witty wickedness and manfu' mischief which even at twa days auld I foresaw would form the striking features of his disposition.'

When Burns was at **Ellisland** Nicol lent him an old bay mare, Peg Nicholson (named after the poor, demented, would-be assassin of King George III in 1776). Burns made many attempts to sell the horse on Nicol's behalf but she was too old and infirm. The mare died in February 1790, and Burns wrote to her erstwhile owner (C.L. p.346) to break the sad news and enclosed the elegy 'Peg Nicholson was a Good Bay Mare' (C.W. p.380).

DUMCRIEFF   NT 102 O36

A handsome mansion, with finely wooded grounds, in Moffat parish, on the right bank of the Moffat Water, 2 miles southeast of **Moffat**. Originally owned by the Murray family, it was the residence of Sir George Clerk (grandfather of the famous physicist Clerk Maxwell) and then, about 1785, John Loudon Macadam of road-making fame. Dr James Currie (1756-1805), the first editor and biographer of Burns, possessed it in the closing decade of the 18th century and sold it a few months before his death to Dr Rogerson, who had been court physician at St Petersburg for almost half a century. Currie purchased the estate on 2nd June 1792 from Colonel William Johnstone who had previously leased it to Macadam. It is thought that Currie spent very little time at Dumcrieff and, indeed, he appears to have almost immediately leased it back to Colonel Johnstone.

It may have been in 1792 that Currie met Burns on one brief occasion, in Dumfries. The following year Currie published an open letter to the Prime Minister, William Pitt, urging him not to embark on war with France.

Although the letter was published under the pseudonym of John Wilson, Currie was in mortal fear of discovery and consequent prosecution under the repressive laws of sedition at the time. He offered Dumcrieff as security for the loan of £1200 from the executors of Theodore Edgars — a sum which Currie deemed sufficient to make good his escape from Britain should his rash political act rebound on him. John Syme, a friend of Currie since their schooldays, was factor for Currie's estate. An advertisement in February 1799, offering growing timber at Dumcrieff for sale, gave Syme's address (the Stamp Office, Dumfries). It has been claimed that Jean Lorimer met Whelpdale, her worthless suitor, at a ball in Dumcrieff given early in 1793 by Colonel Johnstone.

DUMFRIES   NX 97 76

Formerly county town of Dumfriesshire and now the administrative capital of Nithsdale district and Dumfries and Galloway region. A royal burgh since 1186, in the time of Burns it joined with the four other Dumfriesshire burghs in returning a Member to Parliament and, as such, was:

> Maggie by the banks o Nith,
> A dame wi pride eneugh,

in 'The Five Carlins' (C.W. pp.364-6). **Maxwelltown** on the west bank of the Nith, was a separate burgh until 1929 (though included in the parliamentary burgh). A seaport (of no importance after the advent of the railways), market and manufacturing town in Burns's day, it remains the metropolis for the southwest of Scotland to this day. It lies along the **Nith** at that point where it can be bridged, while it was formerly navigable as far as the Caul or weir. The 'mim-mou'd Meg o Nith' has also been dubbed the Queen of the South - 'the cynosure of the south-western counties'. Certainly it has always ranked as the most important place between Ayr and Carlisle or between the Irish Sea and the Lowther Hills. A stone bridge with nine arches (later reduced to six) was erected by Devorgilla, mother of John Baliol, in the 13th century and stands to this day. A bridge suitable for carriages was erected between 1790 and 1795 higher up the river. The subsequent development of Buccleuch and Castle Streets at the close of the 18th and beginning of the 19th centuries shifted the emphasis of the town away from the High Street.

The name is a corruption of the Gaelic *Dun Phreas* 'mound covered by a copse' or 'hill-fort among shrubs'. The slight knoll now occupied by Greyfriars Church was the site of an ancient fort and later a castle. The town motto — 'A Loreburn' was used as a war-cry to rally the townspeople to the Lore or Lower Burn, the stream which formed a natural obstacle to English invaders. A village developed around the fort by the 10th century and gradually grew into a town in the 12th century. A Minorite or Greyfriars' monastery was situated near the head of Friars' Vennel. In 1286 Robert Bruce the Competitor and his son, the Earl of Carrick, captured the castle. The Competitor's grandson, Robert Bruce, halted at Dumfries on 4th February 1306 on his way north from London and met his rival, the Red Comyn, in the church of the Minorites. The men came to blows and Bruce stabbed Comyn. Bruce rushed out of the church crying to his friends 'I doubt I have slain the Red Comyn'. To this Kirkpatrick of **Closeburn** made his famous retort, 'Doubt! I mak siccar!' and with Sir John de Lindsay he rushed into the church and finished off the wounded man. A frenzy seized them and they made a desperate assault on the fortifications at **Castledykes.** This minor victory was, in fact, the first act in the War of Independence. The town was burned by the English before 1448, ravaged by them at many other periods, and razed to the ground in 1536 (for which Lord Maxwell burned Penrith in revenge). Dumfries favoured the Lords of the Congregation against Mary Queen of Scots who retaliated by attacking it in 1565. In 1570 the town was sacked by the English under Lord Scrope and the Earl of Essex.

During the turbulent religious wars of the 17th century Dumfries had its fair share of troubles. The Covenanters occupied the town in November 1666, but in the ensuing generation several adherents of the Covenant were executed on the Whitesands. In 1706 the Cameronians (those Covenanters who resisted the settlement at the Revolution in 1688-9) staged a violent demonstration against the impending Act of Union. Dumfries withstood the Jacobites in 1715 but suffered occupation by the army of Bonnie Prince Charlie in 1745, and was plundered by the Highlanders on their retreat north. Since then Dumfries has 'plenteously participated in the benign effects of peace and enlightenment', as one 19th century writer quaintly put it.

Robert Burns first visited Dumfries on 4th June 1787 at the end of his Border Tour and was made a freeman of the burgh. The following year he settled at **Ellisland** and thus began that very close association between the poet and the town which was to endure until his death in 1796 and which has, indeed, continued to this day. Dumfries is broadly stamped with his name, and his term of residence within the burgh (1791-6) flashed on the popular mind so vividly as to have been at once and till the present day regarded as an epoch — 'the time of Burns'. The places in Dumfries associated with Burns far outweigh those in Ayr, Irvine, Kilmarnock, Mauchline, Tarbolton or Edinburgh. In the following pages the places in Dumfries associated with Burns are discussed first, in alphabetical order, and are followed by an alphabetical list of people whose immortality has been assured by their connections — however tenuous — with the poet.

ASSEMBLY ROOMS

A suite of public rooms at the foot of the **George Inn** Close on Irish Street. Dr Burnside (*First Statistical Account*) describes them as elegant assembly rooms 40 by 24 feet in extent, with separate rooms for playing cards and taking tea. Subscription assemblies (i.e. by admission ticket) were held once a fortnight during the winter months. During the spring and autumn court circuits, the fashionable and well-to-do of the county would regularly gather for balls and exhibitions. It was in connection with one of these gala occasions in 1794 that David McCulloch of **Ardwall** made a point of crossing the street to speak to Burns when the 'county set' cut him dead. Later the Assembly Rooms were transferred to George Street and the original premises were used as Gemmill's Academy. The original Assembly Rooms were erected in the first half of the 18th century, and gave their name to Assembly Street, laid out by the Town Council in 1751. It was in this building that Burns obtained his diploma as a member of the Caledonian Hunt in 1792. Here also he took the oath of allegiance on joining the Dumfries Volunteers (28th March 1795) and was elected to the eight-member management committee of the corps (22nd August 1795).

BURNS HOUSE — 11 BANK STREET

Known as Cavarts Vennel or the Wee Vennel in Burns's time, or less flatteringly (though probably more accurately) as the Stinking Vennel, it runs from the High Street to the Whitesands. It takes its modern name from the number of banks which have, or had, their offices on it from the 19th century onwards. On 11th November 1791 the poet and his family moved from **Ellisland** into the town and took up residence in a house on the north side of the street, near the foot. The poet, with his wife Jean and three sons Robert, Francis and William, lived in three small rooms on the second floor. Robert Chambers provided a graphic description of the poet's first home in the burgh: 'The small central room, about the size of a bed-closet, is the only place he has in which to seclude himself for study. On the ground floor immediately underneath, his friend John Syme has his office for the distribution of stamps. Overhead is an honest blacksmith, called George Haugh, whom Burns treats on a familiar footing as a neighbour. On the opposite side of the street is the poet's landlord, Captain Hamilton, a gentleman of fortune and worth, who admires Burns, and often asks him to a family Sunday dinner.' George Haugh died on 28th January 1838, aged 80.

William Hamilton of Allershaw (1734-1813), scion of an ancient Douglasdale (Lanarkshire) family, owned several properties in the town and was also the poet's landlord when he moved to more spacious accommodation in Mill Street (now Burns Street) in May 1793. Hamilton served as a captain in the Dumfries Volunteers. In the severe floods of November 1795 the Vennel was inundated higher up than Hamilton's house.

The house occupied by the Burns family was next door to the **Coach and Horses** tavern. Access to the Burns apartment was through a long, open pend or doorway, then up a narrow spiral stairway. At the rear of the building was a tiny, part-concealed courtyard just large enough to have stabled the poet's pony. One cow, reserved from the roup at **Ellisland**, was driven into town and had to be sold soon afterwards, due to lack of accessible pasture. The period spent in the Wee Vennel was not the happiest in Burns's life. The earliest letter written from here, and which can be definitely dated, was addressed to Agnes McLehose on 23rd November 1791 (C.L. p.407). From this it is revealed that Burns had just fathered a son on Jenny Clow. He had no sooner settled in Dumfries than he had to go to Edinburgh to sort out this embarrassing matter. On top of that, however, an affair with Anna Park of the **Globe Inn** earlier in the year, while Jean Armour was absent in Ayrshire, resulted in the birth of a daughter who was brought into the household as a 'neebor's bairn' and with remarkable tolerance Jean Armour raised the girl, Elizabeth Burns, as if she had been her own daughter. Rather confusingly, Jean's own daughter, born in 1792, was christened Elizabeth Riddell Burns, in honour of the wife of Burns's friend Robert Riddell of Glenriddell. A letter from the poet to Robert Ainslie (C.L. p.339) - undated but attributed to November 1791 — was written in a fit of depression: 'here must I sit, a monument of the vengeance laid up in store for the wicked, slowly counting every chick of the clock as it slowly — slowly, numbers over these lazy scoundrels of hours, who, d---n them, are ranked up before me, every one at his neighbour's backside, and every one with a burden of anguish on his back, to pour on my devoted head — and there is none to pity me. My wife scolds me! my business torments me, and my sins come staring me in the face, every one telling a more bitter tale than his fellow. When I tell you even [bawdry?] has lost its power to please, you will guess something of my hell within, and all around me.'

Whatever its shortcomings, **Ellisland** must have seemed like paradise compared with the miserable little apartment in Dumfries. The street outside was not known as the Stinking Vennel for nothing; it was disgraced by an open sewer which ran down the middle and debouched into the Nith at the foot. Yet it was in this house that Burns commenced his collaboration with George Thomson on *Select Scottish Airs*, mending old ballads and providing new words for them. In addition, some of his best work was composed here, including 'Ae Fond Kiss'. Among the 60 or so poems and songs written during the Wee Vennel period were 'Thou Gloomy December', 'Bonnie Wee Thing', 'Bessie and her Spinning Wheel', 'Highland Mary', 'Ay Waukin O', 'Willie Wastle', 'The Lea Rig', 'Duncan Gray' and 'Galla Water' (C.W. pp.433-81). About 80 letters written by

Burns in this period are extant, demonstrating that this was a very hectic time for him, as poet and exciseman, both socially and domestically.

In the 19th century the Bank Street house, like much of the neighbouring property, became even less salubrious; by the 1950s it was a slum, scheduled for improvement. By 1969 the property was being considered for demolition to make way for public lavatories. It was saved from this ignominious fate by James Urquhart who purchased it, carried out the necessary repairs and eventually had it reconstructed as a dwelling-house with all modern amenities. In 1976 the Burns flat and the storey above were sold to Robert Laird and converted for use as a family home. A plaque inscribed 'Robert Burns the national poet lived in this house with his family on coming to Dumfries from Ellisland' was erected by William Costen Aitken about 1890. A second plaque bearing a portrait of Burns painted by David Ferguson, was erected by James Urquhart in 1971 and reads: ' Here in the Songhouse of Scotland between November 1791 and May 1793 Robert Burns completed over sixty songs...'

Sadly all attempts to restore the first Burns house to its original condition and furnishings came to nothing, despite valiant attempts by Mr Urquhart to interest the Southern Scottish Counties Burns Association, the Burns Federation, the Town Council, Nithsdale District Council, the National Trust for Scotland and the Secretary of State for Scotland in the project. Incidentally, the Burns connection with Bank Street is alluded to in the Rabbie Burns Cafe, next door to the poet's residence.

BURNS HOUSE, BANK STREET

BURNS HOUSE — 24 BURNS STREET

This substantial red sandstone, two-storey dwellinghouse in Millbrae Vennel (later Mill Street) was also owned by John Hamilton of Allershaw. Following the birth of Elizabeth Riddell Burns on 21st November 1792, the accommodation in the Wee Vennel was increasingly cramped, so the move to a larger house was imperative. In February 1792 Burns was promoted to the Dumfries

Port Division of Excise 'worth twenty pounds a year more than any other Division...' His salary was now £70 a year, with £15-20 extra in perquisites, and once the worry over the enquiry into his political conduct had blown over (January 1793) Burns felt that he could afford a larger house. Sadly, the move coincided with the outbreak of war with France which brought foreign imports to a virtual halt and consequently severely affected Excise emoluments.

Burns suffered a sharp drop in income and soon found himself in arrears of rent. Four letters from the poet to Hamilton of Allershaw are extant (C.L. pp.703-4) and deal almost exclusively with this matter. The first letter, dated 24th March 1794, gives a statement of Burns's payment of £5 in cash, together with allowances totalling £2 3s in respect of a quey calf and some furniture. One can imagine the anguish of Burns, a man who fiercely prided himself on his independence, when he wrote to Hamilton about July 1794 'I assure you, Sir, it is with infinite pain that I have transgressed on your goodness', going on to allude to the unfortunate business with Crombie whose bill he had so rashly discounted — 'I had a sum to pay which my very limited income & large family could ill afford'. On 29th January 1795 he managed to repay three guineas and promised to settle all soon: 'I shall not mention your goodness to me: it is beyond my power to describe... the feelings of my wounded soul at not being able to pay you as I ought'. Hamilton hastily replied, asking if he had in any way offended the poet. Burns replied by return (31st January) and we may read between the lines the bitter memories of the humiliation which debt had brought upon his father: 'It is not possible, most worthy Sir, that you can do any thing to offend any body; my backwardness proceeds alone from the abashing consciousness of my obscure situation in the ranks of life. — Many an evening have I sighed to call in & spend it at your social fireside; but a shyness of appearing obtrusive amid the fashionable visitants occasionally there kept me at a distance'.

BURNS HOUSE

The poet's eldest son, Robert Burns Junior, furnished an interesting account of life in the Mill Street house, indicating that the self-contained house, whose rental was £8 a year, was of the kind then occupied by the better class of burgesses: ['My father and mother] always had a maid-servant, and sat in their parlour. That apartment, together with two bedrooms, was well furnished and carpeted; and when good company assembled, which was often the case, the hospitable board which they surrounded was of a patrician mahogany. There was much rough comfort in the house, not to have been found in those of ordinary citizens; for, besides the spoils of smugglers, the poet received many presents of game and country produce from the rural gentlefolk, besides occasional barrels of oysters from Hill, Cunningham, and other friends in town; so that he possibly was as much envied by some of his neighbours, as he has since been pitied by the general body of his countrymen.'

It would appear that Hamilton could have extracted a much higher rent if he had wished. According to Dr Burnside's report for the *Statistical Account*, a house of that size (three rooms and a kitchen) yielded an average annual rental of £10-12 at that time, and attracted a police tax of 9d in the pound for paving and cleaning the streets. Allan Cunningham, then a twelve year-old apprentice stonemason, has left a vivid account of the poet's return to Dumfries after his disastrous visit to the **Brow:** 'The poet returned on the 18th July 1796 in a small spring-cart. The ascent to his house was steep, and the cart stopped at the foot of the Mill-hole Brae: when he alighted he shook much, and stood with difficulty; he seemed unable to stand upright. He stooped as if in pain, and walked tottering towards his own door: his looks were hollow and ghastly, and those who saw him then expected never to see him in life again.'

BURNS'S STUDY

During his last illness, Burns was confined to the room to the south on the upper floor. From his sick-bed he penned those last, heart-rending lines to his father-in-law, James Armour, soon after his return home on 18th July (C.L. p.722): 'Do, for heaven's sake send Mrs Armour here immediately. My wife is hourly expecting to be put to bed. Good God! what a situation for her to be in, poor girl, without a friend!' and concluding, I think and feel that my strength is so gone that the disorder will prove fatal to me.' On the morning of 21st July the poet died in the smaller of the two bedrooms — definitely not the room with the four-poster bed depicted in so many engravings of the Victorian and later periods.

BURNS'S BEDROOM

Jean Armour Burns continued to reside at that house until her own death 38 years later, in March 1834. John Hamilton sold the property to Dr Maxwell, the poet's physician and friend, and he left it to his son. About 1844 it was sold to Mrs Anna Maria Barker of Langshaw whose trustees, in turn, sold it to Colonel William Nicol Burns, third son of the poet, in 1851. It is not known who were the tenants in the eleven years after Jean Armour's death, but in 1845 the house was let to the Managers of the Industrial School for the accommodation of their schoolmaster. In 1858 Colonel Burns signed a Disposition of Trust, expressing the wish that the house be kept in proper repair as an interesting relic connected with his father's memory. The dwelling-house was to be conveyed to some public body of a permanent character. The Dumfries and Maxwelltown Education Society, tenants since 1845, were formally continued in possession from 1851. If, however, the Society ceased to maintain a Ragged School in the burgh the property was to pass to the Dumfries and Galloway Royal Infirmary.

In 1903 the Education Society let the house to the Town Council on a long lease at a rental only sufficient to pay the annuity of £20 to Colonel Burns's two nieces or their heirs. The last recipient of this annuity was Robert Burns Hutchinson, who died in the United States in August 1944. A caretaker was allowed to occupy the entire house, apart from the small bedroom in which Burns had died, which was transformed into a museum containing relics belonging mainly to the Dumfries Burns Club. When the Boys' Home next door was moved outside the burgh boundary in 1932, the Education Society ceased to comply with the terms of Colonel Burns's disposition and the house automatically passed to the Infirmary. The Town Council lease having expired in 1934, the Directors of the Infirmary decided to take over direct responsibility for the house themselves. The caretaker was moved to a house across the street and Burns House itself was restored, as far as possible, to its late-18th century condition. The house, now entirely given over to a museum, was formally re-opened on 25th January 1935 by Miss Jean Armour Burns Brown, granddaughter of Robert Burns Junior and the last surviving descendant of the poet to reside in the burgh.

The burden of maintenance was too much for the Infirmary which successfully negotiated the transfer of responsibility to the Town Council in July 1944. Burns House is now the property of Nithsdale District Council which administers it through the museums service. The house was extensively renovated in the 1970s. A sandstone portrait bust of the poet was donated by William Ewart M.P. and placed in a niche on the wall of the Ragged School next door. When the school was demolished the bust was removed to a place of safety and is currently stored in the basement of the Old Town Mill which opened in 1986 as the **Robert Burns Centre.**

BURNS MAUSOLEUM

The first resting place of the poet's remains was in the northeast corner of **St Michael's Churchyard**, but eventually the friends and admirers of Burns felt that this arrangement was totally inadequate. John Syme and William Grierson accordingly published a circular on 29th November 1813 aiming at the launch of a public subscription for the erection of a monument at the grave. A meeting for this purpose was held at the George Inn on 16th December, eighteen gentlemen being present. The Rev. Henry Duncan, minister of **Ruthwell**, and William Grierson were appointed joint secretaries of the Mausoleum Committee. Subsequently the appeal became worldwide and donations flooded in from all parts of the British Isles and many of the colonies as well as from India and America. Sir Walter Scott played a notable part in the fund-raising campaign.

After advertisement, about fifty designs were submitted by architects and on 25th April 1815 the plans of Thomas Hunt of London were approved. The job of erecting the proposed Mausoleum was put out to tender, and the contract was awarded to John Milligan, stonemason of Dumfries, whose estimate was £331 8s 6d. James Thomson was appointed superintendent of works. The existing location of the poet's grave being found unsuitable, on account of the crowded nature of that part of the churchyard, a new site was selected and permission was obtained from the poet's family for the removal of his remains. The foundation stone of the Mausoleum was laid with full masonic honours on 5th June 1815 (the actual birthday of King George III).

Meanwhile the designs and models submitted by sculptors for the monument itself were considered and the choice fell upon Peter Turnerelli, an Irish sculptor of Italian descent, working in London. The Committee conferred on 6th June 1815 with Turnerelli whose estimate for full-size figures in marble was 750 guineas, but if reduced to three-quarter size the charge would fall to 600 guineas. Two days later, at a public banquet in the **King's Arms,** the freedom of the burgh was conferred on the architect and the sculptor.

Work began soon afterwards but almost immediately ran into difficulties. Milligan proved to be troublesome; he blatantly disregarded the Committee's written orders and tore up their letter complaining of inefficiency and poor workmanship in the jointing of the granite steps. He placed stones in the dome that did not conform to the contract as regarded thickness and quality, and in the end Hunt was obliged to intervene and closely supervise every stage of the construction.

Turnerelli's model had been criticised because the plough did not resemble the type used in Scotland in the time of Burns. Consequently the Committee went to the trouble of having a model plough constructed by a Mr Smale of Edinburgh and sent to Turnerelli in London for his guidance. Smale charged four guineas for this — much to the disgust of the Committee who felt that a quarter of that sum would have been more reasonable! On 9th August 1816 the Committee inspected progress on site and condemned much of Milligan's handiwork. In particular they took exception to a head of Apollo which Milligan had placed in the centre of the dome. The daisies were not according to Hunt's specifications, although in fairness to Milligan he could not afford to delay the work in progress until details of the daisies came from London. In the end, Thomas McCaig and Alexander Crombie (builder of **Ellisland**) were appointed to arbitrate between the Committee and Milligan, who was awarded an additional payment of £101 16s 2d. At one of the Committee meetings a letter from Milligan to Hunt was read 'of so scurrilous a nature as to be altogether unworthy the notice of the meeting, they determined to treat it with the contempt it deserves.' Work came to a standstill and the impasse was only resolved by negotiating with another contractor. An interdict followed the erection of the iron gates at Milligan's instance and the resulting dispute had to be resolved by the local magistrates. Milligan again began work on the curtain wall but was first interdicted and then dismissed altogether. Hunt prepared drawings for the sarcophagus but great difficulties arose on account of Milligan insisting that he do all the work, although the Committee felt that this could only be executed competently by a trained sculptor.

As if these problems with Milligan were not enough, the Committee also ran into trouble over the money raised by the great public dinner in London on 25th May 1816. In the end, however, a settlement was reached and sufficient funds were forthcoming for the Committee to pay Turnerelli an advance of £220. Despite the fees suggested by Turnerelli he had eventually agreed to emulate the generosity of Hunt who had waived his fee altogether. Turnerelli undertook to carry out the sculpture for whatever sum was left after the Mausoleum was erected. Unfortunately, this was no more than a verbal agreement and when Turnerelli discovered that the balance amounted to little more than half his estimate, he became difficult about the matter. More unpleasantness followed and it was not until September 1817 that the Mausoleum was completed and the sculpture was installed. Poor Turnerelli never received full payment.

Though Turnerelli's bas-relief of the Muse Coila finding her favourite son at the plough and throwing her inspiring mantle over him was widely acclaimed at the time, a later generation were to criticise it, not the least on account of inaccuracies in the poet's garb. By the turn of the century the marble had suffered greatly from atmospheric pollution and exposure to the elements, and about 1910 the figures were repaired to arrest decay by an Edinburgh sculptor, at the request of the Dumfries Burns Club. As a precautionary measure plaster casts of the figures were taken so that the statuary could be exactly reproduced. A decade later, however, the statuary was in a parlous condition, while the Mausoleum itself was scandalously neglected. A restoration fund was launched in 1928 but it failed lamentably to achieve its goal. Originally it was hoped to remodel the statuary in a more durable material such as bronze, but the cost of casting — estimated at over £3000 — was prohibitive. Eventually it was decided to settle for marble, the task being entrusted to Hermon Cawthra who completed the work in 1936, taking the opportunity to correct the more glaring errors in Turnerelli's work. Turnerelli's original figure of Burns was transferred to **Burns House** and was for several years displayed on the upper floor alongside the famous punch-bowl. Subsequently it was withdrawn from the House and ended up in a builder's yard. It was at one time offered to the **Theatre Royal** but no space was available. When Burns's first home in **Bank Street** was restored consideration was given to housing the statue there, but by that time it was too late; the builder had died and his yard had been sold, and the statue has long since disappeared. The Mausoleum was originally intended to have a lengthy Latin inscription, but saner counsels prevailed and this was never implemented.

The mortal remains of the poet were removed from their original lair about midnight on 19th September 1817 by Messrs Grierson, Milligan and Thomson, accompanied by James Bogie, the gardener at **Terraughty**, and assisted by some workmen. Beside the poet lay the coffins of his sons Francis Wallace (1789-1803) and Maxwell (1796-99). Whereas the children's coffins were still almost intact, that of the poet was in an advanced state of decay, revealing the corpse within. At first Burns's cadaver seemed incredibly preserved, 'suggesting one who had just sunk into the slumber of death, the lordly forehead of the dreamless sleeper still rising arched and high, the dome of thought covered with hair still dark as a raven's wing, and the teeth retaining their original regularity and whiteness. The scene was so imposing that most of the workmen stood bare and uncovered, and at the same time felt their frames thrilling with some indefinable emotion as they gazed on the ashes of him whose fame is as wide as the world itself. But the effect was momentary; for when they proceeeded to insert a shell or case below the coffin, the head separated from the trunk and the whole body, with the exception of the bones, crumbled into dust.' (From McDiarmid's *Picture of Dumfries*, quoted by McDowall in *Memorials of St Michael's*.)

BURNS MAUSOLEUM

On 31st March 1834, the night preceding the burial of Jean Armour, the vault of the Mausoleum was opened to prepare for the interment and the opportunity was taken 'by a party of gentlemen' to view the remains of the poet. This group included Provost Murray, the lawyer Archibald Hamilton, Rector McMillan, James Bogie, Andrew Crombie (son of Alexander), John McDiarmid of the *Courier* and Dr Archibald Blacklock who examined the poet's skull and took a plaster cast of it for phrenological purposes. Dr Blacklock reported that the cranium was in a high state of preservation, the bones of the face and palate being also sound. Some small portions of black hair, with a few grey hairs intermixed, were observed while detaching some extraneous matter from the occiput. The skull was taken to the house of Mr Kerr, a plasterer residing in North Queensberry Street, and a plaster matrix taken of it by his assistant James Fraser. 'Two or three tiny tresses that had adhered to the napkin in which the cranium was wrapped were retained, as priceless souvenirs of the illustrious dead.'

This ghoulish work was carried on in the dead of night but by 1 a.m. on the day of Jean's funeral the poet's skull had been replaced in the vault. The poet's skull was last examined in May 1857 when the vault was opened to admit the remains of Burns's eldest son Robert. Little deterioration was evident, and before it was replaced the enclosing lead casket was filled with pitch to preserve the remains for all time.

Soon after the interment of the poet in the Mausoleum the tombstone from the original east wall site was laid in the vault, but subsequently it was deposited in front of the statuary. The inscription on this stone was simple

'In Memory of
ROBERT BURNS
who died the 21st July 1796,
in the 37th year of his age'

though curiously inaccurate, for Burns died in his 38th year. Later inscriptions were added to this slab as they were required, to record the deaths of Maxwell aged 2 years and 9 months, and Francis Wallace aged 14 years. Next comes a record of the re-interment of Burns, followed by the deaths of Jean and Robert Junior. About 1946, when the ceremony marking the 150th anniversary of the poet's death was imminent, the lettering on the slab was recarved by John Urquhart, foreman for J.W. Dods, the monumental sculptor. Two marble tablets were later installed, the one on the left recording the deaths of Lieutenant Colonel James Glencairn Burns (born at Dumfries, 12th August 1794, died at Cheltenham, 18th November 1865) and his family — his wife Sarah Robinson (who died at Neemuch, India on 7th November 1821, aged 24), Jean Isabella, his daughter (died at sea on 5th June 1823 aged 4 years 5 months), Robert Shaw, his son (died at Neemuch on 11th December 1821, aged 18 months), and Mary Beckett, his second wife, (died at Gravesend, Kent on 13th November 1844 aged 52). The tablet on the right recorded the death of Lieutenant Colonel William Nicol Burns (born at Ellisland, 9th April 1791, died at Cheltenham, 21st February 1872) and his wife Catherine Adelaide Crone (died at Kulludghev, India, 29th June 1841). The remains of both James Glencairn and William Nicol were interred in the vault beneath these tablets.

James McClure, a faithful friend of the poet in his declining years and his attendant at his deathbed, died in November 1813, aged 50, and by permission of the Burns family was interred within the precinct of the Mausoleum. His wife Jean Heughan, who died in September 1815 aged 60, was also interred there. A flat stone placed on the right of the entrance to the Mausoleum records that McClure was 'a man who by his punctuality, his integrity, his benevolence, and the uniform uprightness of his character, conferred respectability on the humble station of a letter-carrier. He was the constant and faithful friend of the Poet Burns, and after his death was most active and successful in his endeavours to promote the interest of the family' — a quotation from the preface to Cromek's *Reliques*.

Within the precincts of the Mausoleum two Scotch thistles and four holly bushes were planted, one at each corner, while 'an umbrageous weeping ash furnishes a natural drapery for the tomb behind', to quote McDowall (1876) who went on: 'Among the hundreds of persons from a distance who come here annually to offer the tribute of admiration or pay the meed of a melodious tear, many beg earnestly for a memorial twig, or even leaf or tuft of grass, from the natural garniture of the poet's grave, and if favoured with the same by the keeper, go their way pensive, yet rejoicing.'

The Mausoleum, like its very name (after Mausolos, King of Caria in Asia Minor, c.353 BC), owed everything to the neo-classicism of the early 19th century. Thomas Hunt modelled it consciously on a Grecian temple, with its dome and scroll-topped pillars. In its original form the warm red sandstone of the Dumfries district was left unadorned and was probably more aesthetically satisfying. In the 1880s, however, it was liberally covered with white and blue paint, perhaps with the worthy intention of protecting the fabric against the effects of atmospheric pollution. The result is frankly incongruous, giving St Michael's Churchyard an exotic Mediterranean touch amid the douce freestone of the surrounding tombstones. Moreover, the entrance to the Mausoleum was protected by darkened glass, making it impossible for visitors to look through it. At the time of the Centenary celebrations in 1896 the Mausoleum was repainted in a soft stone colour and plain glass was put in the doorway so that visitors could at least gaze in without requiring the sexton to unlock the doors.

By that time also the trees had become overgrown and unsightly, but they were then removed, and thus restored to the Mausoleum that impression of height and size which had been lost. Philip Sulley, writing in his Centenary handbook *Robert Burns and Dumfries* (1896) hoped that, if the Centenary turned out to be successful 'the Dumfries Burns Club will be able, with the help of stained glass and mellowed light, to make the shrine more in keeping with its illustrious memories. Another tablet, recording the earnest labours and devotion to the Poet of the Rev. Henry Duncan of Ruthwell, of John Syme, of Commelin, Grierson and Rankine, might well and fitly be placed in or near the building'. Neither of these recommendations was implemented.

At the present time, the doors to the Mausoleum are normally kept locked for security reasons, but the key may be obtained on application to the curator of **Burns House** nearby.

BURNS STATUE

Although Dumfries had, in the **Mausoleum**, the earliest memorial to the poet, it lacked a statue sited in a more public place. To be sure, the classical fashion prevailing in the early 19th century preferred ostentatious monuments rather than actual statues — hence the Grecian extravaganzas erected at Alloway and Edinburgh. In 1872 the campaign to have a statue of Burns in George Square, Glasgow was launched and in the same year the idea gained ground in Dumfries following the death of the poet's last surviving son. It was proposed to erect a statue in Church Place at the junction of the High Street and Buccleuch Street, opposite Greyfriars Church, but nothing concrete was done about it until May 1877 when the Town Council adopted the proposal, on the motion of Robert Hamilton, as a formal resolution. A committee was formed, with William McDowall the historian as secretary.

The sum of £500 was raised within a year, but the spectacular crash of the City of Glasgow Bank in 1879 gravely hindered progress. In 1880 a bazaar raised a similar sum and this, together with donations which had accumulated in the interim, gave the committee sufficient funds to bring the project to fruition. Philip Sulley noted that the bulk of the money was raised by the ordinary people of Dumfries, 'the better classes and the nobility being apathetic'. In fairness, however, it should be noted that Lord Rosebery, the Marquis of Queensberry (of boxing rules fame and architect of Oscar Wilde's disgrace) and the Marquis of Bute made generous contributions to the fund. Significantly, the committee was formed by members of the Tam o Shanter and Queen of the South Burns Clubs. The Dumfries Burns Club, content with its private annual symposium, declined to assist. The fund-raising bazaar was held in the Mechanics' Hall from 14th to 17th September 1880 and its chief attraction was an exhibition of Burns relics, by far the largest and richest collection of Burnsiana exhibited prior to the Glasgow Centenary Exhibition of 1896.

Meanwhile, the committee approved the model of the statue, furnished by Amelia Hill, wife of the celebrated painter and photographer, David O. Hill and sister of the eminent painter, Sir Noel Paton. Amelia Hill exhibited portrait busts, animal figures and genre statuettes at the Royal Academy from 1870 onwards and elements of all three specialisations are to be found in the Burns statue, her best-known work. The *Edinburgh Review* published a lengthy description of the statue, which was carved in Carrara marble by Italian craftsmen working from Mrs Hill's original model:

'The figure of Burns is resting against the trunk of a tree, in a half-sitting attitude, which, without taking much from its height, tends to make the figure more graceful and natural. His right hand is laid on his heart, while the other holds a daisy — "the wee, modest, crimson-tippit flower" — his dress is that of a cottar of the period in which he lived, with tailed coat, having large lapelles, long waistcoat, also with lapelles, knee-breeches and shoes, while a plaid falls in easy folds round his body. Luath, his dog, rests his head against the poet's foot. Other accessories, such as the daisies which deck the turf of the tree root, and the mice that gambol careless near, indicate finely that love of and sympathy with nature which formed so conspicuous and overmastering a feature of the poet's character. The shepherd's horn that lies upon the turf suggests, we suppose, the great share which Burns had in the preservation of Scottish airs by his marriage of them to worthy verse. In modelling the figure, in which rustic simplicity, careless grace, homely dignity, and a certain pensive sadness are happily combined, Mrs Hill has striven, and has succeeded, as we believe, in being true to the laws of portraiture. Burns stands before us much as he was, when in some happy moment his Muse was with him in the fields. The cast from the skull of Burns, and the portraits by Nasmyth have, we believe, been her authority for the likeness of the poet.'

BURNS STATUE, DUMFRIES

In due course the statue was shipped from Italy and erected on a grey stone pedestal relieved with appropriate carving. Four marble tablets were set in the sides of the pedestal. The tablet on the south face records that the statue was 'erected by the inhabitants of Dumfries (with the aid of many friends) as a loving tribute to their fellow-townsman, the National Poet of Scotland, 6th April 1882'. Quotations from some of Burns's best-loved poems appear on the other three tablets.

Despite the fulsome tribute quoted from the Edinburgh newspaper, the statue has frequently been criticised. Edward Pinnington in the Art Journal loftily dismissed it as 'the nearest existing approach to a woman's sculptured thought of Burns, and it is an interesting, even if it never was a lofty, embodiment of the poet.' Edward Goodwillie (1911) added, 'The truth is that the statue was Italianized. The clay model was sent to Italy to be cut upon an enlarged scale, and in the process the sculptor's work was bereft of some of its finest features.' Philip Sulley echoed the feelings of his fellow-townsmen when he wrote (1898) 'the expression is stolid, vacant, meaningless, certainly not the inspired, commanding look of Burns. The base is crowded with inartistic, paltry details — a bonnet, shepherd's pipe of an Italian type, mice, daisies and thistle, while the alleged collie defies description.'

The statue was unveiled by the Earl of Rosebery on 6th April 1882, in the presence of a very large crowd which went in procession from Kingholm, via St Michael's Street, the Whitesands, New Bridge to Maxwelltown, up College Street, Portland Place, Glasgow Street, David Street, Terregles Street and Galloway Street, across New Bridge and up Buccleuch Street, Castle Street, George Street, Irving Street, Academy Street, Lovers' Walk, English Street and the High Street to Church Place. Prior to the unveiling ceremony Lord Rosebery was presented with the freedom of the burgh in the Town Hall. A banquet in the Mechanics' Hall, at which Lord Young proposed the 'Immortal Memory', concluded a very busy day.

The statue was originally enclosed in iron railings, but these were removed during the Second World War as part of the metal recovery programme. At the present day the statue occupies a circular site tastefully laid out with lawns and flower-beds. The original panels were removed about 1958 and replaced by the present panels. A few years later the name ROBERT BURNS was carved at the foot of the base by John Urquhart. In the century since the erection of the statue it has been moved on several occasions, during road-widening and redevelopment of Church Place. A display board in the Planning Department shows the various moves of the statue.

BURNS WALK

The poet's favourite walks were along both banks of the Nith upstream of the town. On the west bank he would walk as far as **Lincluden Abbey;** while on the east side he would stroll along a beautifully wooded and secluded path from Martinton Ford known to this day as Burns Walk. This walk terminates just east of that point where the **Cluden Water** enters the Nith, but one may continue back to Nunholm along a minor road, or continue farther upstream along a footpath that skirts the golf course, rejoining the A701 at Dalscone.

BURNS WALK

CASTLEDYKES QUARRY

A quarry on the south side of the town, near the east bank of the **Nith**. The lands of Castledykes take their name from the medieval earthworks nearby, site of a castle erected in the 12th century by King William the Lion. It was here that the first action in the War of Independence took place in 1306. Burns alluded to this in his 'Scots Prologue for Mrs Sutherland' (C.W. p.399):

How here, even here, he first unsheath'd the sword
'Gainst mighty England and her guilty lord.

A report to the English government by a military officer (c.1563-6) regarding the defensive state of Dumfries mentions 'the auld castell of Drumfreis is fyve miles and a half within the mowthe of Nyth, standing upon the syde of the saime, very good for a forte.' This 'auld castell' was about half a mile south of the town and until the early 18th century its remains lay in open countryside. About 1707 part of the Castledykes area was purchased by the Town Council and a quarry developed, from which came much of the stone used in the erection of many fine buildings in Dumfries in the course of the ensuing century. A road was constructed from the foot of St Michael's Street to Kingholm for the convenience of carters doing business at the quarry.

Alexander Crombie Junior (1757-1828), son of the stonemason who built **Ellisland** for Burns, married Charlotte, sister of a fellow-stonemason, Thomas Watson, and established a flourishing business. He obtained a lease of Castledykes Quarry and built a number of country houses, notably the Miller residence at **Dalswinton**. He also had a business in town, as sculptor, monumental mason and manufacturer of ornamental ironwork. Many of the tombstones in **St Michael's Churchyard** were produced by Crombie & Co. It was to this firm that Burns wrote from Ellisland on 8th October 1790 requesting a bar of shoeing iron which cost him 2s 9d. The quarry was worked out by the early 19th century and now makes an interesting feature of the park. A memorial at the upper entrance to the park records the association of Castledykes with Robert Bruce at the beginning of the War of Independence.

CASTLEDYKES VIEW

A house to the south of Wallace's Loaning, formerly known as Castlebank or Castlemilk. It was the residence of Agnes Eleanor Dunlop (c.1750-1825), eldest daughter of Mrs Frances Dunlop of Dunlop, the close friend and confidante of Burns. She married Joseph Elias Perochon, a French royalist *emigre* who set up as a merchant in London, but lost his eyesight. The couple then retired to Dumfries and purchased Castlebank, where Mrs Perochon continued to reside until her death on 16th October 1825. Burns got to know her while she was as yet unmarried and living with her mother at Dunlop House, whither he addressed a letter to her about November 1788. Burns's intemperate remarks about the King and Queen of France, in the long letter he wrote between 20th December 1794 and 12th January 1795 (C.L. pp.212-14) — 'What is there in the delivering over a perjured Blockhead & an unprincipled Prostitute into the hands of the hangman...' — caused Mrs Dunlop so much offence that she broke off her long-running correspondence with the poet. Four of her sons and a grandson fought in the French Revolutionary and Napoleonic Wars, and two of her daughters married French *emigres*.

It is clear that Burns himself never realised the hurt he had caused by his outspoken views of the French Revolution. He wrote three further letters to Mrs Dunlop, uneasy at the lack of response, and the last of these was written only days before his death. Possibly the last words he ever read were the lines which she penned in reply. After Burns's death, a close friendship developed between his widow and Mrs Perochon who was a frequent visitor to the house in Mill Street. Mrs Perochon played an active part in the efforts to benefit the poet's family.

When Burns's remains were removed from their original burial place and interred in the **Mausoleum** Jean gave the burial plot to the Perochons. In a letter of 2nd February 1816 to Agnes Perochon, Jean wrote: 'Much indeed do I already owe to your disinterested friendship; and while a generous public are anxious to do justice to the genius of my husband by building so superb a monument to perpetuate his memory, you have paid the best tribute of your regard by so warmly interesting yourself in behalf of his widow and his children. In this you follow the example of her whose virtues you inherit, and who highly distinguished Mr B. by a friendship which formed one of his first enjoyments.'

COACH AND HORSES INN

A hostelry at 66 Whitesands, on the east bank of the **Nith,** extending round the corner into **Friars Vennel.** In Burns's day it was a place of doubtful repute, especially during the great Whitsun and Martinmas markets when many thousands of cattle were sold, and during the Rood and Candlemas fairs devoted to the sale of horses. Margaret Hog (died 1811), alias Muirland Meg or Monkery Meg, is reputed to have kept a brothel here and inspired the poem 'Muirland Meg' (C.W. p.602).

COUNCIL OFFICES

The administration of the burgh was conducted in premises at the junction of the High Street and Old Union Street, no longer extant but where the offices of Thomas Cook the travel agents now stand. The Council Offices, erected in the 1720s, were entered by the Rainbow Stairs from Old Union Street. They continued in use until about 1830 as the meeting place of the Town Council, with the office of the Town Clerk on the upper floor. It was in this building that Burns received his ticket as an honorary burgess of Dumfries on 4th June 1787 from Provost William Clark.

COUNTY HOTEL

A hotel formerly situated on the west side of the High Street. It is no longer extant, the site being occupied by shops between Binns and Marks & Spencer. In Burns's time it was a two-storey house. A popular belief is that it was the home of Dr William Maxwell, although this has been disproved by Professor Robert Thornton. It may, however, have belonged to the Maxwells of Kirkconnell at one time. In 1798 the building was leased and converted into the Commercial Hotel by a niece of John Paul Jones, Jane Young, who married David Williamson, the 'cruel scoundrel of a Haberdasher' whose demands for payment so worried Burns as he was dying. Prince Charles Edward Stuart used the hotel as his headquarters and held a council of war in one of its chambers, ever afterwards preserved as the Bonnie Prince Charlie Room.

The County Hotel, as it was later renamed, also boasted a Burns Room, meeting place of the Dumfries Burns Club, and the repository of many relics of the poet. It contained the library which had belonged to Miss Jean Armour Burns Brown, great-granddaughter of the poet, as well as busts of Burns in plaster and bronze.

DOCK PARK

The stretch of open ground along the east bank of the **Nith,** extending from the Caul at the Whitesands to **Castledykes.** The Caul or weir across the river marked the upper limit of navigation. The Dumfries Quay occupying the waterfront was owned by the Town Council, but usage declined sharply after the coming of the railway in 1850. Long before that, however, the level ground on this side of the river had taken on the role of a park. The lime trees at the head of the Dock were presented to the town by the Duke of Queensberry in 1748. It was here that the troops stationed in Dumfries drilled, and the Royal Dumfries Volunteers assembled here for their first parade on the afternoon of 26th March 1795. Today it is a park with many recreational facilities, maintained by Nithsdale District Council.

DOCK PARK – CARRONADE IN FOREGROUND

FRIARS VENNEL

Otherwise known as the Bridge Vennel, a narrow street running from Church Place down to the Whitesands. Before the development of Buccleuch Street at the beginning of the 19th century, this was the principal street from the High Street to the New Bridge which was approached up a ramp. Until 1793 the Vennel was extended across the end of the High Street to St Andrew's Street and thence to the Lochmabengate, with only a narrow gap opposite the High Street leading to the New Church (now Greyfriars) and adjacent land. In that year, however, many of the congested older houses were demolished to make way for the development of Castle Street and ultimately Buccleuch Street. Then, as now, the lower end of the Vennel was prone to flooding when the river was in spate. On 24th January 1796 the premises of Mr Thomson (candlemaker) were inundated, but the town house of Thomas Goldie just escaped. Goldie (1748-1823) was the fifth son of John Goldie of **Craigmuie** and, like his father before him, was Commissary of Dumfries. While Burns was a radical in politics, Goldie was on the right-wing of the Tory party and president of the Loyal Natives whose poetical attack on Burns provoked his famous epigram (C.W. p.515). He was also the butt of Burns's epigram 'On Commissary Goldie's Brains' (C.W. p.483). His youngest daughter Jane (1783-1852) never married but was well-known for her charitable works. She was also an authoress of considerable repute, discussing social, religious and political topics with much originality and force in three slim volumes. When she died she bequeathed £300 to provide a park for the people of Maxwelltown. Nothing was done to implement the lady's wishes until 1904, by which date the sum had grown, with interest, to £828 which permitted the purchase of six acres on Nithside for Goldie Park.

GEORGE INN

A hotel, formerly located at the southern end of the High Street, later known successively as the New George Hotel and the Cathron Hotel, but no longer extant. The site is the vacant lot between McDowall's and Iceland Frozen Foods. In the late 18th century the George was one of the principal hotels in the town. In the hotel gardens that swept down towards the **Whitesands** at the rear Williamson's touring company gave theatrical performances before the **Theatre Royal** was established. Some time in April or May 1792 Burns attended a function in the George Inn and from here, at the ungodly hour of 3 a.m., he wrote a letter to Alexander Cunningham (C.L. p.465): 'I am just now devilish drunk — if you doubt it, ask a Mr Campbell whom I have just met with by lucky accident...' As the ensuing letter is perfectly coherent and legible, thanking Cunningham for his generosity to James Clarke of Moffat, it must be assumed that Burns had his tongue in his cheek when he confessed his drunkenness.

It was in a room of this hotel that Glendonwyn (Glendinning) of **Parton** committed suicide. Alexander Cunningham claimed that Glendinning, 'a melancholy person buried near Dumfries', was the subject of Burns's lines 'On a Suicide' (C.W. p.521). Dr Copland Hutchison averred that he had seen Burns write this epitaph and push the paper into the earth over the grave. A letter to Alexander Dalziel on 5th October 1790 (C.L. p.505) mentioned Glendinning's daughter who had been engaged to David Blair of Dumfries: 'Miss G--, after trying a gentle tour in vain for her health, came to the George Inn, in Dumfries, where, in the very room in which her father died, she took her last residence, & there payed the great debt of Nature.' He added that her sister had been so upset at this double tragedy that she had only with the greatest difficulty been 'diverted from a resolution to hang the room... with mourning, & there spend her future days'.

GLOBE INN
Situated at 56 High Street, this tavern was established in 1610 and was one of the more fashionable public-houses by the time Burns came to Dumfries.

In the late 18th century the Globe Inn was the property of William Hyslop of **Lochend**, specifically named in Burns's grace (C.W. p.408):

> Lord, we thank, and Thee alone,
> For temporal gifts we little merit!
> At present we will ask no more —
> Let William Hislop bring the spirit.

William's eldest son John (1770-1835) married Margaret Geddes in 1795 and they took over the running of the Inn. There is a story, probably apocryphal, that Burns intended dining at the Globe with Willie Nicol and Allan Masterton but forgot to order the meal in advance. Meg Hyslop produced a sheep's head which she and her husband intended for themselves. Nicol 'fined' Burns for his neglect by ordering him to compose a suitable grace. When they had eaten, Burns was commanded to compose thanks. The stanzas entitled 'Grace before and after Meat' (C.W. p.409) were the result:

> O Lord, since we have feasted thus,
> Which we so little merit,
> Let Meg now take away the flesh,
> And Jock bring in the spirit!

Chambers, in the fourth volume of *Life and Works of Robert Burns* says: 'As for Burns, he will just have a single glass, and a half-hour's chat beside John Hyslop's fire, and then go quietly home. So he is quickly absorbed in the little narrow close where that vintner maintains his state. There, however, one or two friends have already established themselves, all with precisely the same virtuous intent. They heartily greet the bard. Meg or John bustles about to give him his accustomed place, which no one ever disputes.'

About August 1795 Burns wrote to James Johnson, mainly on matters concerning the *Scots Musical Museum*, but ending on a more personal note. 'Inclosed is a job which I beg you will finish pretty soon. — It is a Bill as you will see, for a tavern. — The Tavern-keeper, Hyslop, is a good honest fellow; & as I lie under particular obligations to him, I request that you may do it for him on the most reasonable terms.' Two subsequent letters, of 23rd September 1795 and March 1796, deal at length on the same matter. Tantalisingly Burns refers therein to 'Hyslop's bill' or 'Hyslop's plate', but does not give the landlord's Christian name although John Hyslop was probably intended.

Similarly Mrs Hyslop is mentioned in two of Burns's letters, but in neither instance is her first name given, though scholars have always assumed that Meg was understood. In August 1795 Burns wrote to William Lorimer (C.L. p.721): 'I called for you yester-night, both at your own house, and at your favorite lady's — Mrs Hyslop of the Globe — but could not find you.' To George Thomson he wrote in April 1796 (C.L. p.677) saying 'This will be delivered to you by a Mrs Hyslop, Landlady of the Globe Tavern here, which for these many years has been my HOWFF, & where our friend Clarke & I have had many a merry squeeze. — I mention this, because she will be a very proper hand to bring that Seal you talk of.'

Helen Anne Park, Jean Hyslop's niece, was employed at the Globe Inn as a barmaid. In June 1790 Jean Armour was absent from home, visiting her relatives in Mauchline. Burns, missing the company and comfort of Bonnie Jean, consorted with Miss Park in her absence. The affair which inspired the lovely song 'Yestreen I Had a Pint o Wine' (C.W. p.407) resulted in the birth of Elizabeth Park at Leith on 22nd March 1791. Nine days later Jean herself gave birth to a son, William Nicol Burns. With remarkable tolerance Jean took in baby Elizabeth and reared her as one of her own family. Tradition has it that she merely commented 'Oor Robbie should have had twa wives'. Nothing at all is known of 'Anna of the gowden locks' apart from this episode, though Maurice Lindsay hints that she 'had other pretty ways to render herself agreeable to the customers at the inn than the serving of wine'.

De Lancey Ferguson says she died giving birth to Elizabeth, while another tradition maintains that she obtained a position as a domestic servant in Leith or Edinburgh, where she married a soldier, and died in giving birth to his child. According to Ovens, 'Anna was also a devotee of the muse, though if so, none of her poetic effusions has survived.' Elizabeth was raised as Betty Burns, grew up to be one of the belles of Dumfries, and is said to have borne a striking likeness to her famous father. She married a soldier named John Thomson and they had a large family, one of whom, Robert Burns Thomson, bore an amazing resemblance to his maternal grandfather, not only in physical appearance but in intellect, humour and a taste for music and poetry. Some of his songs achieved a measure of popularity in the second half of the 19th century. Alone of all the poet's descendants, he was at least touched by the muse's mantle.

Elizabeth Burns Thomson's death certificate (1873) gave her parents' names as 'Robert Burns, Poet' and 'Ann Hislop'. From this William McVittie cast doubt on the existence of Helen Anne Park. To be sure, the fact that the story of her liaison with the poet came from Allan Cunningham (1834) would naturally make one suspect its veracity; but we have the evidence of Maria Riddell's correspondence with Dr Currie (1797), although the lady is not actually named. McVittie deduced from the entry on the death certificate that 'Ann Hislop' must have been a relative of the Hyslops, and not the Maxwell side of the family (through Jean Maxwell, wife of William Hyslop) and speculated as to whether she was a daughter, niece or sister of William Hyslop. It should be noted, however, that the evidence on the death certificate cannot be relied upon at all. The information was supplied to the Registrar by Elizabeth's son who may have had this information on hearsay. Robert Burns Thomson may merely have assumed that the surname was Hislop (sic) and may have simply been ignorant of the statement made by Cunningham, and since followed by other editors and biographers. Similarly the age at the time of death — 83 — led McVittie to deduce that Elizabeth had been born about June 1790 and not March 1791, but here again, ages given on death certificates are frequently inaccurate. The only statement which seems to be true is that Elizabeth Burns was born at Leith; certainly that much was claimed by the lady herself in the details given in the Census returns from 1841 onwards.

By 1797 the tenant of the Globe was Henry Dickson. John and Margaret Hyslop vanish from the scene. Could they, in fact, be the same John Hyslop and Margaret Geddes who bob up in the story of the famous Geddes Burns? This was the name given to a copy of the Kilmarnock Edition which belonged to the Roman Catholic Bishop John Geddes (1735-99). On his death, the book passed by bequest to his niece Margaret Hyslop whose husband, John Hyslop, was a Scottish surgeon living in Finsbury, London. Not only are the identical names too uncanny to be mere coincidence, but Dr and Mrs Hyslop were both dead by 1836 (and it is known that John, son of William Hyslop, died in 1835). The Hyslops had a daughter called Margaret and it was she who parted with the book in 1838, giving it to Dr Henry Goadby prior to his departure for America. It was in this manner that the Geddes Burns came to be in the United States, and is preserved to this day in the Henry E. Huntington Library at San Marino, California.

By the early years of the 19th century the Globe Inn belonged to a Mrs Appleby whose tenant in 1813 was J. Ewing. In February 1829 his widow gave up the tenancy, advertising the Globe 'with commodious dwelling house and garden, extensive stabling and other suitable conveniences.' She was succeeded by Andrew Graham, whose widow Mary Carruthers continued until her death aged 87, in 1860. In turn, she was followed by her daughter, Elizabeth Graham who died in 1870, aged 70. Then her daughter, Mrs Smith, was landlady at the Globe until the 1920s, having worked there for upwards of sixty years. The Inn was then sold to W. D. Mill who was offering bed and breakfast for 6s 6d a night in 1932.

GLOBE INN

Subsequently the Globe was purchased by M. Henry McKerrow, Burgh Chamberlain of Dumfries, President of the Burns Federation (1937-43) and a life-long Burns enthusiast. Mr McKerrow wished to preserve this famous old inn with its close associations with Burns. The present owner is the Midland Bank Pension Fund, but Henry McKerrow's grandson, Gordon, and his wife Maureen are the landlords of the public house. Over the past half century the McKerrow family have acquired many relics of the poet, on display in the bar and the little ground-floor snuggery which was Burns's howff. It retains all the beautiful and original wood panelling of two centuries ago, and still breathes the atmosphere of the period when the poet enjoyed many convivial evenings with his companions.

In an upstairs bedroom two small window panes are inscribed with the poet's diamond stylus. One has a stanza from 'Lovely Polly Stewart' (C.W. p.523), while the other bears a variant stanza from 'Comin Thro the Rye (C.W. p.578):

> Gin a body meet a body
> Coming through the grain.
> Gin a body kiss a body
> The thing's a body's ain.

At least the first stanza of 'At the Globe Tavern' (C.W. p.471) was also inscribed on a window of this inn at one time, as were the three verses of 'Lines Written on Windows of the Globe Tavern' (C.W. pp.568-9).

Considerable development has taken place in the High Street in the years since Burns died and the Globe Inn no longer fronts directly on to the street. It is approached through the Globe Close, a narrow alley which retains the original centuries-old flagstones.

THE GRAMMAR AND WRITING SCHOOL

The nucleus of the present-day Dumfries Academy existed at least as far back as 1481 when Master John Turnbull was described as 'rector of the school of Drumfreis' in a legal document of that date. In those days, and for many years thereafter, it was a one-teacher school. Mr McGeorge, the rector in 1663, combined the multifarious duties of burgh schoolmaster with parish clerk. His salary, for giving instruction in English, Latin and Greek, was a mere £100 Scots per annum, but he had the benefit of quarter days (freewill offerings from the pupils), and fees for proclaiming marriages, baptisms and burials. As late as the mid-18th century the customs and traditions of the school included the annual cock-fight on Fastern's Even (Shrove Tuesday). The admission charge (12 pence Scots) was to be given by the scholars to the under teacher 'to receive and apply to his own use for his pains and trouble'.

By the late 18th century, however, Dumfries had three schools for teaching English, two schools for teaching arithmetic, and the Grammar School which concentrated on the teaching of Latin. The Grammar teacher had a salary of £20 per annum, implemented by 5s a quarter from pupils who were not the children of burgesses. One of the privileges of being a burgess was that education for one's children was free. This was a valuable privilege, indeed, and one that Burns was keen to obtain for his sons. In March 1793 (C.L. p.553) he wrote to the Provost and Bailies of Dumfries: 'Some years ago your good Town did me the honor of making me an Honorary Burgess. — Will your Honors allow me to request that this mark of distinction may extend so far, as to put me on the footing of a real Freeman of the Town, in the Schools?' He bolstered his case by reminding the Council that he had recently been the means of boosting the town's revenues by about £10 in the space of a few weeks, by enforcing the twopenny tax on foreign ale sold within the burgh limits — a levy which had been neglected previously. The poet's petition was granted and Robert Junior was admitted to free education, his brothers following in due course.

James Gray, one of the masters at the school, has left an interesting picture of Burns as a parent: 'In the bosom of his family he spent many a delightful hour in directing the studies of his eldest son, a boy of uncommon talents. I have frequently found him explaining to this youth, then not more than nine years of age, the English poets from Shakespeare to Gray; or storing his mind with examples of heroic virtue, as they live in the pages of our most celebrated English historians.'

Thomas White (1758-1825), for many years mathematics master and latterly rector of the Academy which combined the Grammar School and the other schools in one building from 1802 onwards, served as a second lieutenant in the Dumfries Volunteers and was a very close friend of Burns who inscribed a copy of the 1793 edition of his *Poems* to him. A tradition in the White family speaks of Burns being a regular Saturday guest in their home. The circular ends of the dining-table from White's home, where Burns is said to have regularly taken breakfast, are now on display in **Burns House.** White did much to promote interest in the poet's works, and remained a steadfast friend even in the last months when the poet's revolutionary opinions alienated many of his other friends. White composed a verse tribute to the memory of Burns in 1796. Apart from the 1793 *Poems* Burns presented White with a copy of Voltaire's *La Pucelle.*

The school in which Robert Burns Junior was educated stood on the Greensands, adjacent to Buccleuch Street. Road-widening in connection with the New Bridge, however, meant that the building had to be demolished. David Staig drew up an announcement about this on 18th December 1798 and solicited subscriptions for the construction of the new Academy, opened in 1804. Interestingly over £800 of the first subscriptions came from Kingston, Jamaica.

HOLE I' THE WA' INN

Situated between the High Street and Queensberry Street, this hostelry dates back to 1620 at least, the date on the marriage stone on the front wall giving the names of James Haike and Jean Stot. In Burns's time this part of the town consisted of a back tenement of houses (in the Mid Row), approached by an entry from (the King's High Street). The Mid Row extended to the Rattan Row (now Chapel Street) in one direction, and to Queensberry Square in the other. Although no documentary evidence exists linking Burns with this old inn it is traditionally regarded as one of the ale-houses which he would have frequented. In the late 19th century the proprietor, John Thomson, was an avid collector of Burnsiana and the public bar was a veritable museum of Burns pictures and relics. The most cherished exhibit was the poet's burgess ticket, which Thomson purchased at Sotheby's for £55 in 1904. These relics were transferred to the burgh museum and are now on display in the **Robert Burns Centre.**.

IRISH STREET

The street running parallel to the High Street and connecting the Wee Vennel (now **Bank Street**) with **Friars Vennel.** In the late 18th century the gardens of the houses ran right down to the Whitesands, where there was a footpath called Waterside (later Waterloo Street). Several important people had their town houses here, including Dr John Gilchrist and Provost Wellwood Maxwell. It was at the foot of these gardens in the very early morning of 18th May 1792 that John Lewars and Burns, after an all-night carousal at the **Globe Inn,** encountered two servants of Wellwood Maxwell in the wash-house. As a result of his drunken and disorderly behaviour, occasioning actual bodily assault of one of the girls, John Lewars was charged with 'crimes of a heinous nature'. Remarkably, Burns was kept out of the affair. Jean Murdoch, the servant who was assaulted, mentioned 'John Lewars and another person whom the declarant does not know'. It was 'the other man' who finally dragged Lewars away, begging the girls to say nothing of what had happened. Lewars himself, however, referred to Burns being with him, in his own statement, but could recollect nothing on account of his 'inebriety'. Fortunately for Lewars, the Procurator Fiscal, David Newall, with the consent of the magistrates, 'deserted this process pro loco et tempore' after a plea of mitigation was entered.

IRISH STREET – FORMER HOME OF COLONEL DE PEYSTER

JERUSALEM TAVERN

An old inn situated in the Long Close running west of the High Street. It is no longer extant but stood to the north of the present Royal Bank building in the High Street. It was from this tavern, one Monday evening in May 1794, that Burns sent his friend John Syme a dozen bottles of porter with the lines:

> O had the Malt thy strength of mind,
> Or Hops the flavour of thy wit;
> 'Twere Drink for first of Humankind,
> A Gift that e'en for SYME were fit.—

KING'S ARMS

One of the oldest and, in its heyday, the most fashionable, of the town's hotels, it stood at the south end of the High Street where Boots the Chemists are now located. It was the main coaching inn of Dumfries and had a large pend leading to a side entrance of the hotel, with extensive stabling towards Shakespeare Street. Even earlier, in the 17th century, it was the town's leading commercial hotel, in the days when Mrs McKill was the landlady. Her establishment was so much frequented by the civic authorities that she might have put upon her sign-board 'Patronised by the Provost, Bailies and Town Council' (McDowall). Robert Fergusson, the poet, paid a visit to Dumfries in 1773 and is said to have foregathered with John Mayne, a local poet best remembered for his verses on the Siller Gun, at the King's Arms. In the verses composed by Fergusson in honour of that occasion he mentions the Bushby family, later immortalised in the poems of Burns. It was from the King's Arms, on 6th February 1829, that William Hare narrowly escaped a lynch mob. Hare had escaped the gallows by turning king's evidence against his body-snatching accomplice Burke, but the mob felt that he should not escape his just deserts. Hare had arrived in Dumfries on his way to Portpatrick and thence to his native Ireland. A graphic account of the ugly scenes, when the mob took over Dumfries and would have torn Hare limb from limb, is given by McDowall in his *History of Dumfries*.

Significantly, Burns only frequented the King's Arms on business, as it was very much an aristocratic establishment whose clientele included the nobility and country gentry. Nevertheless, it was on a window-pane at the King's Arms that Burns scratched the lines generally entitled 'Kirk and State Excisemen' (C.W. p.363):

> Ye men of wit and wealth, why all this sneering
> 'Gainst poor Excisemen? Give the cause a hearing.

This poem is thought to have been composed in 1789, shortly after Burns was appointed an officer of the Excise. The poem 'On the Commemoration of Rodney's Victory' (C.W. p.484) was probably composed extempore at a celebration in the King's Arms, shortly after news was received of the defeat of the French navy off Dominica in the West Indies in April 1792. It is likely that Collector Mitchell held his Excise dinners at this hotel. The King's Arms was also the venue for the meetings of the Loyal Natives. On the King's birthday 1793 the club met at three o' clock in the afternoon and received the blue sashes embroidered 'God Save the King', which the members' wives had made to mark the occasion. After partaking of an elegant dinner no fewer than fourteen loyal and well-adapted toasts were drunk before the final bumper 'God bless every branch of the Royal Family!' which brought the celebration to a rousing climax.

On another occasion Andrew Turner, 'a vain coxcomb of an English commercial traveller' tried to patronise Burns over a bottle of wine in the King's Arms. Burns was asked by his friends, whose party had been interrupted by Turner, to give an example of his impromptu versifying. On hearing the Englishman's age and name he produced the lines beginning 'In Se'enteen Hunder'n Forty-Nine' (C.W. p.363).

LIBRARIES

The location of the first public library in Dumfries is unknown; in the police rolls of the period it is listed as 'Dumfries library-room' but no address is given. It was established in September 1792 and Burns, who seems to have played a leading part in its formation, based on his experiences in running the library of the Monkland Friendly Society at **Dunscore,** was admitted a member on 5th March 1793. A minute of the proceedings stated that the committee had 'by a great majority, resolved to offer him a share of the library free of the usual admission money (10s 6d) out of respect and esteem for his merits as a literary man'. Burns responded on 30th March by presenting four books to the library — *Humphrey Clinker, Julia de Roubigne,* Knox's *History of the Reformation* and De Lolme's *British Constitution.* The last-named was inscribed by the poet on the fly-leaf: 'Mr Burns presents this book to the library, and begs they will take it as a creed of British liberty till they find a better. — R.B.' Nowadays no one would take these sentiments amiss, but in 1793, when a paranoid government found sedition in any voice of dissent, such an expression was open to misinterpretation and could easily have landed the poet in the gravest trouble, leading to his dismissal from his Excise post. Burns soon thought better of his rashness and, hurrying the following morning to the home of William Thomson with whom the books had been deposited, he asked for the De Lolme, saying that he was afraid that he had written something in it which might bring him into trouble. On the volume being produced, Burns glued the fly-leaf to the frontispiece in order to seal up his seditious secret.

This volume, like many other books in the original library, passed into the hands of the Dumfries and Maxwelltown Mechanics' Institution and is now in the **Robert Burns Centre**. The offending fly-leaf has now been unstuck and is on prominent display.

William Thomson was later Provost of Dumfries on three different occasions. During his second term in office, on 15th March 1825, a meeting in the Trades Hall decided on the establishment of the Dumfries and Maxwelltown Mechanics' Institute. Among the members of the founding committee, in addition to Provost Thomson, were William Grierson and the Rev. Dr Henry Duncan, both of whom had played a prominent part in perpetuating the memory of Burns in Dumfries. The library and reading room were opened in 1826 and a large lecture hall was added in 1861. By the end of the 19th century the library of the Mechanics' Institute contained nearly 8000 volumes, including the books which had belonged to the original library. In 1898 Andrew Carnegie offered £10,000 to the burgh provided it embraced the Free Libraries Act and furnished a site. A site was donated by Thomas McKie and his sister who laid the foundation stone on 13th October 1899. The library, which opened in 1903, was named in memory of the late William Ewart, M.P. for the Dumfries burghs and chief architect of the Free Libraries Act. The Ewart Library boasts a comprehensive holding of books by and pertaining to Burns. The extensive library of Burnsiana formed by A.J. Craig of Glendyne, formerly housed in the Ewart Library, may now be consulted in the Regional Archives, opposite **Burns House.**

LOREBURN CHURCH

A church in Loreburn Street, where the first Secession congregation in Dumfries was established in 1759. Known originally as the General Associate or Anti-Burgher Congregation, it became known as the Loreburn Street United Associate or Secession Congregation in 1820, later Loreburn Presbyterian Church and then, in 1900, Loreburn United Free Church. At the union of the churches in 1929 Loreburn voted to carry on in the old tradition as the United Free Church Continuing and thereafter as the United Free Church in Scotland. The first minister of the Congregation was the Rev. Thomas Herbertson, succeeded in 1765 by the Rev. William Inglis, a native of Leslie in Fife.

PLAQUE ON WALL OF LOREBURN CHURCH

Although the Burns family had a pew in **St Michael's** the poet was a frequent visitor to the 'Whig Meeting House' as it was popularly known at the time. Burns is said to have first made the acquaintance of Mr Inglis when the latter visited David Cullie at the **Isle** where Burns lodged in

1788 while **Ellisland** was being built. At a public dinner, during a lull in the conversation, someone shouted, 'Tell us, Mr Burns, why you go to the Whig Meeting House on a Sunday night?' As Burns paid no heed, the speaker persisted, thinking he had cornered the poet. In the end, however, Burns rose to his feet and replied, 'I go to hear Mr Inglis because he preaches what he believes, and practises what he preaches'.

Burns was also a regular visitor at the Loreburn manse. On one occasion when the poet was expected, the children were warned to behave, with the caution 'Mr Burns is coming: if you don't behave, he may write a poem about you!' Burns may, indeed, have written a poem about Elizabeth Inglis, the minister's younger daughter. At least, she is the only lady whose initials fit the extempore epigram on 'Miss E.I---, a Lady of a figure indicating amazonian strength' (C.W. p.533). Mr Inglis visited the poet during his last illness.

MIDSTEEPLE

Located in the cente of the High Street and a prominent landmark of the town. In 1697 the tack or lease of the Customs and Foreign Excise of Scotland was purchased at public auction by the Convention of Royal Burghs for £33,000. Each burgh having been offered a share in proportion to the amount of tax paid by it, the Town Council of Dumfries took part in the venture, but later sold its share to Sir Robert Dickson of Inveresk and John Sharpe of Hoddam. This transaction outraged the townspeople who threatened legal action against the Council. In the end, however, the matter was settled amicably by arbitration, it being decided that Dickson and Sharpe could retain their bargain provided they paid 20,000 merks into the burgh purse.

It was resolved to put this windfall to good use and a new town-house with a steeple was proposed. This decision was taken on 30th April 1703 and a committee to implement it was formed. John Moffat, a Liverpool architect, originally submitted a design, but this was rejected and in 1705 Tobias Bachup of Alloa was consulted. Bachup offered to complete the design, provide the necessary materials and labour, and see the project through to the end. The foundation stone was laid on 30th May 1705 and the work completed by 1707, the total cost amounting to about £1700. John Bancroft of Stockport supplied the clock for the spire, at a cost of £21, and the four dial plates were painted by John Chandley of Cheadle for £11. Three bells for the steeple were cast by George Barclay of Edinburgh. A guardhouse and tron (weights and measures office) occupied the ground floor. On the first floor were meeting rooms and Council offices, while prison cells occupied the second floor.

In Burns's time the Midsteeple was used as the Court House and the meeting place of the County Commissioners, prior to the establishment of the Court House in Buccleuch Street in 1816. Thomas Wilson (1750-1825) — 'Blin' Tam' — was the bellringer for 63 years, 'summoning the lieges to labour and repose' by ringing the bells at 6 a.m., 6 p.m. and 10 p.m. To mark the Octocentenary of the Burgh a carillon system was presented by Noel Dinwiddie and included the melody of 'Auld Lang Syne'. The Midsteeple is now occupied by the offices of the Registrar of Births, Marriages and Deaths.

Burns immortalised this building in his patriotic song 'Does Haughty Gaul Invasion Threat?' (C.W. p.537):

> Who will not sing God Save the King
> Shall hang as high's the steeple;
> But while we sing God Save the King,
> We'll ne'er forget the people!

The poet's body was removed from his house and lay in the courtroom of the Midsteeple until Monday 25th July 1796 and his funeral about mid-day. Unfortunately the only eye-witness account of the poet's lying in state was furnished many years later by Allan Cunningham — hardly the most reliable of witnesses at the best of times. Cunningham was only twelve years old at the time and the following account must be regarded with caution:

'He lay in a plain unadorned coffin, with a linen sheet drawn over his face, and on the bed and around his body herbs and flowers were thickly strewn. He was wasted somewhat by long illness, but death had not increased the swarthy hue of his face, which was uncommonly dark and deeply marked, but his broad and open brow was pale and serene, and around it his sable hair lay in masses, slightly touched with grey. The room in which he lay was plain and neat. We stood and gazed on him in silence for the space of several minutes. We went, and others succeeded us — man following man patiently and orderly — not a question was asked, not a whisper was heard.'

MIDSTEEPLE: A plaque above the door marks Burns's Bicentenary, 1959

NITH PLACE

The fashionable quarter of the town in the late 18th century, prior to the development of Castle Street. William Grierson (1733-1813) moved from Upper Nithsdale into the town in the 1750s and set up as a merchant in the High Street. When he prospered he purchased a house in Nith Place, which had been developed in the middle of the century. The Grierson family were still residing in the High Street, just below the **Midsteeple,** when William Junior was born in 1773 but they moved to Nith Place while he was still a small boy. William kept a diary from 1794 until 1811, published in 1981 with notes by John Davies, under the title *Apostle to Burns.* Despite this title, however, the Grierson diaries make no mention of the poet prior to the day of his death. It is odd that Burns did not cross Grierson's path, in view of the facts that they attended the same church, were entertained at the same theatre and had quite a few friends in common. Entries in the diaries mention Dr Mundell, William McCraken, James Gracie and there are frequent and lengthy references in 1795 to the Royal Dumfries Volunteers drilling at the Dock. On the other hand, the diaries make no mention of John Syme, with whom Grierson was closely associated in the campaign for the erection of the **Mausoleum,** and the diary entry for Monday 25th July 1796 contains an unusually perceptive opinion of the poet's private character and behaviour, which suggests that Grierson and Burns were on intimate terms. Certainly there can be no doubt of the tremendous efforts made by Grierson on behalf of the poet's widow and family, and later the Mausoleum.

OLD BRIDGE HOUSE

Situated on the west bank of the Nith at the end of the old bridge built by Devorgilla Baliol. In 1662 it was described as 'new biggit' by James Birkmyre, barrel-maker. In Burns's day it functioned as an inn serving the Brig-En', a lawless village beyond the jurisdiction of the Town Council, but gradually developed to become the separate burgh of **Maxwelltown.** It was one of the hostelries frequented by the poet. The Old Bridge House has been beautifully preserved and now operates as a museum devoted to Old Dumfries. The Old or Devorgilla's Bridge is the oldest surviving multiple-arch bridge in Scotland and dates from 1431, although an earlier wooden bridge was founded by the mother of John Baliol in the 13th century. The New Bridge farther upstream was designed by Thomas Boyd, architect of **Ellisland,** in 1792 and completed in 1794. The Dumfries approach required the construction of Buccleuch Street on a raised causeway bridging Brewery Street. The chief promoter of the New Bridge and other developments in the last two decades of the 18th century was David Staig.

BRIDGE HOUSE, MAXWELLTOWN

PLAINSTANES

That portion of the High Street in the vicinity of the fountain, at the junction of the High Street and English Street. The name was derived from the flagstones paving the main square of the town. It was here, in the autumn of 1794, that David McCulloch of **Ardwall** had his famous encounter with Burns while on his way to a ball in the old Assembly Rooms. William Grierson Junior, the 'Apostle to Burns', was born in a house over his father's drapery business here in 1773 (between Binn's department store and Bank Street). A tobacconist's shop was operated near here by Robert Mundell, brother of Dr James Mundell, and brother-in-law of Gabriel Richardson, friends of the poet. A coffee house (on the site now occupied by Burton's) was built by the Town Council as a mercantile exchange and meeting place for the business community. At the Plainstanes end of Queensberry Street was the town house of the Charteris family of Amisfield (rebuilt in 1876).

QUEENSBERRY SQUARE

The open space where Great King Street approaches the High Street at right angles. In Burns's day its principal feature was the monument to Charles, duke of Queensberry, erected in 1778 to a design by Robert Adam. Thomas Boyd and Alexander Crombie, both involved in the design and erection of **Ellisland,** were responsible for the construction of this monument. The square itself was laid out in 1770 at a cost of over £700, for the purpose of providing a public market. During the French Revolutionary Wars it was also employed as a ceremonial parade ground by the Royal Dumfries Volunteers. It was here, on the King's Birthday (4th June 1795), that the Volunteers paraded with Grant's regiment of Highland Fencibles. The Volunteers then marched into the centre of the Square and received their Colours, two banners having been embroidered by Mrs De Peyster and other wives of the Volunteers. The Colours were consecrated by the Rev. Dr Burnside. According to Grierson's diary: 'After that the Volunteers marched from the centre of the Fencibles till near the place where they were drawn up and fired three rounds and were answered each time by the Fencibles. Both the Volunteers and the Fencibles made a very fine appearance and fired remarkably well. The Volunteers dined together in the King's Arms and at six o'clock went up with the Magistrates to the court house to drink His Majesty's health. There was none of the inhabitants invited to the Court House as was customary, which offended the people very much, it being such an old custom.'

After the presentation of the Colours the Volunteers were addressed by their commandant, Colonel De Peyster. The text of his speech, together with the sermon preached by Dr Burnside, were reproduced in full in Grierson's diary. The Trades Hall on the south side of the Square was not built until 1804.

ROBERT BURNS CENTRE

This exhibition centre, with its multi-projector audio-visual theatre, diorama and exhibits devoted to Robert Burns, was opened in 1986 by HRH the Princess Alexandra. It contains a bookshop, restaurant and display areas on ground and upper floor. Many of the relics formerly displayed in **Burns House** have been transferred to this location. Admission is free, but there is a small charge for the audio-visual theatre. The Centre was formerly the old Town Mill of Dumfries, erected in 1781 to a design by Thomas Smeaton on the site of a mill and granaries which had been destroyed by fire the previous year. It was in use as a corn mill until 1911, using water from the nearby Nith to power the grinding wheel. In 1911, however, it was converted into a hydro-electric station. The giant flywheel from the electricity works is preserved opposite the Centre. In 1987 it was proposed to construct a dock between the Centre and the river for the permanent exhibition of the replica of Patrick Miller's first steamboat, after it was incorporated in the maritime exhibit at the Glasgow Garden Festival of 1988.

ROBERT BURNS CENTRE

ST MARY'S CHAPEL

A small chapel in English Street, serving the Episcopalian congregation. From 1772 until 1818 the clergyman in charge of this chapel was the Rev. William Babington. Trinity College, Dublin conferred the doctorate of divinity on him in 1781. He was also, for 28 years, Chairman of the Dumfries and Galloway Royal Infirmary. At the end of a letter to Mrs Dunlop, dated 13th March 1794 (C.L. p.209) Burns added an epigram 'In answer to one who affirmed of a well-known Character here, Dr Babbington(sic), that there was Falsehood in his very looks -

<blockquote>
That there is Falsehood in his looks,
I must & will deny;
They say, their Master is a KNAVE —
And sure they do not lie.—
</blockquote>

A polished variant of it was later published (C.W. p.514). Burns had his tongue in his cheek when he composed this epigram, for Dr Babington was one of the best-loved figures in the town, and numbered Syme, Bushby, McMurdo and Colonel De Peyster as close friends and members of his congregation. Dr Babington's wife, Janet Maitland (1748-1814), belonged to one of the oldest Dumfriesshire families. His second son, the Rev. Charles Maitland Babington, succeeded him as Episcopal clergyman and served his congregation for 22 years, till his death in 1841. His wife Lilias (1778-1827) was a daughter of Provost David Staig and sister of Jessie Staig.

ST MICHAEL'S CHURCH

The civil parish of Dumfries was divided into three ecclesiastical parishes, of Greyfriars, St Mary and St Michael. The last-named covered that portion of the town in which the poet resided, so it was natural that his family should attend divine worship in St Michael's Church. Following the Reformation St Michael's, formerly the Catholic church, became the parish church of Dumfries, Ninian Dalyell being the first minister. At least three churches are believed to have stood on the site prior to the erection of the present handsome red sandstone building in 1746 and the adjacent burial ground is thought to have been in use for nine centuries. Dr Thomas Mutter, former minister of Auchtermuchty, was the nominal incumbent of St Michael's when the Burns family moved into the town; but he had been too ill to officiate since 1780 and his duties were effectively carried out by William Burnside. Mutter died on 26th December 1793 and Dr Burnside then took over and remained in office until his own death on 6th January 1806 at the age of 55. Dr Burnside is best remembered for compiling a folio manuscript of 172 pages for Sir John Sinclair, a digest of which was published in the *Statistical Account*. Oddly enough, the only reference to Dr Burnside by Burns occurs in a letter to Willie Nicol from Mauchline on 18th June 1787 (C.L. pp.343-4), following his return to Mossgiel after his Border Tour: 'I am quite charmed with Dumfries folks. — Mr Burnside the Clergyman, in particular, is a man whom I shall ever gratefully remember; and his wife, Gude forgie me, I had almost broke the tenth commandment on her account. —Simplicity, elegance, good sense, sweetness of disposition, good humour, kind hospitality, are the constituents of her manner and heart; in short — but if I say one word more about her, I shall be directly in love with her.' This paragon was Anne Hutton (1759-1838).

The poet first appears in the Sitting Book of St Michael's in 1794. Under pew 80 were listed William Hyslop (2), Robert Mitchell's wife (1), John Caird (2), Hugh Walker and Robert Burns (1). By 1797, however, J. Little had replaced Burns. On the other hand, under pew 18, was listed Mrs Burns (3) from that year onwards, alongside Mr Hyslop (3) and Mr Lewars (2). It seems probable that Burns took up his sitting in St Michael's either because of his move to **Burns Street,** or because of Dr Burnside's translation from the New Church to St Michael's. Burns is said to have carved his initials 'R.B.' on the pew, although it seems more likely that this embellishment was added posthumously, after the manner of so many other Burns relics which were deliberately engraved or marked to establish their provenance.

In 1869 the entire interior of the church was refurnished, the original square pews being then replaced by open seats of the modern pattern. 'A great improvement was thus effected', wrote McDowall, 'but unfortunately during the process a precious memorial was cleared away like the ordinary timber among which it stood; this was Burns's Pew in the south-west, which was occupied by the poet and his family.' McDowall added that by the exercise of a little ingenuity the pew could have been harmonised to a great extent with the other wood-work. 'Any appearance of anomaly that remained would have been far more than compensated for by the preservation of such an interesting memento of Burns and Jean Armour.' The location of this pew, however, is indicated by a brass plaque set in the pillar nearby. The pew was in the care of the Burgh Museum until recent years, but has since mysteriously disappeared. It seems incredible that such a bulky relic of the poet could have been mislaid!

None of the accounts of Burns's funeral actually mentions the clergyman who officiated at it, but it is assumed that Dr Burnside conducted the burial service. The poet's funeral was the most spectacular demonstration ever seen in Dumfries up to that time, all the more impressive on account of its spontaneity and the very short amount of time allowed for its preparation. William Grierson's diary noted:

'In respect to the memory of such a genius as Mr Burns, his funeral was uncommonly splendid. The military here consisted of the Cinque Ports Cavalry and Angus-shire Fencibles, who, having handsomely tendered their services, lined the streets on both sides from the Court-house to the burial ground... Order of procession: — The firing party, which consisted of twenty of the Royal Dumfries Volunteers... in full uniform, with crapes on the left arm, marched in front with their arms reversed, moving in a slow and solemn time to the Dead March in Saul, which was played by the military band belonging to the Cinque Ports Cavalry. Next to the firing party was the band, then the bier or corpse supported by six of the Volunteers, who changed at intervals. The relations of the deceased and a number of the respectable inhabitants of both town and country followed next. Then the remainder of the Volunteers followed in rank and the procession closed with a guard of Angus-shire Fencibles. The great bells of the churches tolled at intervals during the time of the procession. When arrived at the churchyard gate, the funeral party formed two lines, and leaned their heads on the firelocks pointed to the ground. Through this space the corpse was carried and borne to the grave. The party then drew up alongside of it, and fired three volleys over the coffin when deposited in the earth. Thus closed a ceremony which on the whole presented a solemn, grand, and affecting spectacle, and accorded with the general sorrow and regret for the loss of a man whose like we can scarce see again.' This account follows very closely that which was published in the *Dumfries Journal* and which may, in fact, have been written by Grierson as well.

ST. MICHAEL'S

Allan Cunningham, recalling the most dramatic episode of his youth almost forty years later, estimated the number of mourners at 12,000. 'Not a word was heard; and although all could not be near, and many could not see, when the earth closed on their darling poet for ever there was no rude impatience shewn. It was an impressive and mournful sight to see men of all ranks and persuasions and opinions mingling as brothers and stepping down the street of Dumfries with the remains of him who had sang of their loves and joys and domestic endearments with a truth and tenderness which none perhaps equalled. I found myself at the brink of the Poet's grave. There was a pause among the mourners as if loath to part with his remains; and when he was at last lowered and the first shovelful of earth sounded on the coffin lid I looked up and saw tears on many cheeks where tears were not usual. The Volunteers fired three straggling volleys. The earth was heaped up, the green sod laid over him, and the multitude stood gazing on the grave for some minutes space, and then melted silently away.'

The piece of ground first occupied by the remains of the poet is thought to have been purchased by him some time before his death, although no entry to this effect has been found in the Kirk Session records. At a meeting of the Session on 21st October 1796, some months after the burial, it was minuted that 'a petition was read and agreed to in favour of Bailie Robert and the deceased

Robert Burns for two burying-grounds, as in the petitions of this date; and the clerk was appointed to register them in the books kept for that purpose; the above burying-grounds to be paid for at the rate of one guinea each, together with clerk's and beadle's dues.'

Following the removal of Burns's remains to the site of the proposed **Mausoleum** on the night of 19th September 1815, the vacant lair was given by Jean Burns to Mrs Perochon. In more recent times a simple plaque has been affixed to the railings: 'Site of Original Grave of Robert Burns'.

A stone pedestal in the Churchyard, south of the church near the footpath leading to the Mausoleum bears a diagrammatic plaque showing the location of the graves of people associated with Burns:

1 Dr and Mrs Burnside
2 Thomas Goldie   **Craigmuie**
3 Robert Cutlar
  Wauchop Riddell
4 Dr John Harley   1742- 1803. A surgeon who served in
      the same Volunteer company as Burns
      and was a friend of Syme, Gracie and
      Lewars.

5 William and Jean
  Hyslop   **Lochend**
6 John Bushby   **Tinwald Downs**
7 James Gracie
8 Mrs Perochon   **Castledykes View**
9 Robert Jackson
10 John Lewars   **Ryedale Cottage**
11 Rev. William Inglis   **Loreburn Church**
12 Francis Shortt   **Courance**
13 David Staig
  Jessie Staig
14 George Gray   1736-1810. A fellow Exciseman
15 John Mitchell
16 The Mausoleum
17 James McClure   **Mausoleum** precinct
18 Jessie Lewars
19 Adam Rankine
20 Dr James Crichton★
21 Robert Mundell   brother of Dr James Mundell of
      Rosebank
22 Col. Archibald McMurdo   a son of John McMurdo of **Drumlanrig**
23 Gabriel Richardson
24 John McDiarmid   1789-1852. Editor of the *Courier* and an
      authority on Burns
25 Col. De Peyster   **Mavis Grove**
26 George Haugh   **Bank Street**
27 Frances Every Miller★
28 William Smith
29 William Wallace★   1772-1818
30 David Williamson   'cruel scoundrel of a Haberdasher'
31 Capt. John Hamilton   **Bank Street**

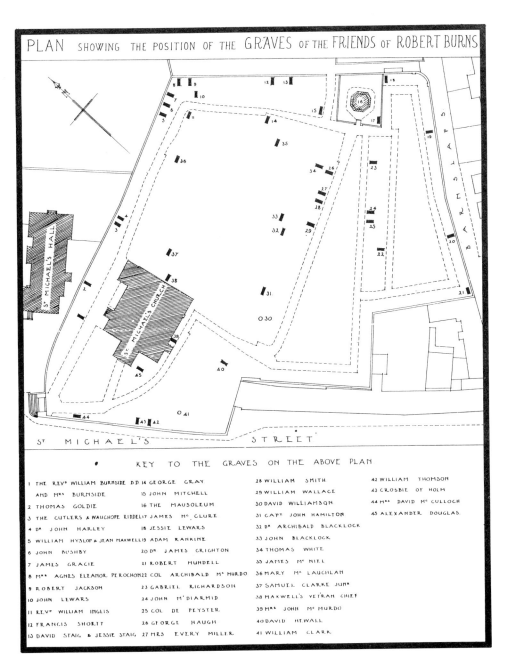

PLAN SHOWING THE POSITION OF THE GRAVES OF THE FRIENDS OF ROBERT BURNS

KEY TO THE GRAVES ON THE ABOVE PLAN

1 THE REVᵈ WILLIAM BURNSIDE D.D
  AND MRˢ BURNSIDE
2 THOMAS GOLDIE
3 THE CUTLERS & WAUCHOPE RIDDEL
4 Dᴿ JOHN HARLEY
5 WILLIAM HYSLOP & JEAN MAXWELLIS
6 JOHN BUSHBY
7 JAMES GRACIE
8 Mᴿˢ AGNES ELEANOR PEROCHON
9 ROBERT JACKSON
10 JOHN LEWARS
11 REVᵈ WILLIAM INGLIS
12 FRANCIS SHORTT
13 DAVID STAIG & JESSIE STAIG

14 GEORGE GRAY
15 JOHN MITCHELL
16 THE MAUSOLEUM
17 JAMES Mᶜ CLURE
18 JESSIE LEWARS
19 ADAM RANKINE
20 Dᴿ JAMES CRICHTON
21 ROBERT HUNDELL
22 COL ARCHIBALD Mᶜ MURDO
23 GABRIEL RICHARDSON
24 JOHN M'DIARMID
25 COL DE PEYSTER
26 GEORGE HAUGH
27 MRS EVERY MILLER

28 WILLIAM SMITH
29 WILLIAM WALLACE
30 DAVID WILLIAMSON
31 CAPTᴺ JOHN HAMILTON
32 Dᴿ ARCHIBALD BLACKLOCK
33 JOHN BLACKLOCK
34 THOMAS WHITE
35 JAMES Mᶜ NIEL
36 MARY Mᶜ LAUCHLAM
37 SAMUEL CLARKE JUNᴿ
38 MAXWELL'S VETRAN CHIEF
39 MRˢ JOHN Mᶜ MURDO
40 DAVID HEWALL
41 WILLIAM CLARK

42 WILLIAM THOMSON
43 CROSBIE OF HOLM
44 Mᴿˢ DAVID Mᶜ CULLOCH
45 ALEXANDER DOUGLAS.

32 Dr Archibald Blacklock	1791-1875. Examined Burns's skull, 1834
33 John Blacklock*	1726-1806. Father of the above
34 Thomas White	**Grammar School**
35 James McNeil	**Craigs**
36 Mary McLauchlan*	1789-1860.
37 Samuel Clark, Jr.	1769-1814.
38 John Maxwell	**Terraughty**
39 Jane Blair McMurdo	**Drumlanrig**
40 David Newall	
41 William Clark	The Provost (1786-8) from whom Burns received his burgess ticket in June 1787
42 William Thomson	1770-1847. Recipient of books from Burns for the **Library**
43 Andrew Crosbie	**Holm**
44 Janet McCulloch	1740-1824. Wife of David McCulloch of **Ardwall**
45 Alexander Douglas	

Biographical details of the people in the above list will be found under the name of their house or business premises (indicated in bold lettering), or in the biographical notes later in the Dumfries section of this book, if not otherwise indicated. Some of the 'friends' of Burns noted on this plaque have only a very tenuous link with the poet, noted in the column opposite their names above. In some cases, indeed, the connection with Burns himself is non-existent. These names, denoted by an asterisk, are explained below. Conversely, there are many other people buried in this churchyard with far better claims on the poet's acquaintance but who are not included in this plaque, e.g. Dr Babington, James Bogie, Jock Brodie, John Lawson, William McCraken, James Nicholson and the architect Thomas Boyd. Boyd's tombstone is one of the simplest and least pretentious in the graveyard, but it could equally have been said of him, as it was of Sir Christopher Wren in St Paul's, 'If you wish to see his memorial, look around you', for many of the fine tombs in St Michael's, like so many of the landmarks in the town itself, were to his credit.

Robert Cutlar kept a shop below the porch of the **Midsteeple** in the mid-18th century. He would be otherwise lost to posterity, but for the fact that his wife Sarah was a Fergusson of **Craigdarroch.** Miss Wauchop Riddell (1752-79) was the sixth daughter of Robert Riddell of Glenriddell and Jean Fergusson of Craigdarroch and first cousin to Captain Robert Riddell of Glenriddell and **Friars' Carse,** friend of the poet. Dr James Crichton, a pioneer of the China trade, was living in Macau and Canton throughout the entire period when Burns was in Dumfries and apparently owes his association with the poet solely to the fact that he retired to **Friars' Carse** in 1812, dying there in 1823. There is, however, absolutely no record of Dr Crichton having the slightest interest in Burns. He was not involved in the Mausoleum fund, nor a subscriber to it. Frances Every was the second wife of Major William Miller of **Dalswinton** who married her some time after his first wife, Jessie Staig, died in 1801. Mary McLauchlan was only six or seven years old when Burns died, so it cannot be claimed that she had first-hand knowledge or memory of him. Early in the 19th century, however, she was a servant to James McClure who had tended the poet on his death-bed, and for this reason some writers have mistakenly associated her in these ministrations. When McClure died in 1813 Mary was taken into service by Jean Armour who regarded her more as a companion than as a servant.

No account of St Michael's Churchyard would be complete without mentioning the tombstone of Robert Anderson, painter and glazier, who died on 24th May 1792 at the age of 80. On this stone is an epitaph:

> They may make epitaphs who can,
> I say here lyes an honest man

This couplet is popularly attributed to Burns. McDowall comments 'an inscription which professes to be no epitaph, and is yet a very happy effort in that line'.

ORIGINAL GRAVE OF BURNS

STAKEFORD

A small estate on the west bank of the **Nith,** now part of the Lincluden housing estate. The mother of Dr James Currie was born in this neighbourhood, and in 1792 Burns's future biographer himself purchased a half share in Stakeford and its teinds. The estate bordered the river, and Burns must often have walked across Currie's land while strolling along the west bank to Lincluden. John Syme, a friend of Dr Currie from their schooldays, acted as his factor and in 1792 offered to lease Stakeford to John Lewars on his behalf, but Lewars turned it down.

THEATRE ROYAL

Situated on Shakespeare Street, it has the distinction of being the only surviving Georgian theatre in Scotland. When Burns settled in Dumfries theatrical entertainments were given by itinerant companies in the old **Assembly Rooms.** One such company, which performed at Dumfries in 1789-90, was managed by George Stephens Sutherland, to whom Burns sent a Prologue (C.W. p.376) with a note: 'Jogging home yester night, it occurred to me that as your next night is the first night of the New Year, a few lines allusive to the Season, by way of Prologue, Interlude or what you please, might take very well...' Burns sent a copy to his brother on 11th January 1790 reporting that Sutherland had 'spouted to his Audience with great applause' (C.L. p.358). The following

March Burns composed a 'Scots Prologue for Mrs Sutherland' (C.W. p.399) which she delivered on her benefit night. Sutherland was sufficiently encouraged by the response of his audiences to make approaches to certain influential gentlemen in the district, with a view to securing a permanent theatre. Burns himself, an avid patron of dramatic performances, discussed this matter with Willie Nicol to whom he wrote on 2nd February 1790 (C.L. pp.346-8):

'Our theatrical company, of which you must have heard, leave us in a week. Their merit and character are indeed very great, both on the stage and in private life; not a worthless creature among them; and their encouragement has been accordingly. Their usual run is from eighteen to twenty-five pounds a night; seldom less than the one, and the house will hold no more than the other. There have been repeated instances of sending away six, and eight, and ten pounds in a night for want of room. A new theatre is to be built by subscription; the first stone is to be laid on Friday first to come. Three hundred guineas have been raised by thirty subscribers, and thirty more might have been got if wanted. The manager, Mr Sutherland, was introduced to me by a friend from Ayr; and a worthier or clever fellow I have rarely met with. Some of our clergy have slipt in by stealth now and then...'

A meeting of the subscribers took place on 18th February 1790, at which Sutherland announced that he had feued a portion of the gardens at East Barnraws (now Queen Street) as a site. A design, based on that of the Theatre Royal, Bristol, was submitted to Thomas Boyd who drew up the plans. The Founding Deed for the Theatre was drafted in the name of Robert Riddell of Glenriddell, to whom was granted by Thomas and William Bushby land 'on the South East side of the street called the Barnraws, or Shakespeare Street'. Riddell was to pay £5 a year to Thomas Bushby, who was also entitled to two 'Brass Tickets' which gave him free admission to all performances (except benefit nights). Each of the original subscribers of ten guineas or more was similarly granted free admission, receiving as a token of this a silver medal which had a vignette of the Theatre on the obverse and the subscriber's name engraved on the reverse.

Burns was too optimistic about the funds raised, for the original capital was exhausted before the work was completed. A further £500 had to be raised before the Theatre was ready. John Brown Williamson, actor - manager formerly with the Theatre Royal in the Haymarket, London, was appointed to manage the Theatre, with Sutherland as his assistant. The opening ceremony, on Saturday 29th September 1792, was reported by the *Weekly Journal:* 'The united elegance and accommodation of the house reflected equal honour on the liberality and taste of the proprietors, and design and execution of the artists, and conspired with the abilities of the performers in giving universal satisfaction to a crowded and polite audience. In a word, it is allowed by persons of first taste and opportunities that this is the handsomest provincial theatre in Scotland.' This report added that Mr Boyd was the architect, and that the scenery was designed by Alexander Nasmyth. Nasmyth, best remembered for painting the portrait of Burns five years previously, received 100 guineas for his work. At that time, Nasmyth was down on his luck. His open advocacy of parliamentary reform alienated his wealthy Edinburgh clientele and it seems likely that he secured the theatrical commission through the good offices of Burns. A sketch is preserved in the National Gallery of Scotland entitled 'Design for a scene for the Dumfries Theatre, done at the desire of Robert Burns, by Alexander Nasmyth'.

The Theatre was designed in the classical fashion then prevailing, with a pillared portico. The interior consisted of a pit, a dress circle of boxes arranged in a horseshoe and, above and behind that, the gallery. Seats in these areas cost 2s, 3s and 1s respectively. Behind the boxes ran a semi-circular passage, off which opened the doors to the boxes. Each box was divided into compartments containing several seats. The baize-covered door to each box had an oval glass panel in the centre, and was tastefully festooned by crimson curtains. The Theatre was capable of accommodating up to 600 people. The Theatre was enlarged in 1830 and rebuilt in 1876 to improve and beautify it in the prevailing Victorian taste. By that time it belonged to Thomas McKie who maintained it 'not as a source of profit but out of public spirit'. In 1911 it was converted to a cinema, a far more lucrative venture than the legitimate stage at that time. In this guise it continued until 1954 when it became a casualty of television. The building was closed until 1st October 1960 when it re-opened as a theatre again, under the auspices of the Guild of Players, and has flourished ever since.

From its inception, the Theatre Royal was keenly patronised by Burns who was on the free list of patrons, thanks to his great friend Robert Riddell. The Theatre had only been open for a month, however, when there occurred the so-called 'Ca Ira' incident. In a letter to Mrs Dunlop, dated 6th December 1792 (C.L. pp.201-2), he comments on the Republican spirit in Dumfries: '... in our Theatre here, "God save the king" has met with some groans and hisses, while Ca ira has been repeatedly called for. — For me, I am a *Placeman*, you know; a very humble one indeed, Heaven knows, but still so much so as to gag me from joining in the cry.'

Despite this disavowal, however, Burns was widely rumoured to be involved in the call for the French Republican song, during the performance of 30th October 1792 and this was included in the charge of disaffection laid against him by a person or persons unknown. Robert Graham of Fintry wrote to Burns at the beginning of January 1793 apprising him of the charge and seeking an explanation. The poet replied on 5th January (C.L. pp.436-8), denying involvement in, or knowledge of, Republican or Reform movements in Dumfries. 'I was in the playhouse one night, when Ca ira was called for. — I was in the middle of the pit, & from the Pit the clamour rose. One or two individuals with whom I occasionally associate were of the party, but I neither knew of the Plot, nor joined in the Plot; nor ever opened my lips to hiss, or huzza, that, or any other Political tune whatever...' On a happier note, Burns was closely associated with the earliest years of the Theatre. A playbill for the New (*sic*) Theatre, Dumfries is extant, dated 26th November 1792, 'for the benefit of Miss Fontenelle'. The evening's entertainment, which began with Wycherley's *Country Girl* and concluded with a re-enactment of Drake's victory over the Spanish Armada 'with Fire Ships, &c., &c.', had as its high point 'A new Occasional Address written by Mr R. Burns called The Rights of Woman' (C.W. pp.471-2). These lines, mirrored on fellow-Exciseman Tom Paine's *Rights of Man*, place Burns in the very forefront of the feminist movement, although, in view of the subsequent furore about his political proclivities, Burns may have regretted the closing lines:

Let Majesty your first attention summon,
Ah! ca ira! THE MAJESTY OF WOMAN!

Louisa Fontenelle (1773-99) played at Dumfries with George Sutherland's touring company in the winters of 1792 and 1793 and three years later married Williamson with whom she migrated to the United States. She died of yellow fever at Charleston, South Carolina on 30th October 1799. She is said to have been a lady of immense charm and beauty and Burns was obviously captivated by her. He sent a copy of the 'Rights of Woman' to her with a highly complimentary letter (C.L. p.682) beginning 'To you, Madam, on our humble Dumfries boards, I have been more indebted for entertainment, than ever I was in prouder Theatres.' A shorter letter, written soon afterwards, sought her permission before sending the poem for publication. For Miss Fontenelle Burns also composed, the following year, the prologue beginning 'Still anxious to Secure your partial Favor' (C.W. p.508) and enclosed a copy with a letter written about 1st December 1793 (C.L. p.683). The stanzas beginning 'Sweet naivete of feature' (C.W. p.509) were probably sent to Miss Fontenelle at the same time.

Williamson's theatrical company was touring Cumbria in 1794 when the entire troupe were thrown into Whitehaven jail by the Earl of Lonsdale on a vagrancy charge. Burns used this incident to hit back at Maria Riddell and Lord Lonsdale in the lines 'From Esopus to Maria' (C.W. p.539). Esopus was an actor in imperial Rome.

Many famous actors and actresses appeared on the stage of the Theatre Royal. In October 1794 Mrs Stephen Kemble (1763-1841) took the eponymous role in George Colman's romantic drama *Yarico* and inspired a quatrain from Burns (C.W. p.526):

Kemble, thou cur'st my unbelief
Of Moses and his rod:
At Yarico's sweet notes of grief
The rock with tears had flow'd.

In the winter season of 1792-3 the leading actor was F.J. Guion, with whom Burns was on good terms, although this was not signified by any poem. The *Dumfries Weekly Journal* of Tuesday 8th January 1793 contained an announcement regarding Guion's benefit night on the following Friday, when *The Way to Keep Him* and the farce *The Old Maid* were to be staged. Burns referred to this event in two letters. One, to David Staig (C.L. p.552), invited the Provost and his family to grace Mr Guion's boxes. The other, to Maria Riddell (C.L. p.602), reminded her of her promise to honour his friend Guion on his benefit night. 'I have the pleasure to know Mr G. well. His merit as an actor is generally acknowledged. He has genius and worth which would do honour to patronage.'

A bronze plaque, with a bas-relief portrait based on the Nasmyth bust by a local artist, Ian Douglas, is to be found on the facade of the theatre.

THEATRE ROYAL, DUMFRIES

WEST BARNRAWS

That part of the ancient thoroughfare known as the Barnraws now known as **Irish Street,** as opposed to the East Barnraws (Queen Street) which led to the **Theatre Royal.** Here stood the town house of John McMurdo of Drumlanrig which he had built in 1793 when he moved into Dumfries. McMurdo also purchased a small country estate called **Hardriggs** near **Annan** before he moved to **Mavis Grove** in 1820. No correspondence from Burns to McMurdo exists after 1793, and it is assumed that this was due to the fact that McMurdo, being resident in the town, saw Burns daily.

BIOGRAPHICAL NOTES

Below are enumerated several people with whom Burns came in contact in Dumfries, but whose homes or premises cannot be precisely located.

ROBERT ANDERSON

Burns recorded that his jemmy boots, ruined by rain on Loch Ken during his Galloway Tour with Syme, had been purchased from Robert Anderson at a cost of £1 2s. There is no trace of Robert Anderson, although there were several shoemakers and leatherworkers of that surname in Dumfries in the late 18th century. Many of the craftsmen plying these trades lived in **Friars Vennel** and included Deacon David Anderson, chief of the craft, who died in 1791. Several generations of Andersons, employed as shoemakers in the Vennel, are recorded. From **Ellisland** on 5th May 1789 Burns wrote to his brother William (C.L. p.516): 'Anderson I hope will have your shoes ready to send by the waggon tomorrow. I forgot to mention the circumstance of making them pumps; but I suppose good calf shoes will be no great mistake.'

FRANCIS ARMSTRONG

A Dumfries wine merchant, possibly the father of the merchant Christopher Armstrong and the dyer Robert Armstrong who flourished in the early 19th century. John Syme narrates that a great rise on rum took place in June 1796. Francis Armstrong had several casks or puncheons and asked Burns in his official capacity to gauge and prove the spirit. Burns tested the spirit and found it to be above proof (due to evaporation). Armstrong wished to reduce the spirit so water was procured for the purpose. The wine merchant and the Exciseman were engaged in watering the rum when Syme caught them in the act and was suitably indignant at this business, and promised to blackguard it with an epigram. Burns promised to retaliate in similar vein. Syme later claimed to have written the following lines extempore:

> In beneficent times the blest mandate was given —
> 'Let the Pitchers with water be filled.'
> And forthwith the fluid, by the bounty of Heaven,
> Into Wine, that cheers Man, was distilled —
> But see the vile arts of an Armstrong & Burns —
> When a Puncheon of Spirits has spunk; —
> The choice liquor with water is drenched till it turns
> A potion too base to be drunk —

Frederick Kent (*Burns Chronicle*, 1932) suggested that Burns, not Syme, was the author of this epigram, on the grounds that Syme is not known to have penned a line of verse in the whole of his long life, the substance and manner indicate Burns, and if Syme had written it one would have expected an instant and devastating rejoinder. Syme probably let it stand as it had been sent to him by his friend, one who playfully represented him as suddenly verse-articulate. Nevertheless, this poem has not been admitted to the canon. It is to be found in the manuscript collection of Burns epigrams compiled by John Syme and now in the Hornel Collection at Kirkcudbright.

JAMES BOGIE (1778-1861)

Much of his life was spent at **Terraughty** where he was employed as gardener to John Maxwell 'the Maxwells' vet'ran chief'. As a youth he had known Burns well, during the latter's visits to Terraughty. His father, also named James (1717-93), was head gardener at Terraughty before him. James Junior played a prominent part in the campaigns to provide for the poet's widow and family, and later in the **Mausoleum** project. On a more practical level, however, he was in charge of the arrangements in 1815 when the remains of the poet were removed from their original lair and re-interred. During his latter years he was employed as groundsman at **St Michael's** and resided in a cottage of that name near the churchyard. James Bogie was one of the chief mourners at the funeral of Jean Armour on 1st April 1834 and helped to place her coffin in the grave dug within the vault of the Mausoleum.

JOHN 'JOCK' BRODIE (1777-1875)

Born and brought up in a house in **Friars Vennel,** he later resided in Townhead Street. In his boyhood he often ran errands for the Burns family when they lived in nearby **Bank Street** and was about nineteen years old when Burns died. *The Gallovidian* (1903) contains a sketch of Brodie, one of the more kenspeckle characters of Dumfries in the 19th century. Brodie made a living as a general dealer, though he also had a reputation as a poacher. A.J. Armstrong, in his sketch, comments of Brodie that 'His knowledge of the poet and his wife he valued but did not parade. He never gave it away for nothing.' The writer recalled an incident one day in the Dumfries Curiosity Shop run by W.G. Gibson when Brodie and the shopkeeper were discoursing on the subject of 'brocks, stoats and moudies'. The auctioneer Andrew Stewart and an American gentleman entered the shop. Stewart had been looking all over the town for Brodie, whom he wished to introduce to the American as someone who had actually known Burns.

Brodie responded with the following description of the poet: 'Rob was a long lingle fallah wi a loot an his een gied through ye like gemlits, his broos were gey aften doon, an he looked like ane that cared mair for ither folk than he did for his sel' an his ain.' When questioned about Jean Armour, Jock replied, 'She was weel-faured and kind, only a wee bit thowless; a better-natured woman I never saw. She needed, for Rob was nae saunct!'

Mrs E. Kirkland of Dumfries Ladies Burns Club, a great-granddaughter of Jock Brodie, has several anecdotes which have been handed down through her family and concern her ancestor and the poet.

One day Burns was walking down the street and coming towards him was the minister and an elder. When they were opposite Burns they both turned and shouted 'Baa!'. Burns turned to them and retorted:

> Mr Auld and Elder Blair
> Oh guid manners, ye are bare.
> Like twa sheep amang folk's kye
> Juist ca' 'Baa' as folk gae by.

No minister named Auld is recorded in Dumfries and the only Blairs were the family of Mrs John McMurdo. The story seems hardly likely. Another tale concerns a stay at a gamekeeper's cottage, when Burns was asked to say grace before the last meal. By this time Burns was sick of rabbit served at every meal, hence the grace:

> Rabbits young and rabbits old,
> Rabbits hot and rabbits cold,
> Rabbits black and rabbits grey,
> Thank the Lord I'm gaein away.

According to Mrs Kirkland Jock gave Burns the drinking vessel made from half a coconut, now preserved in **Burns House.** Two wooden vessels in the same museum are alleged to have been given by the poet to Jock. Mrs Kirkland adds, 'It has been said that Bonny Jean gave Jock Brodie the musket belonging to Burns, and Jock would never part with it. Two years after his death in 1875 the gun was offered for sale in a Dumfries gun-shop.' It is not known, however, whether this musket is the one which was purchased in recent years and is now on display in **Burns House.**

Jock also claimed to own the poet's basket-hilted Highland broadsword, despite the fact that no such sword was ever in Burns's possession. Brodie also played a questionable role in the manufacture and distribution of spurious Burns relics. He purchased two swords at the roup of Dr William Maxwell in 1834, paying 7s 8d and 8s respectively for them. One of these was the Highland broadsword subsequently acquired by 'Honest Allan' Cunningham and thereafter paraded as Burns's sword. The other was apparently retained by Brodie himself and similarly paraded. More seriously, Brodie was implicated in the farce of the poet's pistols, which caused such a furore in the national press in 1859. The truth was exposed by the *Glasgow Herald* on 8th February 1859. The pistols had been purchased at the Maxwell sale and subsequently sold on to

Cunningham for £5. The purchaser at the auction was given as 'Jock Brodie, a kind of broker, game-dealer, sportsman and perhaps poacher in a small way; but though decent, he was not a person of any consideration.' The *Herald* was equally dismissive of the pistols — 'a very common pair they are'. Wellwood Anderson subsequently questioned Brodie about this episode and eventually wrung an admission from him that no one had ever told him that they were the poet's pistols at all. The sale record reveals that he paid 15s 6d for them, and sold them half an hour after the sale to Cunningham's son Peter for £5 — a very handsome profit on the transaction.

Brodie was also the perpetrator of another brace of Burns's pistols (now on display at the Birthplace Museum, Alloway). If the Cunningham pistols were indeed 'a very common pair', then this brace is beneath contempt. They are typical of the very cheap pistols turned out in countless thousands in the late 18th century and possess no merit, technically or intrinsically. Their sole claim to fame lies in their butts which bear the initials R.B. in pokerwork. They are displayed with a letter from Mrs Brodie, dated 28th May 1875, certifying that the pistols were given to her husband John by Burns at his decease. Brodie himself had died at Dumfries on 4th May that year, at the advanced age of 98.

In view of his part in the promotion of spurious relics, Brodie's claims regarding the drinking vessels and musket must be regarded with caution and also cast some shadow of doubt on his other tales concerning the poet and his wife. Neither his epigram nor his grace, quoted above, have been admitted to the canon.

SAMUEL CLARK, JUNIOR (1769-1814)

Like his father before him, a solicitor in Dumfries and conjunct Commissary Clerk as well as Clerk of the Peace for the County. He married Mary Wight in 1798 and had fourteen children. He was a good friend of Burns who seems to have been more than usually convivial in his company. Clark was with Burns on that memorable occasion in July 1794 when the poet's ambivalent toast 'May our success in the present war be equal to the justice of our cause' roused the ire of Captain (later Major) Dods. Burns wrote to Clark the following morning begging him to intercede with Dods and ensure that word of the incident did not get back to his superiors in the Excise. Clark was also the recipient of an earlier letter asking him to use his influence with William Corbet (Supervisor-General of Excise) in correcting the prejudices in the Excise Office, Edinburgh 'against me as being a drunken dissipated character. — I might be all this, you know, & yet be an honest fellow, but you know that I am an honest fellow and am nothing of this.'

ALEXANDER DOUGLAS (1742-97)

Son of the wig-maker, David Douglas, he was a general merchant in the town and kept a hostelry in the High Street, which Burns used to visit both as a customer and in a professional capacity. His daughter (Mrs Thomas Watson) distinctly remembered Burns coming to her father's house one day on Excise business, just after she and the servant had been making potato starch, then an interdicted trade, in the kitchen. Burns could not help seeing the illicit article, as it lay exposed in an ashet on the window-sill; and having learned what it was, he, with a warning shake of his head, said, 'Lassie, ye sin and fear not: take this out of my sight!'

JOHN DRUMMOND

A native of Crieff, he spent four years as a clerk in a Stirling bank before coming to Dumfries as clerk in the branch of the Paisley Union Bank about 1791. Burns was a customer of this bank, and sent its draft for £32 to John Ballantine from **Ellisland** in September 1791 (C.L. p.104), adding, 'I would have sent a servant all the way with the money, but the Banker in Dumfries who manages for the Paisley people assured me, that you banking-folks hold Draughts on one another, as equal to cash.—' Rather than the manager, Mr Wylie, the banker in question was probably John Drummond whom Burns obviously got to know very well, both professionally and socially.

When the Paisley Union Bank closed its Dumfries branch during the recession following the outbreak of the war with France, Drummond was made redundant. On 25th August 1793, therefore, Burns wrote to Mrs Dunlop (C.L. p.206) asking if she were acquainted with any of the principals of the new Royal Bank about to be established in Glasgow and soliciting her help in obtaining a position there for Drummond, 'an uncommonly clever worthy young fellow, an intimate friend of mine'.

ALEXANDER FINDLATER (1754-1839)

Born at Burntisland, Fife, the fourth son of an Excise officer, James F. Findlater, and named after his grandfather, the Rev. Alexander Findlater of Hamilton. He entered the Excise in 1774, was appointed Examiner in June 1790 and became Supervisor at Dumfries the following April. He was promoted to General Supervisor in 1797 and then moved to Edinburgh. He succeeded William Corbet as Collector at Glasgow (1811-25). He had been Supervisor at Dumfries about six months when Burns moved into the town and was thus, for the last years of the poet's life, his immediate superior in the Excise. His connection with Burns, however, dated back to the time when the poet had become an Exciseman. Later he was to write: 'In all that time the superintendence of his behaviour as an officer of the revenue, was a branch of my especial province, and it may be supposed I would not be an inattentive observer of the *general* conduct of a man and a poet so celebrated by his countrymen.'

This is borne out by the fact that Burns wrote to him as far back as October 1789 from **Ellisland,** taking him up on a promise to carry letters for him to and from Glasgow — an illegal, though common, evasion of the Postmaster General's monopoly. Later the same month (C.L. p.539) Burns thanked him for 'this uncommon instance of kindness & friendship' — the excellent character reference which Findlater supplied to Corbet. The minutes of the Justices of the Peace Quarter Sessions for Dumfriesshire, dated 27th October 1789, show that both Burns and Findlater appeared before the magistrates and were sworn, the one as an Excise officer, and the other as 'an extraordinary officer of the Customs' in addition to his Excise duties. From Ellisland, probably some time in 1790, Burns sent Findlater a parcel of new-laid eggs. Findlater was the recipient of nine letters in all up to September 1794, and only two of them actually deal with Excise business. In a copy of Thomson's *Select Scotish Airs*, which Burns presented to Findlater early in May 1793, were written the words 'A pledge of rooted Friendship, well watered with many a bottle of good WINE ', showing that Burns and Findlater associated not just on a professional plane. After his friend's death Findlater robustly defended his memory against the calumnies of Heron and Currie, and contributed a lengthy testimonial for the preface to Peterkin's edition of 1814. He also wrote at length and in great detail refuting similar allegations which appeared in Allan Cunningham's edition of 1834. His rebuttal of Cunningham's charges were published in the *Glasgow Courier* of 29th January 1835.

Burns referred to Findlater in several of his letters to other correspondents. Burns put Findlater on the subscription list for Dr Anderson's magazine *The Bee*. Findlater was the recipient of the verse epistle beginning 'Dear Sir, our Lucky humbly begs' (C.W. p.378), probably composed about February 1790.

JAMES GRACIE (1756-1814)

Born at New Abbey, he was a prominent businessman in Dumfries. For more than twenty years he was Treasurer or Dean of Guild and one of the principal magistrates of the town. When the Royal Dumfries Volunteers were formed, Gracie was appointed captain. For some years the manager of the Bank of Scotland's Dumfries branch at 94 Irish Street, he founded in 1804 the Dumfries Commercial Bank with his son James and John Stott as partners. The bank, however, failed in 1808 with a deficiency of ten shillings in the pound. Three different types of one-guinea banknotes are known, as well as a five-pound note. The man whom Burns apostrophized as 'Gracie, thou art a man of worth' (C.W. p.420) died a bankrupt on 23rd March 1814. At Burns's behest, Gracie became a subscriber to Johnson's *Musical Museum* about August 1795. Two brief notes from Burns to Gracie are extant (C.L. p.582). The first, written about April 1791, dealt with the vexatious matter of Alexander Crombie's bill and it is clear that Gracie, in his capacity as bank manager, had shown remarkable forbearance. The second, written from the **Brow** on 13th July 1796, declined Gracie's kind offer of a convalescent outing in his carriage.

ROBERT JACKSON (1743-1810)

Apart from Burns himself, the leading literary figure of Dumfries in the late 18th century. About 1776 he founded the *Dumfries Magazine*, the town's first periodical, an octavo publication 'well got up externally... but signally lacking in topics of local interest'. In 1777 he dropped it in favour of a newspaper, the *Dumfries Weekly Journal*. After Jackson's death the paper had several proprietors before it passed into the hands of the Rev. Henry Duncan who closed it down in 1833. Although McDowall dismissed its local reportage as 'extremely scant', it remains a goldmine of information about the events and people of Dumfries in the late 18th and early 19th centuries and is the chief source for details of those connected with Burns. To this paper goes the credit for having published the earliest memoir of Burns, by Maria Riddell of **Woodley Park**. Three of Burns's poems were published in the Journal in his lifetime: 'Adown Winding Nith' (C.W. p.497) and 'Address spoken by Miss Fontenelle' (C.W. p.508) were both published in the issue of 3rd December 1793, while 'Does Haughty Gaul Invasion Threat' (C.W. p.537) appeared in the number of 5th May 1795. Burns was a frequent and welcome guest at Jackson's home. Oddly enough, the Journal made little mention of Burns himself — even the memorable fact that Dumfries acquired such a celebrity as a citizen towards the close of 1791 received no mention. An account for 10s in respect of the advertisement in the *Journal* for the sale of stock at Ellisland is extant. Mrs Jackson, Jane Cochrane, was also a close friend of the poet.

Jackson was later Provost of Dumfries on three separate occasions (1797-9, 1800-2 and 1809-10).

JOHN LAWSON (1767-1809)

A wine merchant whose premises are believed to have been in Irish Street on the west side between Bank Street and Friars Vennel. This old shop was demolished in the 1950s. In the 'Election Ballad' (C.W. pp.402-6) at the close of the contest for the Dumfries Burghs in 1790, addressed to Robert Graham of Fintry, Burns speaks of Sir Robert Lawrie as:

... that baron bold,
'Mid Lawson's port entrench'd his hold,
And threaten'd worse damnation.

JESSIE LEWARS (1778-1855)

The sister of John Lewars Junior and last of Burns's heroines. After the death of her father, John Lewars Senior (Supervisor of Excise in Dumfries), she moved in with her brother who had a house in Millbrae Vennel, across the street from the house occupied by the poet's family from 1793 onwards. As John was an Excise colleague as well as nearest neighbour, a close friendship developed between the two families. It was in the Lewars' house that Burns heard Jessie singing the old ballad 'The Robin cam to the Wren's Nest' and wrote for this air the song 'O Wert Thou in the Cauld Blast' (C.W. p.567). According to McDowall, Jessie made the poet's house a second home, 'her affectionate nature, artless manners, and acquired accomplishments rendering her a favourite guest with its inmates. Burns's hours of ease received new zest from her society; she helped to soothe his sorrows by playing on the piano those sweet Scotch airs to which many of his own lyrics had been lovingly wedded; and when the poet lay on his death-bed, she was to him one seraph left on earth, of which he wrote prophetically in the celebrated epigram penned by him in her praise'. The lines referred to were part of the 'Versicles to Jessie Lewars' (C.W. p.566). During his last illness Burns was nursed by the eighteen year-old Jessie. Tradition maintains that 'O, Lay thy Loof' (C.W. p.552) was written as a tribute to Jessie Lewars, although Burns actually sent it to James Johnson in May 1795. She certainly inspired the song 'Here's a Health to Ane I Loe Dear' (C.W. p.565). The second stanza conveys the hopelessness of the dying poet's passion:

> Altho thou maun never be mine,
> Altho even hope is denied,
> 'Tis sweeter for thee despairing
> Than ought in the world beside, Jessie —
> Than ought in the world beside!

This song was sent to George Thomson in April 1796 and a copy went to Alexander Cunningham on 12th July 'as the last I made or probably will make for some time.' Burns died just nine days later. In June of that year Burns wrote to James Johnson (C.L. p.303) '... my wife has a very particular friend of hers, a young lady who sings well, to whom she wishes to present the Scots Musical Museum. If you have a spare copy, will you be obliging as to send it by the very first Fly, as I am anxious to have it soon.' Johnson promptly sent the set of volumes and Burns inscribed the back of the title page of the first volume on 26th June with twelve lines of verse, beginning 'Thine be the volumes, Jessie fair' (C.W. p.567). After Burns's death a month later, Jessie took charge of the poet's four sons for some time. The poet's widow had no closer or more trusted friend than Jessie Lewars. In June 1799 Jessie married James Thomson, a Dumfries solicitor, and had five sons and two daughters. A neighbour in death as in life, Jessie's tomb is close to the **Mausoleum.**

JESSIE LEWARS' TOMB IN ST. MICHAEL'S KIRKYARD

WILLIAM McCRAKEN (1757-1818)

A lawyer in Dumfries, he was lampooned along with Burns, Maxwell and Syme in the verses circulated by the Loyal Natives:

With Cracken, the attorney, and Mundell, the quack.

McCraken was embroiled with Syme in the legal afairs of James Maxwell of **Kirkconnell,** elder brother of Dr William Maxwell, which was probably enough to have him branded as a 'Jacobin' — a term which was bandied about as freely in 1794-5 as 'Commie' in America during the McCarthy era. Significantly, McCraken was one of the first to join the Dumfries Volunteers and served on the management committee. McCraken lived at Lochvale. His tombstone in **St Michael's** shows that his wife Clementina died very young, and records laconically: 'She was near two years a wife; had two sons, William and James; the youngest predeceased her 32 days, the eldest survived her 22 hours, and was buried with her.'

WILLIAM McCRAKEN'S TOMB IN ST. MICHAEL'S KIRKYARD

SIMON McKENZIE

A lawyer in Dumfries, he held office as Town Clerk in 1795. He is a shadowy figure, no biographical details being known; but the *Dumfries Weekly Journal* from 1788 onwards contains many advertisements which reveal that he acted also in the capacity of estate agent. He was tentatively identified by Kinsley as the recipient of 'Remorseful Apology' (C.W. p.568), which he dates to January 1796. The tone of remorse after a drunken quarrel had misled previous editors into thinking that these lines had been addressed to Maria Riddell after the 'Rape of the Sabines' incident, but this verse epistle was sub-titled 'Sent to A Gentleman Whom He Had Offended' which clearly rules out a female recipient. Simon McKenzie attended the inaugural meeting of the Royal Dumfries Volunteers on 31st January 1795, at which Burns was also present. Whatever the truth of the matter, Simon McKenzie played a prominent part in the campaigns to provide for the poet's widow and family, and subsequently for the erection of a suitable memorial.

HUGH MARQUES (born 1765)
A fellow Exciseman, whom Burns entered as a subscriber to *The Bee* in November 1790. He came to Dumfries in September 1790 and was appointed to the Woodhouse Division (Gretna). He was subsequently promoted and transferred out of the Dumfries area. He became Port Supervisor at Leith and lived long enough to enjoy his pension for 20 years. There was no connection between him and the local worthy nicknamed the Marquis who kept a public house in a close of that name, long since demolished and now untraceable, inspiring the extempore mock epitaph (C.W. p.521):
> Here lies a mock Marquis, whose titles were shamm'd,
> If ever he rise, it will be to be damn'd.
According to Allan Cunningham (1834) 'This personage was landlord of a respectable public-house... and the little court or alley where his change-house stood is still called the Marquis's Close'.

JOHN MITCHELL (1731-1806)
A native of Aberdeenshire, he studied for the ministry but never completed the course. Instead he entered the Excise service and was successively stationed in Fraserburgh and Kilmarnock before being appointed Collector at Dumfries in 1788. He remained there until 1802 when he became Collector at Haddington and retired two years later. Burns had taken Excise instruction in 1788 and obtained his commission. A letter from Robert Graham of Fintry was the means of introducing Burns to Collector Mitchell. Writing on 13th May 1789 (C.L. p.428) to Graham, Burns said: 'I waited on Collector Mitchell with your letter.- It happened to be Collection-day, so he was very throng, but he received me with the utmost politeness and made me promise to call on him soon.' On 31st July Burns again wrote to Graham: 'Mr Mitchel did not wait my calling on him, but sent me a kind letter giving me a hint of the business, and on my waiting on him yesterday, he entered with the most friendly ardour into my views and interests.' Mitchell apparently agreed to transfer the present incumbent of the Excise division in which Burns lived so that Burns could have the appointment — a move which has led to Burns being accused of pulling strings to the disadvantage of a fellow Exciseman. Burns heard that he had got the appointment about two weeks later, although he did not actually commence work until the beginning of September 1789. Burns later acknowledged the invaluable help of Mitchell and Findlater in breaking him in.

Burns's first extant letter to Mitchell was written from **Ellisland** in September 1790 and illustrates the problems that faced an Exciseman in doing his duty without fear or favour. Burns had reported Thomas Johnston of **Mirecleugh** for illicit maltings and though Johnston was fined, his conviction was suspended until his appeal could be investigated. This led to Burns compiling a detailed answer to Johnston's petition (C.L. pp.564-5) containing more than a hint of the exasperation he felt at justice being impeded by the intervention of Johnston's powerful friends. As it so happened, they were Burns's friends also — Fergusson of **Craigdarroch** and Riddell of Glenriddell. The only other letters from Burns to Mitchell were brief notes, seeking permission for leave of absence to attend his brother Gilbert's wedding, and dealing with Excise accounts.

From the Globe Inn on 4th September 1790 (C.L. pp.433-4) Burns wrote to Graham, telling him that he had asked Mitchell to get him transferred to Dumfries itself. 'I own I have some wayward feelings at appearing as a simple Gauger in a Country where I am only known by fame.' It was Mitchell who broke to Burns the news that the Excise Board had ordered an enquiry into his political conduct, but it was also Mitchell who recommended Burns to take over as Supervisor of the Galloway District from McFarlane when the latter became ill. Late in 1795 Burns sent a verse epistle 'To Collector Mitchell' (C.W. p.561) which began with the line 'Friend of the Poet tried and leal', which ever afterwards stuck as an epithet to Mitchell. It is clear that Burns consulted Mitchell on poetic as well as Excise matters. In a letter to John Leven, General Supervisor of Excise in March 1792 (C.L. p.614), Burns wrote: 'Mr Mitchel mentioned to you a ballad, which I composed and sung at one of his Excise Court dinners'. The ballad was, of course, 'The Deil's Awa wi th'Exciseman'. After Mitchell's death a collection of poems and songs in Burns's handwriting was found among his papers, obviously sent to him for his comments. Mitchell's family subsequently lost these precious manuscripts.

ROBERT MOORE

Described in the *Dumfries Weekly Journal* of 13th March 1798 as a bricklayer, his sole claim to fame lies in the fact that he was prosecuted by Burns for a breach of Excise regulations. On 26th October 1789 he received notification from Burns (C.L. p.543) that he had been fined £1 for making bricks without entry. This brief letter is the sole surviving example of Burns's dealings with the general public in his capacity as an Excise officer. The craft of brickmaking was relatively new to Scotland at that time and it is interesting to note that it had been introduced from France by James Maxwell of **Kirkconnell** (father of Dr William Maxwell) in the 1750s following his return from Jacobite exile. Nothing else is known about Moore, although it is believed that his premises were in the **Ryedale** area, possibly near the present Cargenholm Hotel.

DAVID NEWALL

A Dumfries lawyer and businessman who owned a number of properties in and around the town. His tombstone in **St Michael's** is exasperatingly devoid of dates and other useful details, but he flourished in Dumfries in the late 18th and early 19th centuries. His son Adam was a property developer who left his mark in Newall Terrace, Rae Street (his mother's maiden name) and Catherine Street (his sister's name). David Newall owned the house at **Isle** where Burns and Jean Armour lodged while waiting for the completion of **Ellisland** in 1788. David practised law in Dumfries and became Procurator Fiscal, but also speculated in property and collaborated with his son Adam in land deals and property development. Adam Newall was for many years a successful wine merchant in Bordeaux and only retired to Dumfries at the end of his career, so it must be deduced that his involvement in the property ventures was merely a front for his lawyer father. Burns is reputed to have been a frequent visitor to his town house called Bushybank (untraceable and no longer extant), where his daughter Catherine (later wife of the Rev. Charles Maitland Babington) would play on the piano old Scottish airs that Burns collected and to which he composed fresh lyrics. The only extant letters from Burns to David Newall (C.L. pp.544-5) dealt mainly with business matters regarding the building of Ellisland, but Newall was also the recipient of at least one of Burns's poems, a copy of 'The Five Carlins' (C.W. p.364).

JAMES NICHOLSON

A snuff-dealer and tobacconist, he succeeded his father Jonah Nicholson in this business on the latter's death in 1780. His young wife Agnes Haining died in May 1800, leaving six children, but nothing is known of the later career of her grieving husband. Burns was apparently a customer.

MATTHEW PENN

A Dumfries lawyer who would be totally unknown and forgotten but for the fact that he acted on behalf of David Williamson in attempting to recover a debt from the poet, incurred over the cost of his Volunteer uniform.   During the second critical week of Burns's sojourn at the **Brow**

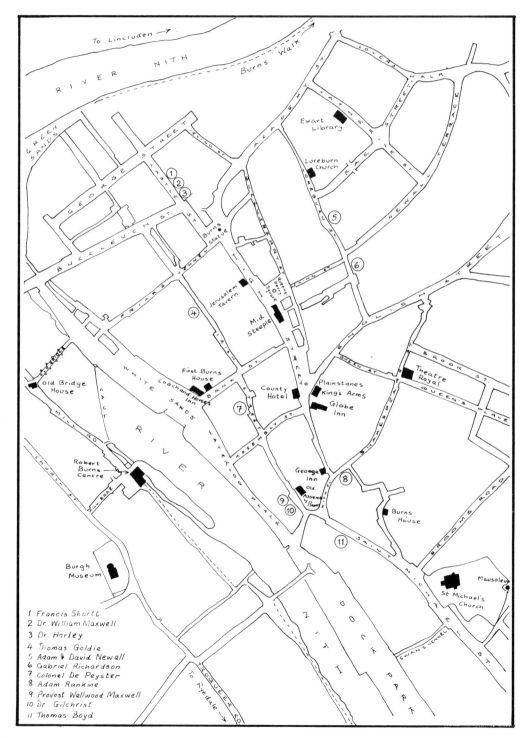

1 Francis Shortt
2 Dr. William Maxwell
3 Dr. Harley
4 Thomas Goldie
5 Adam & David Newall
6 Gabriel Richardson
7 Colonel De Peyster
8 Adam Rankine
9 Provost Wellwood Maxwell
10 Dr. Gilchrist
11 Thomas Boyd

he received a letter from Penn demanding payment of £7 4s, which was due to Williamson. In fairness to the latter it appears that the account, with others which were over-due, had been given by Williamson to Penn to chase up. Penn's letter contained no threat, but Burns's mind was so unhinged with disease that the missive appeared to him to be very menacing. Had he been in good health his knowledge of business practice would have kept matters in their true perspective; as matters stood, however, Penn's innocuous letter told on him with devastating force. This explains the hysterical letter from the poet to his cousin James Burness at Montrose on 12th July 1796 (C.W. p.63) saying that Williamson, taking it into his head that Burns was dying, 'has commenced a process against me & will infallibly put my emaciated body into jail'. Virtually the same words were used in Burns's letter to George Thomson, written on the same date (C.W. p.679). According to Dr Burnside's manuscript history of Dumfries, in 1790, out of 70 committed to jail, no fewer than 23 were committed for debt. Of these 13 were resident in Dumfries and the others came from the county and the Stewartry.

NICHOL RAE

Franklyn Bliss Snyder (p.360) reproduces a bill for clothing for the poet's family, amounting to £2 5s, supplied by this tailor. He is otherwise unknown to posterity, although he may have been a son of George Rae, Deacon of the Tailors, who died in 1783 aged 68. The close in which Nichol Rae plied his trade was on the site of the southern boundary of the Munches Street car park.

ADAM RANKINE (1777-1859)

Described by McDowall as 'an active, bustling, enterprising and warm-hearted gentleman'. Few men in the first half of the 19th century took so prominent a part in local affairs, though he is chiefly remembered for having founded the Dumfries Artillery Volunteers in 1804, when war with France was renewed after the collapse of the Peace of Amiens. His wife Sarah was a sister of Simon McKenzie. He was born in New Galloway and came to Dumfries as a youth. As well as being captain in the Volunteers, he was a bailie and in the latter capacity saved the burgh from bankruptcy. He was also governor of the Dumfries Savings Bank. Although included among the 'Friends of Burns' listed on the tablet in **St Michael's,** it is unlikely that Rankine, only eighteen years old when Burns died, could have had more than passing acquaintance with the poet; but he took a leading role in the **Mausoleum** campaign and interested himself in the welfare of the poet's family.

GABRIEL RICHARDSON (1759-1820)

A native of the parish of Kirkpatrick-Juxta, he was born in humble circumstances on the lands of Kellobank which had once belonged to his ancestors. By some misfortune, however, the family estate had to be sold and the Richardsons reduced to the status of landless farm-labourers. By dint of sheer hard work, Richardson picked himself up. Moving into Dumfries, he became a brewer and merchant, a leading councillor in the burgh and eventually its Provost (1802-3). Between the families of the poet and Richardson there was a great deal of intimacy. Gabriel and Burns were the same age, and their eldest sons John and Robert both started at the **Grammar School** on the same day. The former grew up to be an explorer and naturalist, eventually knighted. In his professional capacity Burns had the task of surveying Richardson's brewery. When Gabriel complained that he was unfairly taxed on his ale, when compared with the products of brewers outside the burgh, Burns took up the case and wrote to Provost Staig in January 1793 (C.L. pp.552-3) to rectify this injustice. Burns composed a mock epitaph (C.W. p.483):

> Here Brewer Gabriel's fire's extinct,
>   And empty all his barrels:
> He's blest — if as he brew'd, he drink —
>   In upright, honest morals.

This was inscribed on a glass goblet, for long in the possession of the Richardson family. Burns was a regular visitor to the Richardson home in **Nith Place** on Sunday evenings. Sir John Richardson, the Arctic explorer, was only nine years old when Burns died, but he had vivid memories of the poet. He recalled how, on one occasion, Burns had pointed out some of the Paraphrases which he most admired and urged the boy to memorise them. He was eight years old when he and young Robert Burns were enrolled by their fathers at the school. John never forgot the poet's bright smile and flashing eye when he turned to his friend Gabriel and said 'I wonder which of them will be the greatest man.' As a boy, Robert Junior showed immense promise, but though he obtained a clerkship in the Board of Inland Revenue at Somerset House in 1804, his civil service career was undistinguished.

THOMAS SMITH (1764-1825)

Born at Dumfries, he was educated at Edinburgh University and after graduating in 1785 went to Alloa Seminary. In 1789 he was licensed to preach by the Presbytery of Dumfries and ordained the following year.

Later in 1790 he received a call from the congregation of Mecklenburgh County, North Carolina, but declined it and worked for ten years as a home missionary. In 1800, however, he emigrated to the United States where he did missionary and supply work for eleven years. He was then appointed minister of a United Presbyterian congregation in Huntingdon, Pennsylvania where he remained till his death. Smith was doing missionary work in Auchinleck parish in July 1791 when Burns sent him a copy of 'Wilt Thou be my Dearie' (C.W. p.512) and 'O wat ye wha's in yon Town' (C.W. p.541), with a long letter which was conveyed privately by the Rev. Mr Ferrier of Paisley (C.L. p.585).

WILLIAM SMITH (1782-1866)

A barber and perfumier with premises in English Street, opposite the **King's Arms,** which made his place of business a fashionable resort for distinguished visitors to the town, as well as to the actors at the **Theatre Royal** nearby. Edmund Kean, the celebrated actor, was one of his clientele. He was also a town councillor and for some time Burgh Treasurer. The story has gained ground that Robert Burns was also among his customers, but McDowall merely states that 'When quite a youth, he frequently saw Robert Burns, of whose appearance he retained a distinct recollection. He has told us that the poet's eyes were something wonderful — piercing and lustrous, like orbs of fire; the only eyes he ever saw at all comparable with them being those of Kean.' Smith would only have been about fourteen years old at the time of the poet's death.

DAVID STAIG (1740-1824)

For upwards of forty years he was Dumfries agent of the Bank of Scotland and the most powerful man in the burgh in his day. At Michaelmas 1783 he was elected Provost, and from then until 1817 he held the chief office no fewer than nine times. Shrewd, inventive, enterprising, politic, fond of power, not insensible to flattery, warm-hearted and virtuous, using his influence so far as his judgment went for the advancement of the public good. But for the law at the time, which prevented anyone from being provost for more than a year or two at a time, he would undoubtedly have held office for life. Under his administration Dumfries got its first paving, cleansing, lighting and police, followed by sweeping reform of the civic revenues (1788). The new Academy, the shipping quay, the new bridge over the Nith and the first regular mail-coach service were all due to his energy and drive.

Four letters from Burns to David Staig are extant, three on relatively personal matters and the fourth a formal petition addressed to him in his capacity as Provost. On 1st March 1790 Burns wrote (C.L. p.551) enclosing a copy of the Scots Prologue for Mrs Sutherland's benefit night (C.W. p.399). That Staig shared the poet's interest in the **Theatre** is shown in the letter of 10th January 1793 inviting the Staig family to attend Guion's benefit night. The third letter, however, shows how

Burns the Exciseman used his expertise to promote the revenue of the burgh by overhauling the application of the local beer tax. His suggestions were adopted soon afterwards and considerably benefited the burgh's income — a matter of which Staig was gently reminded in the fourth letter by which Burns sought for his children the free education which was one of the privileges enjoyed by burgesses.

Provost Staig was also referred to in the Election Ballad of 1790 (C.W. p.404) as:

> Redoubted Staig, who set at nought
> The wildest savage Tory.

In his letter of 10th January 1793 Burns referred to Staig's wife and daughters, and promised that when Staig was made Commissioner of Customs he would 'write a congratulatory Ode on the subject, that every one of your charming Girls as she is married shall have an Epithalamium & your Lady shall command my Muse on any theme she pleases.' Lilias Staig (1778-1827) married the Rev. Charles Maitland Babington of **St Mary's Chapel,** but Burns was dead before her marriage took place. Her elder sister Jessie is noted separately below.

JANET 'JESSIE' STAIG (1775-1801)

Writing to Mrs Dunlop in September 1794 (C.L. p.211), Burns sympathised with 'the leading man in our Borough' whose daughter, 'a lovely creature of sixteen, was given over by the Physician, who openly said that she had but few hours to live' and went on to describe how Dr Maxwell had saved her life. Jessie was actually nineteen at the time, but as a result Burns composed the epigram:

> Maxwell, if merit here you crave,
> That merit I deny;
> You save fair Jessie from the grave!
> An Angel could not die.

Sadly, the Angel died seven years later. She was the first wife of Major William Miller, Royal Horse Guards, the son of Patrick Miller of **Dalswinton.** Burns wrote a short letter to Jessie in the spring of 1793 (C.L. p.688), enclosing the poem 'Young Jessie' (C.W. p.486).

JAMES SWAN

The Council Minutes contain an interesting sequence of entries in 1794-7 pertaining to this local businessman who had premises in Queensberry Square in 1798, but who is otherwise unknown. On 22nd September 1794 he was elected a merchant councillor. Exactly a week later an entry states 'James Swan who is son of the deceased Swan ----- a burgess of Dumfries, was in like manner admitted a burgess and freeman... and was subsequently elected a bailie on the same date.' It is clear that James Swan was able to exert a great deal of influence in promoting himself. Within a week, a man not a burgess was elected a merchant councillor and so hurriedly made a burgess and freeman that the clerk did not know his father's name, and then with indecent haste raised to the dignity of the magistracy, truly a meteoric elevation in the municipal firmament. Subsequent entries in the Minutes, however, show that he was re-elected a bailie (22nd September 1795), then merely retained on the Council, no longer a bailie (3rd October 1796) and finally voted off the Council (2nd October 1797). He might have remained in oblivion, had it not been for an epigram by Burns (C.W. p.534). This was prefaced by a note by John Syme concerning the election of the magistrates for Dumfries in 1794. 'John McMurdo, Esqr. was chosen Provost and a Mr Swan one of the Baillies: and at the Entertainment usually given on the occasion Burns, seeing the Provost's Supporters on the Bench, took his pencil and wrote the following:

> Baillie Swan, Baillie Swan,
> Let you do what you can,
> God ha' mercy on honest Dumfries:
> But e'er the year's done,
> Good Lord! Provost John
> Will find that his Swans are but *Geese.*

WILLIAM THOMSON (1770-1847)

A Dumfries lawyer, he was for many years Sheriff Clerk of Dumfriesshire and also Provost of the burgh in 1819-21, 1823-5 and 1826-7. He played a leading role in the formation of the town's first **Library** and later in the foundation of the Mechanics' Institute. He owned property at Woodhouse and later at Moat and, about 1826, became President of the Dumfries Gas Company. Apart from the incident involving the indiscreet inscription on the fly-leaf of De Lolme's *British Constitution*, Burns was not himself connected to Thomson. After the poet's death, however, Thomson was appointed Factor loco tutoris on behalf of the poet's children. A letter from Syme to Alexander Cunningham in April 1798 discusses this appointment and adds that Thomson was 'a sedate and intelligent young man married to a Niece of McMurdo.' Thornton, in *William Maxwell to Robert Burns*, infers that Thomson was not, like Maxwell and Syme, a personal friend of the poet: 'Their voice of warm intimacy and sympathetic understanding was not his voice of sober business and·frosty law.' Moreover, Thornton points out that Thomson adopted a high-handed approach in his dealings with Dr Currie and with the publishers Cadell & Davies, and this is certainly borne out in the surviving correspondence between Thomson and the publishers.

Letters from Currie to the publishers from May 1798 indicate that the poet's biographer had had more of the lawyer than he could stomach. In fairness to Thomson, he shouldered the responsibility of carrying out the day-to-day business of seeing that the poet's widow and children were properly looked after, and while others got so much of the credit, it was Thomson who laboured quietly behind the scenes to execute their decisions. He continued to act in this capacity until 1815, by which time none of the poet's children was still a minor. Although Thomson was not a member of the **Mausoleum** Committee (as were Maxwell and Syme, the executors with whom he mostly dealt), he was a founder member of the Dumfries Burns Club and, as 'Provost Thomson' his signature appears on the famous punch-bowl inaugurated in January 1820. William Thomson was also a member of the Dumfries Volunteers and must have come into close contact with Burns in that context.

AGNES 'NANIE' WELSH

An innkeeper in Dumfries, from whose establishment Burns wrote a brief, undated note to Alexander Findlater, inviting him to join 'Simm, Hyslop, & a stranger to whom you will like to be known.' Nothing else is known of her, although a Mrs Agnes Welsh donated five shillings to the Voluntary Subscription for the Defence of the County in 1798.

JOHN WELSH

In 'Election Ballad' (C.W. pp.402-6) occur the lines:

> And Welsh, who ne'er yet flinch'd his ground,
> High-wav'd his magnum-bonum round
> With Cyclopeian fury.

The man who brandished his half-gallon bottle in this dramatic fashion was described in a footnote in the Chambers-Wallace edition as 'Sheriff of the County', a fact queried by Maurice Lindsay who noted in his *Encyclopaedia* that Sir James Fergusson had told him that there was no Sheriff of Dumfriesshire by that name. In fact, John Welsh, was Sheriff-substitute and in that capacity witnessed the induction of Burns into the Excise on 27th October 1789 at the Quarter Sessions of the Peace.

DAVID WILLIAMSON (1766-1824)

A draper in Dumfries, he supplied Burns with his Volunteer uniform, the non-payment for which caused the poet such anguish on his deathbed. As previously noted under Matthew Penn, the lawyer whose letter so upset Burns, Williamson has unfairly come down to posterity as the 'cruel scoundrel of a Haberdasher' mentioned in the letters to James Burness and George Thomson, written from the **Brow** on 12th July 1796. Williamson had a more felicitous connection with that other local celebrity, John Paul Jones, for his wife Jane Young was a niece of the American admiral. Through the influence of the United States government, Mrs Williamson succeeded in obtaining the residue of her uncle's estate, amounting to about £700, and with this money she obtained a lease of the Commercial Hotel, later known as the **County Hotel.**

MISS WOODS

Nothing is known about this young lady, other than that she assisted a Miss McMurdo in the running of a boarding school for girls in Dumfries. Miss McMurdo and her boarders occupied three pews in **St Michael's** (about eight persons to each pew) which gives some idea of the size of the school. Miss Woods may have been the sister of John Woods, recorded as an innkeeper in Dumfries in the early years of the 19th century. Burns's young Excise colleague, John Lewars, however, was apparently infatuated with Miss Woods, hence the reference in 'The Hue and Cry of John Lewars (C.W. p.468):

> A thief, and a murderer! stop her who can!
> Look well to your lives and your goods!
> Good people, ye know not the hazard you run,
> 'Tis the far-famed and much-noted Woods.

DUNKITTERICK   NX 489 716

A place in Minnigaff parish in the Stewartry on the eastern fringe of **Kirroughtree** Forest, just off the A712 about seven miles northeast of **Newton Stewart.** The shepherd's cottage, for long a ruin, has been partially restored in memory of Alexander Murray (1775-1813) who was born there. The Galloway shepherd boy who became the leading linguist and Oriental scholar of his day was minister of **Urr** from 1806 till 1813, and was appointed Professor of Oriental Languages at Edinburgh University a year before his death. A tall granite obelisk marks his grave in Greyfriars kirkyard, Edinburgh, but monuments also exist in his native Galloway. One stands on a hill near the Grey Mare's Tail waterfall at Talnotry in his native parish (NX 488 719), while the other stands on an eminence overlooking the A75, near **Cardoness Castle** in Anwoth parish (NX 587 558). Murray was introduced to Burns in Dumfries about 1795 and submitted some of his vernacular poems for criticism, as he was contemplating getting them published. Burns advised him as tactfully as possible that the poems were better left unpublished, saying that he would be ashamed to acknowledge them when he could judge and write better. Murray took this advice and abandoned his muse, concentrating instead on languages for which he had a phenomenal aptitude.

DUNSCORE   NX 866 844

A village and parish of Nithsdale. The village, formerly known as Cottack, is nine miles northwest of Dumfries. The parish contains **Ellisland** and **Friars' Carse.** The village itself has associations with the poet. It was in a house on the Main Street, formerly a tailor's shop, that the library of the Monkland Friendly Society, founded by Burns and Riddell in March 1789, operated until its closure on 2nd February 1931. It took its original name from Monkland Cottage where it was originally located. Later it moved to Hopeside before finally settling in the Main Street. Because the account of Dunscore parish written by the minister was inadequate, Riddell prevailed upon Burns to give Sir John Sinclair a separate note of the Library for publication in his *Statistical Account.* This was sent to Sir John in the form of a letter (C.L. pp.586-7) which Burns signed 'A Peasant'. The identity of the writer, however, was revealed in the letter which Riddell enclosed with it when sending it to Sir John: 'Mr Burns was so good as to take the whole charge of this small concern. He was treasurer, librarian, and censor of this little society, who will long have a grateful sense of this public spirit and exertions for their improvement and information.' Burns's contribution was published as an appendix to Volume III (pp.598-600). Many of the books were purchased from Peter Hill in Edinburgh, and Burns's letters to the bookseller contain numerous references to orders for the library. Sometimes Burns was reduced to devious ploys in order to influence the choice of reading matter. Thus, in a letter of 2nd March 1790 (C.L. p.317), when he was forced by the vote of the majority of subscribers to order an additional copy of Watson's *Body of Divinity,* he neatly side-stepped this: 'This last heavy Performance is so much admired by many of our Members, that they will not be content with one Copy, so Captain Riddel our President & Patron agreed with me to give you private instructions not to send Watson, but to say that you could not procure a Copy of the book so cheap as the one you sent formerly & therefore you wait farther Orders.'

According to Burns's account, the members entered into a three-year agreement, each paying 5s on entry and sixpence at each meeting, held on the last Saturday of the month. This gave them the funds to buy books. The library boasted some 150 volumes when the agreement expired. The books were then sold by auction, but only among members, 'and each man had his share of the common stock, in money or books, as he chose to be a purchaser or not.' This implies that the library was dispersed and it may be that a closing-down sale of this sort took place when the library moved from its original location. Nevertheless, the library in the Main Street continued to have many of the original volumes at the time of its closure, and these are now preserved at **Ellisland** which also has some interesting records of the subscribers from 1860 to 1931.

The King's Arms Hotel, a coaching inn in Burns's time, is still extant though no longer licensed. Burns kept his horse in the stables under the inn, while attending church or engaged on Excise duties in the village. As regards the latter, Allan Cunningham had the following anecdote: The poet and a brother Exciseman one day suddenly entered a widow woman's shop in Dunscore, and made a seizure of smuggled tobacco. 'Jenny,' said the poet, 'I expected this would be the upshot. Here, Lewars, take note of the number of rolls as I count them. Now, Jock, did you ever hear an auld wife numbering her threads before check-reels were invented? Thou's ane, and thou's no ane, and thou's ane a' out — listen.' As he handed out the rolls he went on with his humorous enumeration, but dropping every other roll into Janet's lap. Lewars took the desired note with much gravity, and saw, as if he saw not, the merciful conduct of his companion. Similar stories of Burns's compassionate dealing with breaches of Excise regulations are noted under **Kirkpatrick Durham** and **Thornhill.**

DUNSCORE CHURCH

Situated in the middle of this large parish, on the south side of the village. The present Gothic edifice (850 sittings) was erected in 1823 and is not the church in which Burns worshipped from 1788 till 1791. Little trace of the original structure is extant, as the present parish church was built on the same site. In the old church Burns writhed under the Whiggish sermons of the Rev. Joseph Kirkpatrick. To Mrs Dunlop on 22nd June 1789 (C.L. pp.173-4) he wrote: 'I have just heard the Rev. Joseph Kirkpatrick give a sermon. He is a man famous for his benevolence, and I revere him; but from such ideas of my Creator, good Lord deliver me!' The ensuing passage shows how deeply Burns thought and cared about religion. On 9th February 1790 he wrote to Willie Nicol (C.L. p.347) at length regarding the petty politics involving Kirkpatrick and his fellow divines. In a letter to Alexander Cunningham in March 1791 (C.L. p.462) Burns described the minister as 'one vast constellation of dullness, and from his weekly zenith rays out his contradictory stupidity to the no small edification and enlightenment of the heavy and opaque pericraniums of his gaping Admirers.'

On one occasion, however, Mr Kirkpatrick's sermon goaded Burns into more public action. Burns, a secret Jacobite in sentiment if not in politics, was revolted by the 'harsh political prejudice' in the diatribe by Kirkpatrick from the pulpit at the centenary celebrations of the Glorious Revolution of 1688. This induced the poet to write a polemical essay calling for moderation and a proper perspective on the House of Stuart, concluding by drawing a parallel between the rebels of 1688 and the Americans of 1776. This essay, which shows Burns as a political thinker of considerable courage and originality, was published in the Edinburgh *Evening Courant* of 22nd November 1788 under the pseudonym of 'A Briton'.

The Rev. Joseph Kirkpatrick (1750-1824) was ordained minister of Dunscore in 1777 and moved to Wamphray in 1806 where he remained until his death. He married Anne McMillan, daughter of the minister of Torthorwald. Robert Riddell of Glenriddell shared the poet's assessment of Kirkpatrick, when he expressed his extreme dissatisfaction of the Dunscore parish account sent to Sir John Sinclair for publication in the *Statistical Account* — 'the worst account yet printed, except the parish of Terregles. Much more may be said of Dunscore, but the ignorance and stupidity of the minister is such, and so great a Mule is he, that no good can be done with him.' The only letter from Burns to Kirkpatrick was written on or about 22nd October 1791 when the poet and his family were about to leave the parish, and was merely a formal note observing the social niceties.

In the kirkyard, to the south of the church, is the grave of James White, the retired Jamaican planter whose advice as to the route he should take to Jamaica delayed Burns's voyage to the West Indies and thus ultimately prevented his sailing at all.

In the west of the parish lies the farm of Craigenputtock, where Thomas Carlyle, the 'Sage of Chelsea' wrote his celebrated *Essay on Burns*, still highly regarded for its perceptive analysis and criticism. From Craigenputtock Hill Carlyle and his American friend, Ralph Waldo Emerson, looked down on Dunscore church. Carlyle summed up his philosophy in these simple words: 'Christ died on the tree; that built Dunscore Kirk yonder; that brought you and me together. Time has only a relative existence.' The famous preacher Edward Irving held a service in the churchyard before a crowd too large to be accommodated in the church itself. Carlyle was one of the congregation on that occasion.

DUNSCORE PARISH CHURCH

DUNSCORE OLD KIRKYARD   NX 926 834
' The original parish burial ground lies not far from **Ellisland**. Travelling northwards on the
A76 turn left off the main road about half a mile south of Ellisland. 200 yards along the minor
road to Dunscore via Throughgate, the burial ground is just off to the right. It contains the flat
tombstone of Robert Riddell of Glenriddell who died on 21st April 1794. The adjoining tomb is
that of Sir Robert Grierson of Lag, the persecutor of the Covenanters.

DUNSKEY   NX 001 559
An estate and mansion in Portpatrick parish, Wigtownshire, deriving its name from an old
castle (now ruined) half a mile south of Portpatrick. The mansion, however, stands near the head
of Dunskey Glen 1.25 miles north of the town, amid extensive wooded policies. It was built in 1706,
but considerably extended and improved in 1830. It was the ancestral home of the Blair family.
In 1770 the Blair heiress married James Hunter of Robertland, Ayr, a leading merchant banker,
who thereafter added Blair to his surname. He was Member of Parliament for Edinburgh from
1780 till 1784 and subsequently Lord Provost, being created a Baronet in 1786. He seems to have
been to Edinburgh what David Staig was to Dumfries, and many of the improvements carried
out in the Age of Enlightenment were instituted during his term of office. Hunter Square and Blair
Street were named after him. Burns was cordially received by Sir James Hunter Blair on his arrival
in Edinburgh. His death the following year inspired 'Elegy on the Death of Sir James Hunter Blair'
(C.W. p.281); even Burns himself admitted that it was 'just mediocre'.
Major Sir David Hunter Blair of Dunskey, second baronet, was mentioned in the 'Second
Heron Election Ballad' (C.W. p.546) as
the wild Scot o Galloway Sogering, gunpowther Blair!
His younger brother, James Hunter Blair of Peninghame, was MP for Wigtownshire in the 1820s.

ECCLEFECHAN   NY 193 745
A village in Hoddam parish, Annandale, 6 miles southeast of Lockerbie and 20 miles northwest
of Carlisle. In Burns's day it was an important stage on the mail-coach route between Carlisle and
Glasgow which had been inaugurated in July 1788. It was the birthplace, on 4th December 1795,
of Thomas Carlyle who immortalised it as Entepfuhl in *Sartor Resartus*. Most of the original 18th
century houses and cottages were built by the father and uncle of Carlyle, who were employed there
as stonemasons. The house in which Carlyle himself was born, on the west side of the main street
near the south end of the village, is now preserved as a museum. The house in which Carlyle and
his family grew up was in Carlyle's Close nearby, the local abattoir in the 19th century. The graveyard
contains not only the tombs of the Carlyle family, but also the last resting places of Archibald Arnott
(1772-1855), Napoleon's physician on St Helena, and Robert Peal (1692-1749), great-grandfather
of Sir Robert Peel, the prime minister.
The father of Willie Nicol was a tailor in Ecclefechan before moving to **Dumbretton**. In the
winter of 1794-5 Burns was employed as acting Supervisor and his duties took him to Ecclefechan,
where he was caught in the great snow-storm of 6th-8th February 1795. During the resulting period
of enforced inactivity he wrote at length to George Thomson (C.L. p.671): 'I came yesternight
to this unfortunate, wicked, little village.' To add to his misfortune, 'since dinner, a Scraper has
been torturing Catgut, in sounds that would have insulted the dying agonies of a Sow under the
hands of a Butcher... I have been in a dilemma, either to get drunk, to forget these miseries; or
to hang myself, to get rid of these miseries:— like a prudent man (a character congenial to my every
thought, word & deed) I, of two evils have chosen the least, & am very drunk — at your service!'
That Burns had his tongue in his cheek is evident from the rest of the letter which discussed musical
matters in some detail and included a transcription of 'O Wat Ye wha's in Yon Town' (C.W. p.541).
It has been postulated that the 'Jeanie' referred to in this song was Jean, daughter of John Scott,
the innkeeper and postmaster of Ecclefechan, rather than Jean Armour or Jean Lorimer, the other

alternatives. There is no doubt regarding the young lady's identity in 'Epigram on Miss Jean Scott' (C.W. p.541) which is said to have been inscribed by Burns on a window-pane of the local coaching inn. Jean's father was appointed postmaster of Ecclefechan when the office was established in July 1788, as a result of the mail-coach route then inaugurated. Her brother Walter was the mail-coach contractor in the early 19th century.

Allan Cunningham states that during the poet's first visit to Annandale an old song called 'The Lass of Ecclefechan' was sung to him. A version of this ancient ditty is preserved in *The Merry Muses*, but later Burns 'rendered the language more delicate, and the sentiments less warm' (C.W. p.571). The traditional ballad 'The Trogger' (C.W. p.604) was reworked by Burns and largely inspired by a wager of John Lewars that Burns 'could not get a word to clink with Ecclefechan' which they were visiting at the time. The last stanza, however, contains the lines:

> Then up we raise, and took the road
> An in by Ecclefechan,
> Where brandy-stoup we gart it clink,
> And the strang-beer ream the quech in.

And so John Lewars lost his bet.

ELLISLAND   NX 929 838

A small farm (170 acres) in Dunscore parish, Nithsdale, on the right bank of the **Nith**, 5.75 miles north of Dumfries. It is about a quarter of a mile down a farm road, east of the A76. It was rented by Burns for £50 a year from Whitsunday 1788 till December 1791, his landlord being Patrick Miller of **Dalswinton.** The estate in general was in a run-down condition when Miller purchased it, and Ellisland was no exception. As far back as 14th January 1787 Burns was contemplating a return to the farming life and wrote on that date to John Ballantine (C.L. p.100): 'My generous friend, Mr Peter Miller, brother to the Justice Clerk, has been talking with me about a lease of some farm or other in an estate called Dasswinton which he has lately bought near Dumfries. — Some life-rented, embittering Recollections whisper me that I will be happier any where than in my old neighborhood, but Mr Miller is no Judge of land; and though I dare say he means to favour me, yet he may give me, in his opinion, an advantageous bargain that may ruin me...' Little did he then realise how true this would be. The matter was shelved until the end of September 1787 when Burns wrote to Miller to signify his interest, and on 20th October he re-iterated his intentions (C.L. p.242): 'I want to be a farmer in a small farm, about a plough-gang, in a pleasant country, under the auspices of a good landlord. I shall certainly be able to ride to Dalswinton about middle of next week...'

Again, the business dragged on, Burns being in Edinburgh during the ensuing winter. On 3rd March 1788 he wrote letters to both Miller and his old friend Robert Ainslie saying that he had visited Ellisland with John Tennant of Glenconner whose report he enclosed to Miller (C.L. pp.242-3). Significantly Burns proposed to make entry at Martinmas rather than Whitsunday because the farm was so worn out, although he undertook to pay for the grass and houses 'whatever they deserve' for the summer. He wished also to have the lease at the present rent of £50 for three years: 'The lands are so exhausted, that to enter to the full rent would throw me under a disheartening load of debt...' Four days later, however, he wrote in more jubilant mood to Robert Muir (C.L. p.89): 'I took old Glenconner with me to Mr Millar's farm, and he was so pleased with it, that I have wrote an offer to Mr Millar, which if he accepts, I shall sit down a plain farmer, the happiest of lives when a Man can live by it.'

Miller gave Burns £300 with which to build a farmhouse and fence the fields. The rental was fixed at £50 per annum for the first three years, rising to £75 a year for the rest of the 76-year lease. Burns was to take possession at Whitsunday (25th May 1788). The erection of the farmhouse was unduly protracted and cost Burns much heartache. It was not completed until the spring of 1789, although it was sufficiently advanced for Burns to bring Jean Armour down from Mauchline by

November 1788. Burns began working on the farm on 11th or 12th June 1788. The first letter he wrote from 'Ellesland' (*sic*) was to Mrs Dunlop and dated 13th June (C.L. pp.147-8): 'This is the second day, my honored Friend, that I have been on my farm. — A solitary Inmate of an old, smoky SPENCE; far from every Object I love or by whom I am belov'd...' Sometime between 11th and 30th June Burns also wrote the verse epistle to Hugh Parker (C.W. p.322), complaining of the uncouth clime and the peat-smoke in the hut:

> The red peat gleams, a fiery kernel
> Enhusked by a fog infernal.

Two of the four extant letters from Burns to Jean Armour were written during this period (C.L. pp.477-8), the first on 12th September: 'I received your kind letter with a pleasure which no letter but one from you could have given me. — I dreamed of you the whole night last; but alas! I fear it will be three weeks yet, ere I can hope for the happiness of seeing you...' Burns commuted between Ellisland and Mossgiel in the autumn of 1788. A second letter to Jean, dated 14th October (the day of the first steamboat trial), told her to get ready for Nithsdale as fast as possible. Even then, they were not to occupy Ellisland itself, but were to lodge in David Newall's house at the **Isle.**

To Ainslie a few day's later he expressed his doubts about the venture (C.L. p.336): 'I am not entirely sure of my farm's doing well.— I hope for the best: but I have my Excise commission in my pocket...' By the end of July 1789 he confesed to Robert Graham (C.L. p.425) 'I am deliberating whether I had not better give up farming altogether.' By 11th January 1790 he had had enough. 'This Farm has undone my enjoyment of myself', he complained to his brother Gilbert, 'It is a ruinous affair on all hands. But let it go to hell! I'll fight it out and be off with it. (C.L. p.358). By now his career in the Excise promised to be more lucrative and less of a gamble, even although it was involving him in up to 200 miles riding every week. The die was cast on 27th January 1790 when Burns was placed on the list of officers eligible for promotion to Examiner or Supervisor. The following July he was transferred to the Dumfries Third Division.

Thereafter he was keen to divest himself of what had proved to be a bad bargain. Fortunately he was allowed to get out of the lease because the farmer of the adjacent property, **Laggan** offered Miller £1,900 for Ellisland. In the autumn of 1791 Burns wrote to Peter Hill (C.W. p.320): 'I have sold to My Landlord the lease of my farm, & as I roup off every thing then, I have a mind to take a week's excursion to see old acquaintances.' After discussing his excellent prospects in the Excise, he went on: 'I have not been so lucky in my farming. Mr Miller's kindness has been just such another as Creech's was...' Obviously relations between Burns and Miller were pretty strained by that time, although they put the matter behind them and eventually resumed friendly terms.

On 25th August Burns's crops were auctioned. Over thirty people engaged in a drunken riot for three hours after the roup. 'Such a scene of drunkenness was hardly ever seen in this country', he wrote to Thomas Sloan (C.W. p.104), 'Nor was the scene much better in the house. No fighting, indeed, but folks lieing drunk on the floor, & decanting, untill both my dogs got so drunk by attending them, that they could not stand.— You will easily guess how I enjoyed the scene as I was no farther over than you used to see me.' The Ellisland lease was formally renounced on 10th September 1791 but the Burns family continued to occupy the house until 11th November when they moved to Dumfries.   The five-roomed farmhouse, with outbuildings, was erected by Alexander Crombie, supervised by Thomas Boyd the Dumfries architect. The work dragged on interminably, as can be seen from the letters to the latter (C.L. p.513). The first, dated 8th February 1789, began: 'I see at last, some signs of your executing my house within the current year...' while a second, written on 1st March on his return from Edinburgh expressed a great deal of surprise 'at finding my house still lying like Babylon in the prophecies of Isaiah'. [And Babylon, the glory of kingdoms, the beauty of the Chaldees' excellency, shall be as when God overthrew Sodom and Gomorrah. It shall never be inhabited, neither shall it be dwelt in from generation to generation.] The account between Burns and Boyd was not settled till June 1791 — barely two months before Burns extricated himself from Ellisland.

ELLISLAND

Burns had to start from scratch with unimproved ground, which he set about liming and clearing of stones. It is thought that he also re-organised the old rigs or ploughing ridges into straight 15-foot rigs to facilitate drainage through surface run-off. William Clark was hired as a ploughman, while Elizabeth Smith was taken on as a farm servant. Burns later switched from arable farming to dairying, leaving Jean and the farm- servants to cope with the milking and making of butter and cheeses while he concentrated on his Excise duties. He kept about ten cows as well as heifers and calves, five horses and several pet sheep. William Clark, however, stated that during the period of his employment Burns had a dozen milch cows and only three horses.

Despite the arduous labours of farming and Excise duties, Burns found time for literary pursuits. Some 230 of the 700 extant letters of the poet were written during the period of his tenancy (not all, of course, actually written from there). Some editors have ascribed the song 'I Hae a Wife o my ain' (C.W. p.450) to the period when Burns set up home with Bonnie Jean at Ellisland but Kinsley, on internal evidence, dated it more accurately to 1792. Nevertheless, the Ellisland period was to see numerous poems and songs, beginning in June 1788 with 'Epistle to Hugh Parker' (C.W. p.322), 'Verses in Friars' Carse Hermitage' (C.W. p.324) and the verse epistle to Alexander Cunningham on 27th July (C.W. p.328). The beautiful love songs 'Of A' the Airts' and 'O, Were I on Parnassus Hill' (C.W. p.329) were both composed 'out of compliment to Mrs Burns' in the summer of 1788 when the poet would gaze longingly to the Cumnock Hills beyond which dwelled his young wife. Many old ballads were reworked and fragments mended and rewritten, including 'Auld Lang Syne' (C.W. p.341). There were essays in occasional odes, such as that on the departed Regency Bill (C.W. p.352), as well as the political ballads for the parliamentary elections of 1789 and 1790. That very moving song 'Thou Lingering Star' (C.W. p.372) was composed in the barnyard about the third anniversary of Mary Campbell's death.

On the morning of 19th April 1789 as he was out at an early hour, sowing in the fields, Burns heard a shot and presently saw a poor little wounded hare, which 'set my humanity in tears and my indignation in arms' as he wrote to Mrs Dunlop (C.L. p.171). The ode on the Wounded Hare (C.W. p.354) was the result. James Thomson, a neighbour, stated that having shot and wounded a hare he saw it run past Burns. 'He cursed me and said that he would not mind throwing me in the water — and I'll warrant he could hae done it, though I was but young and strong.'

Undoubtedly the greatest product of his muse in this period, however, was 'Tam o Shanter' (C.W. pp.410-15), arguably Burns's masterpiece. It was composed for Captain Francis Grose to accompany an engraving of Alloway Kirk, and was published in the second volume of Antiquities of Scotland in April 1791. It was written in fulfilment of a promise to Grose in 1789, but not carried out before the winter of 1790. About November of that year Burns sent the first fragment to Mrs Dunlop, and sent a copy of the completed work by carrier at the beginning of December. Grose's copy was sent by post on 1st December, accompanied by a letter: 'I am not, God knows, vain of my Composition...' (C.L. p.559).

The poet's correspondence disproves the local tradition that Burns composed his mock-epic in the course of a single day. McDowall gives a rather fanciful account of the composition, in Burns in Dumfriesshire: 'For one day at least all prosaic business must be set aside, that the poet may, by doing full justice to his theme, gratify his friend. He is seen in the forenoon pacing to and fro along his favourite walk southward of the house, beside the river. Some hours afterwards Mrs Burns, with her two children, Robert and Francis Wallace, join him; but perceiving that he is deeply absorbed — "busy crooning to himsel" — she, guided by true womanly tact, retires with her little prattlers, and from behind some lang yellow broom growing upon the bank, she keeps a loving look-out, unperceived by the poet. He becomes increasingly excited; his manner is that of a pythoness, so strange and wild are his gesticulations, and, though now at the remote end of the promenade, she can perceive that he is "agonized with an ungovernable access of joy". It is his masterpiece of Tam o Shanter with which he is busy. He is so far advanced with it that heroic Tam has been brought in full sight of the fantastic dancers, and then the poet bursts out with the apostrophe so loud that his listening wife hears every line —

> Now, Tam! o Tam! had thae been queans,
> A' plump and strapping in their teens

'The fine frenzy of Burns continued till the poem was completed, and, lest the glow of his first fresh conceptions should in any degree cool down, he, with a sod-dyke for desk, committed the poem to paper. Then, returning to the house, he read it in triumph to Bonnie Jean. Even as the farm-yard of Ellisland witnessed the agonizing throes in which the poet's most pathetic effusion was produced, so this walk of his, trodden by hosts of admiring visitors, was the scene of his most joyful ecstasy and of his proudest achievement'. 'Tam o Shanter', says Alexander Smith, with pardonable exaggeration, 'was written in a day — since Bruce fought Bannockburn, the best single day's work done in Scotland.' The legend is maintained by a plaque affixed to the gate leading to the footpath along the Nith south of the farmhouse.

In the autumn of 1790 Burns was visited by Sir Egerton Brydges and Dr Ramsay of Ochtertyre. The latter left a vivid account of his meeting with the poet: 'We fell into conversation directly and soon got into the mare magnum of poetry. He told me that he had now gotten a story for a drama, which he was to call Rob Macquechan's Elshon, from a popular story of Robert Bruce being defeated on the Water of Cairn, when the heel of his boot having loosened in flight he applied to Robert Macquechan to fit it, who, to make sure, ran his awl nine inches up the King's heel.' That Burns had ambitions to become a playwright was also revealed in a letter to Lady Elizabeth Cunningham on 23rd December 1789 (C.L. pp.498-9): 'I have some thoughts of the Drama.— Considering the favorite things of the day... does not your Ladyship think that a Scotish Audience would be better pleased with the Affectation, Whim & Folly of their own native growth...?'

In 1805 John Morine of Laggan sold Ellisland to a Mr Taylor who dismantled and remodelled the steading, although the farmhouse is today much as it was in the poet's time. The parlour, in particular, is thought to have remained unchanged since it was built. The names of John Gillespie (an Excise colleague) and Jean Lorimer (whom he was courting) are scratched on one of the window-panes, along with Burns's favourite line from Pope: 'An honest man's the noblest work of God,' which unfortunately was vandalised with a piece of flint about March 1876.

Ellisland was farmed until 1921 when it was bought by George Williamson, a former President of the Edinburgh Burns Club, and presented to the nation by John Wilson Williamson in 1929. The land is now let for grazing, but the farmhouse has been restored and contains a museum of Burns relics in the poet's old parlour, together with accommodation for the resident curators. The kitchen contains part of the range on which Jean did her cooking and the 'swee' from which pots were suspended. Beside the range is the Carron oven which Burns installed especially for his wife. The ceiling still has the hooks from which cured hams were hung.

Beside the farmhouse the granary was restored and opened in 1979 as a museum of farming life, with displays mounted by the Country Life section of the Royal Museum of Scotland. This includes a life-size figure of Burns in 18th century farming costume, scattering oats from a sowing-sheet over his left arm. The fields would have been tilled with a plough very similar to that on display, a replica of the Chilcarroch plough preserved in Stranraer Museum. Other items on display include a swing plough, a flail, smiddy implements and joinery tools.

FINGLAND   NX 670 903
Farmhouse in Dalry parish, Kirkcudbrightshire, on the south side of Fingland Hill and just north of the stream called Fingland Lane. It is approached by an unfenced farm road northwest of the minor road running between the B729 at Auchenstroan, and the B7000 at Barlaes Cottage. In this remote upland farmhouse, about 1763, was born Margaret 'Peggy' Chalmers. Her mother was a sister of Gavin Hamilton's stepmother. Peggy's father later fell on hard times and was forced to sell Fingland and take a lease of a farm near Mauchline in Ayrshire. She is thought to have been the recipient of the undated letter (probably January 1787) beginning 'My dear Countrywoman' (C.L. p.230). She was a young lady of great culture and accomplishment, both literary and musical, and Burns, who met her at Mauchline, was captivated by her. Including the undated letter, Burns wrote twelve letters still extant. Towards the end of her life she told Thomas Campbell, the poet, that Burns had proposed to her, but she tactfully declined him and they had remained on good terms. She may have been the 'Miss (who) flew off in a tangent of female dignity and reserve' referred to in a letter to James Smith on 30th June 1787 (C.L. p.122). Margaret played the piano and often sang for the blind Dr Blacklock. In December 1788 Peggy married Lewis Hay, a partner in the banking house of Forbes, Hunter & Co. After her husband's death in 1800 she settled at Pau, where she died in 1843. She was the subject of 'My Peggy's Charms' (C.W. p.297) and 'Where, Braving Angry Winter's Storms' (C.W. p.298), which he sent to her about December 1787. Burns wished to publish them but she demurred on the grounds that she would easily be identified and thereby embarrassed. Publication was, indeed, delayed till 1802. It is generally agreed that Peggy Chalmers was one of the only two intellectually able women with whom Burns enjoyed close friendship (the other being Maria Riddell).

FRIARS' CARSE   NX 925 849
Estate and mansion house in Dunscore parish, Nithsdale, on the west bank of the **Nith** not far from **Dalswinton,** 6 miles north of Dumfries and just over a mile south of Auldgirth on the A76 from which it is approached along a private road. It was the site in pre-Reformation times of a cell of Melrose Abbey and in the avenue leading to the mansion were several sculptured stones believed to have come from the friary. Passing at the Reformation to the Kirkpatricks, then the proprietors of **Ellisland,** it went in 1634 to the Maxwells of Tinwald. Bonnie Annie Laurie died

here on 5th April 1764 at the age of 81. In 1784, following his marriage to Elizabeth Kennedy of Manchester, Captain Robert Riddell of Glenriddell purchased Friars' Carse and settled there. Built about 1774, on a piece of rising ground, round which the Nith makes a graceful curve, the mansion was often visited by Burns during his tenancy of Ellisland. Riddell (1755-94) retired from the Army in 1782 on half-pay and devoted the rest of his life to that of a country gentleman. He inherited **Glenriddell** in 1788 but sold the ancestral estate and continued to live at Friars' Carse.

It is not known precisely how and when Burns met Robert Riddell, but it seems likely that Patrick Miller effected the introduction about the time the poet settled at Ellisland on 11th June 1788. Certainly within a fortnight he had met Riddell and established a good relationship, to the extent that Burns was favoured with a key to the Hermitage — a little summer house designed by Riddell in allusion to the estate's monastic origins. It was here, on 28th June, that Burns composed the lines beginning 'Thou whom chance may hither lead' (C.W. p.324). This was but the first of several poems inspired by the friendship between Burns and Riddell. Robert Riddell possessed considerable musical talent and composed a number of airs, for which Burns wrote the lyrics of 'The Whistle' (C.W. p.368), 'Nithsdale's Welcome Home' (C.W. p.377), 'The Blue-eyed Lassie' (C.W. p.333) and 'The Day Returns' (C.W. p.333). Riddell's collection of reels was published by James Johnson of Edinburgh about 1785 and demonstrated his passion for collecting traditional Scottish music, a passion which he shared with the poet.

In September 1788 the friendship was cemented by 'The Day Returns' (C.W. p.333), 'Composed out of compliment to one of the happiest and worthiest married couples in the world, Robert Riddel, Esq. of Glenriddel, and his lady. At their fire-side I have enjoyed more pleasant evenings than at all the houses of fashionable people in this country put together.' 'Answer to an Invitation' (C.W. p.370) may have referred to the drinking contest at which Burns was an observer and subsequently composed 'The Whistle' (C.W. p.368). The contest took place at Friars' Carse on 16th October 1789, the prize being a small ebony whistle brought to Scotland by a Dane in the service of Prince George of Denmark who married Princess (later Queen) Anne in 1683. He lost it in a drinking contest to Sir Robert Laurie, first baronet of **Maxwelton**, one of whose daughters married Walter Riddell of Glenriddell. The whistle thus passed into the Riddell family. Sir Robert Laurie, third baronet, attempted to emulate his grandfather in this contest with Robert Riddell and Alexander Fergusson of **Craigdarroch**. The lastnamed consumed upwards of five bottles of claret before blowing the victory blast. John McMurdo of **Drumlanrig** judged the contest. The 'good Scottish King' referred to in the third line of the ballad was James VI whose daughter Anne also married a Prince George of Denmark, but that event took place almost a century earlier than the union which had brought the whistle to Scotland.

It was also at Friars' Carse, in July 1789, that Burns was introduced to Captain Francis Grose (1731-91), the famous antiquary who was then gathering material in Annandale and Nithsdale for the two-volume *Antiquities of Scotland*. Their meeting was described by the poet in a letter to Mrs Dunlop on 17th July 1789 (C.L. p.176) and, of course, it also inspired the lines beginning 'Hear, Land o Cakes, and brither Scots' (C.W. p.373). 'Tam o Shanter' (C.W. p.410) was composed for publication in Grose's work. The lines 'On Captain Grose' and 'Epigram on Francis Grose the Antiquary' (C.W. p.415) were further fruits of this friendship.

Robert Riddell himself was the inspiration of the fragment of 1791 'On Glenriddell's Fox Breaking his Chain' (C.W. p.426). Riddell kept a pet fox in a dog-kennel — something which Burns with his libertarian principles abhorred. When the fox escaped the poet seized the opportunity to compose these lines on the theme of liberty. Riddell was also sent a verse epistle in 1791 thanking him for the loan of a newspaper (C.W.p.427) and the rhyming reply to a note, beginning 'Dear Sir, at onie time or tide' (C.W. p.428). Riddell joined with Burns in promoting the Monkland Friendly Society library in **Dunscore**. Burns later compiled two volumes of poetic and prose manuscripts for his friend, and this collection came to be known as the Glenriddell MS. Only the volume of poems, however, was actually handed over to Riddell. Riddell also had a copy of the *Scots Musical Museum* interleaved with annotations, most of which were made by Burns.

In April 1793 Burns sent Riddell a copy of the latest edition of his poems, with the inscription: 'When you and I, dear Sir, have passed that bourne whence no traveller returns, should the volumes survive us, I wish the future Reader of this Page to be informed that they were the pledge of Friendship, ardent and grateful on my part, as it was kind and generous on yours.' Riddell also shared the poet's views on political reform, as mentioned in Burns's justification of his actions to the Excise authorities. A polemical essay signed 'Cato' was written by Riddell and sent to Burns to pass on to the Editor of the *Gazetteer*, where it was later published.

The relationship was broken, however, at the end of December 1793, as a result of the drunken incident known as 'the Rape of the Sabines'. Burns, egged on by some of the gentlemen present, led an all-too-exuberant romp against the ladies. Tradition, wholly unsupported by any eye-witness account, maintains that the menfolk had been discussing the Rape of the Sabines over their port after dinner, and that on rejoining the ladies in the drawing-room they staged a re-enactment that was too realistic for good taste, Burns's victim being his hostess, Mrs Elizabeth Riddell. The poet was ordered from the house in disgrace. The following day he wrote a letter to Mrs Riddell (C.L. p.697) which began: 'I daresay this is the first epistle you ever received from this nether world. I write you from the regions of Hell, amid the horrors of the damned...' The ensuing dozen lines constitute the most poetic description of a hangover ever penned.

FRIARS' CARSE

Sadly, Mrs Riddell, who had a reputation for a narrow and unforgiving nature, never relented and the rift between Burns and the Riddells merely widened, and eventually dragged Maria Riddell into the dispute as well. Robert Riddell died in April 1794 at the early age of 39 before the breach could be healed. His erstwhile friend's death, however, inspired Burns to write to John Clark of **Locharwoods** on 21st April (C.W. p.706), grieving at the loss 'of the *man I loved.*' and enclosing the 'Sonnet on the Death of Robert Riddell' (C.W. p.513). A few weeks later Burns wrote to one of Riddell's sisters, probably Eleanor (although Sophy has also been suggested), seeking her intercession with Elizabeth Riddell so that the poet could retrieve the Glenriddell MS. This appeal had the desired effect, and the collection was returned to him in due course. Riddell himself was the recipient of nine extant letters from the poet (including the prose preface to the Glenriddell MS and the inscription on the 1793 poems). Posterity has dealt rather harshly with Riddell, largely on account of the estrangement which arose from an incident in which he was by no means blameless. He was a man of culture and wide-ranging interests which included numismatics, a hobby which was humorously referred to in the 'Election Ballad' of 1790 (C.W. pp.402-6):

> Glenriddel, skill'd in rusty coins
> Blew up each Tory's dark designs,
> And bared the treason under.

After Riddell's untimely death his widow could have allowed Friars' Carse to go to his younger brother Walter who, under the terms of Robert's will, would have had to pay the widow an annuity. But Elizabeth Riddell heartily detested her brother-in-law and refused to exercise this option, so the property had to be sold. This curious episode was described in a letter of 18th June (C.L. pp.710-11) from Burns to John McLeod of Colbecks who had written to the poet on 16th May enquiring about the sale of the estate, as he had expressed an interest in buying it. William Stewart of **Closeburn** was appointed by Riddell's trustees to value the estate and from him Burns obtained information which should have helped McLeod make a competitive bid. The estate was sold to a Captain Smith and in 1810 it was purchased by Provost John Crichton of Sanquhar, acting on behalf of his brother Dr James Crichton, the pioneer of the China trade, who took up residence in 1812 when he retired from Canton and married the heiress of Lag, Miss Elizabeth Grierson. The estate was acquired in 1895 by the Crichton Royal Institution, the mental hospital in Dumfries which was founded by Mrs Crichton in her late husband's memory. It now belongs to the Post Office Fellowship of Remembrance.

The original Hermitage, in the grounds at the south of the estate, suffered neglect after Riddell's death. When Cromek visited it in 1810 he found it in a derelict condition, and the window on which Burns had inscribed lines to the memory of Robert Riddell (C.W. p.513) in his characteristic fashion had been removed. The Hermitage was rebuilt in 1874 but at the time of writing is in urgent need of repair. In July 1793 William Shepherd of Liverpool, a close friend of Dr James Currie, visited Friars' Carse to call on Currie's sister who happened to be staying with the Riddells at the time. Shepherd has left an interesting description of the estate in a letter dated 19th July 1793. He mentioned the beautiful walks along the Nith and that salmon and trout were caught for supper. He also commented on the largest and tallest oak he had ever seen.

The Riddells were connected by marriage with the Fergussons of **Craigdarroch**, the Lauries of **Maxwelton**, the Gordons of **Kenmure** and Deborah Duff Davies, noted under **Drungans Lodge**.

GALLOWAY HOUSE   NX 478 452

The family seat of the Earls of Galloway, in Sorbie parish, Wigtownshire, about 10 miles southeast of Wigtown, about half a mile south of the village of Garlieston and approached by a private road off the B7063. The mansion was built in 1740-5, a plain large edifice with projecting wings, a fine conservatory and beautiful gardens commanding magnificent views of Wigtown Bay and the Solway Firth. Sir Alexander Stewart of Garlies was created Lord Garlies in 1607 and Earl of Galloway in 1623. The former title was subsequently used as a courtesy title by the eldest son of the earl. The handsome wooded policies were planted in 1790 and in the late 18th century the library of the house was far-famed for its size and prodigious quantity of books. Burns never visited this celebrated mansion, but he and Syme caught a glimpse of it across Wigtown Bay, when they were travelling back from **Gatehouse** to **Kirkcudbright** on 1st August 1793. The sight of such opulence roused the poet's ire, hence the epigrams against the Earl of Galloway (C.W. p.494) beginning:

What dost thou in that mansion fair?
Flit, Galloway, and find
Some narrow, dirty, dungeon cave,
The picture of thy mind.

When he heard, rightly or wrongly, that the Earl resented this, Burns retaliated with:

Spare me thy vengeance, Gallowa!
In quiet let me live:
I ask no kindness at thy hand,
For thou has none to give.

John Stewart, seventh Earl (1736-1806), was a Scottish representative peer from 1774 till 1790. Apart from these bitter epigrams Burns savagely lampooned the Earl in the Election Ballads. Following the death of General Stewart in January 1795, there was a parliamentary by-election and the Earl championed the Tory candidate, Gordon of **Balmaghie.** Burns is said to have heartily detested the Earl on account of his High Tory politics; certainly there was no other reason for the poet's antagonism, and it was oddly at variance with all other published references to the Earl who was noted for his great piety and generosity to his servants. The Earl himself was later quoted as saying 'it would not become him, when his good old master the King despised and disregarded the paltry attacks of a Peter Pindar, to feel himself hurt by those of a licentious, rhyming ploughman.'

GARLIES   NX 423 692
Ruined castle in Minnigaff parish, Kirkcudbrightshire, 2.5 miles northeast of Newton Stewart. Take the minor road (the Old Edinburgh Road) out of Minnigaff, then cross the Penkill Burn and take the right-hand turn along the west bank of the burn almost due north about a mile to Garlies Wood.

From the latter half of the 13th century the castle was the stronghold of the Stewarts, later Earls of Galloway. It was raised to a barony by King James VI in 1607, although even by that time it was in a ruined state. It provided the courtesy title for the eldest son of the Earl of Galloway from 1623 onwards. The writ for the parliamentary by-election, occasioned by the death of General Stewart in January 1795 was issued and entrusted to Lord Garlies, Lord Lieutenant of the Stewartry who, as George Stewart, also sat in the House of Commons. In 'The Election' (C.W. p.545) Burns asks:

An whare is our King's Lord Lieutenant,
Sae famed for his gratefu return?
The billie is getting his Questions
To say at St Stephens the morn!

'St Stephens' was an allusion to the Palace of Westminster. In the third ballad, sub-titled 'John Bushby's Lamentation' (C.W. p.547), this incident is again referred to:

An there had na been the Yerl himself,
O, there had been nae play!
But Garlies was to London gane,
And say the kye might stray.

The village of Garliestown or Garlieston, to the north of **Galloway House,** was laid out in 1759 by the then Lord Garlies (later seventh Earl of Galloway). The Lord Garlies of the Election Ballad succeeded as eighth Earl in 1806.

GATEHOUSE OF FLEET   NX 60 55
A town in the southwest of the Stewartry on the Water of Fleet, 9 miles west of **Kirkcudbright.** Gatehouse proper is in the parish of Girthon, but the suburb of Fleet Street was developed on the west bank, in Anwoth parish, at the end of the 18th century. The village sprang up, about the middle of the century, from a single cottage at the gate to **Cally House,** hence its curious name. It rose dramatically in importance as a manufacturing town, with four cotton factories, several bobbin

factories, a brewery, soapworks, tanneries, a wine company, sawmills, numerous handlooms and a wide range of workshops. The navigation of the Fleet was improved by cutting a canal enabling vessels to come right up to the town. At the height of its prosperity Gatehouse was made a burgh of barony in 1795. Twenty years later, however, the boom collapsed suddenly at the end of the Napoleonic Wars

Burns and Syme visited Gatehouse during their first Galloway Tour and spent the night of 31st July 1793 at the Murray Arms Hotel. At that time Thomas Muir, one of the leaders of the Friends of the People whose convention the previous December had so alarmed the Government, was a fugitive from justice, and passed through Gatehouse on his way to **Portpatrick** where he was arrested a few days later while trying to get a boat to take him to Ireland and safety. The views of Muir and his friends, demanding universal suffrage and parliamentary reform, were akin to those of Burns himself and he was undoubtedly aware of the furore over Muir's abortive flight. The poet's thoughts at this critical time turned to memories of his visit, six years earlier, to the field of Bannockburn. Bruce's troops marched to the tune of an ancient ballad 'Hey Tutti Taitie'. Pietro Urbani begged Burns to make 'soft verses' for it. 'I had no idea of giving myself any trouble on the subject, till the accidental recollection of that glorious struggle for Freedom , associated with the glowing ideas of some other struggles of the same nature, *not quite so ancient*, roused my rhyming Mania.' he wrote to George Thomson about the end of August (C.L. pp,638-9) enclosing the words of 'Robert Bruce's March to Bannockburn', more popularly known nowadays by its opening words 'Scots Wha Hae' (C.W. p.500). The phrase which Burns italicised was a none too subtle reference to the persecution of Muir and Palmer, whose trial on charges of sedition was taking place in Edinburgh before the notorious Lord Braxfield by the time the letter was written. The patriotic song of liberty which was later regarded as Scotland's national anthem was actually composed in the Murray Arms Hotel.

GATESLACK   NX 892 024

A farm in Durisdeer parish, Nithsdale about a mile south of Durisdeer village on the minor road from Carronbridge. It gives its name to a pass through the Lowther Hills following the Kirk Burn, along which lay a Roman road. It is referred to in 'The Braw Wooer' (C.W. p.556).

GIRTHEAD   NY 109 932

A farm in Johnstone parish, Annandale on the east bank of the Annan Water north of its confluence with Dalmakethar Burn. Though only about half a mile east of the A74 north of Johnstonebridge, it can only be approached by the minor road running parallel to the main road, with access near Dinwoodie Mains. The farm was the property of the Lawson family. William Lawson (1752-1819), succeeded his father Hugh as laird of Girthead in 1771 and took a prominent part in county politics, becoming a Justice of the Peace. In this role he was a witness to the induction of Burns as an Excise officer at the County Quarter Sessions in Dumfries on 27th October 1789.

GLENCAIRN

A parish on the western border of Nithsdale, containing the village of Moniaive, and taking its name from the valley of Cairn Water which, in its lower reaches, is known as **Cluden Water.** The parish contains **Craigdarroch, Dalgonar** and **Maxwelton.** The parish is chiefly of interest as the source of the title of Burns's earliest patron. In the late 14th century Sir William Cunningham of Kilmaurs married Margaret, daughter and co-heiress of Sir Robert Dennieston and thereby acquired the lands of Glencairn. His grandson, Alexander, was created Lord Kilmaurs in 1445, and Earl of Glencairn in 1488. James Cunningham, fourteenth Earl of Glencairn (1750-91) has been immortalised as Burns's patron, details of whom will be found in the companion volume The *Ayrshire Book of Burns-Lore.* The poet named his third surviving son James Glencairn (1794) after the Earl.

GLENKENS

The northern district of the Stewartry, consisting mainly of the basin of the River Ken and comprising the parishes of Carsphairn, Dalry, Balmaclellan and Kells. It is justly celebrated for its picturesque scenery. Dr Robert Trotter, 'the Muir Doctor', took Burns on a conducted tour of the Glenkens, during his three-day stay at Kenmure. Trotter shared with Gordon of **Kenmure** and the Rev. Dr John Gillespie a penchant for cock-fighting. The district is mentioned in the Third Heron Election Ballad (C.W. p.548):

> And frae Glenkens cam to our aid
> A chief o doughty deed!

GLENLEE   NX 609 802

A mansion in Kells parish, Kirkcudbrightshire, near the right bank of the Ken, three miles northwest of New Galloway. It lies just southwest of the A762 opposite the Holm of Dalry. Much enlarged in 1822, it stands in a level park adorned with fine old oaks. It was the seat of William Miller, father of Patrick Miller of **Dalswinton** who was born there in 1731. Patrick's elder brother Thomas (1717-89) was called to the bar in 1742, became Lord Justice Clerk with the title of Lord Barskimming in 1766, and afterwards President of the Court of Session, assuming the judicial title of Lord Glenlee and receiving a baronetcy. Lord Barskimming took his title from the family's Ayrshire estate. In 'The Vision' (C.W. p.117). Burns describes this estate and is said by Maurice Lindsay to allude to Sir Thomas in the line:

> An aged Judge, I saw him rove
> Dispensing good

although it is generally understood that Alexander Boswell (1707-82) was meant. Sir William Miller (1755-1846) succeeded to the baronetcy in 1789 and is thus referred to as 'Barskimming's guid knight' in the Second Heron Election Ballad (C.W. p.546). Sir William also took the title of Lord Glenlee on his elevation to the bench.

GLENLEE MILL   NX 602 815

A watermill on the west bank of Coom Burn, just off the minor road running south to Glenlee. A footpath running east from the Mill joins the A762, south of the junction with the A713. The tenant of Glenlee Mill was James Kennedy who wrote two letters to Burns. On 24th September 1789 he discussed the school of **Dunscore** while the letter of 19th October 1789 made further enquiries about Dunscore school and asked Burns for his Greek Grammar. No letters from Burns to Kennedy, however, are extant.

GLENRIDDELL   NX 846 858

The ancestral home of the Riddell family in Glencairn parish, Nithsdale, it was no longer occupied by the middle of the 18th century and is now a picturesque ruin on a knoll just to the south of Snade farm, about half a mile west of the ford across the Cairn Water. Robert Riddell's mother Anne Riddell of Glenriddell was heiress of the estate and married her cousin Walter Riddell of Newhouse, best remembered as a hostage (along with the Provost of Dumfries) taken by the Jacobite Army in 1745. Robert Riddell was the eldest son of this union, and inherited Glenriddell on the death of his father in 1788. By that time, of course, he had purchased the estate of **Friars' Carse**. He then sold Glenriddell, but retained the name as his title.

GOLDIELEA   NX 931 735

An estate, with a mansion, in Troqueer parish, Nithsdale, three miles southwest of Dumfries. It lies north of the A711, about three miles from Beewsing, and about a mile west of the ICI works at Cargenbridge. The mansion was originally called **Holm** and was the residence of Andrew Crosbie, the Whig Provost of Dumfries who was taken hostage, with Walter Riddell of Newhouse, by Prince Charles Edward Stuart in 1745. Crosbie's son later sold it to Lieutenant-Colonel Thomas Goldie who renamed it Goldielea, in compliment to himself and his wife whose maiden name was Leigh. Early in 1792, the grandson and namesake of Walter Riddell of Newhouse, the younger brother of Robert Riddell of Glenriddell, purchased the estate and then renamed it **Woodley Park** as a tribute to his wife Maria whose maiden name was Woodley. Walter Riddell, however, was forced to sell it back to Colonel Goldie two years later. More probably, he never actually completed the purchase in the first instance. In his letter to John McLeod of Colbecks (C.L. p.710) Burns wrote: 'In the mean time, Wattie has sold his Woodleypark to Colonel Goldie, the last Proprietor. Wattie gave £16000 for it; laid out better than £2000 more on it; & has sold it for £15000. So much for Master Wattie's sense & Management which, entre nous, are about the same pitch as his worth.'

GOLDIELEA

Certainly Walter Riddell advertised the house and estate for sale in the *Edinburgh Evening Courant* where it was described as 'fit for the accommodation of a genteel family', consisting of a dining-parlour and drawing-room of equal dimensions (nearly 16ft by 24, and 12 in height), a library, and large breakfasting parlour, kitchen, servants' hall and other conveniences on the first floor; with eight bedrooms above, besides dressing rooms and servants' apartments. The farms on the estate brought in rents of £460 per annum and the whole property amounted to 'rather more than 600 English acres'.

Colonel Goldie restored the name of Goldielea by which it has been known ever since. It was subsequently owned by James Newall and at the beginning of the 20th century was the residence of Balfour Browne, KC. Colonel (later Major-General) Goldie was briefly mentioned in the Second Heron Election Ballad (C.W. p.546) as 'Colonel Tam'.

HALLEATHS
NY 096 825

Formerly a mansion in Lochmaben parish, Annandale, 1.75 miles east of the town, but now occupied by a tile factory and a caravan park. It was about half a mile north of the A709. The house was greatly enlarged by David Bryce in 1866. In Burns's time it was owned by William Gordon, who leased it in May 1795 to Walter and Maria Riddell. From there, Maria healed the breach between herself and Burns, sending him a card of good wishes, which he acknowledged. 'The health you wished me,' he wrote about June or July (C.L. p.610), 'is I think flown from me for ever.' But he showed that the muses had not quite forsaken him for he enclosed 'some detached stanzas' for the song entitled 'Now Spring Has Clad the Grove in Green' (C.W. pp.554-5). Subsequent letters from Burns to Maria at Halleaths in November of that year show the poet in very low spirits, hoping that she would never experience such a loss as his — a reference to the death of his daughter Elizabeth Riddell Burns that September.

There is no evidence that Burns ever visited Maria at Halleaths, but their correspondence gradually improved after she moved there. In the summer of 1795 Maria wrote to him about one of the estate-workers at Halleaths named Shaw. He was anxious to improve himself but did not know how to go about it. Could Burns advise her on whether she should use her influence to get the young man appointed as a tide-waiter. Burns's reply was very detailed and helpful (C.L. pp.609-10). Soon after the poet's death Walter Riddell went to the West Indies to recover his fortune, but never returned. Maria gave up the lease of Halleaths and went to London.

HARDRIGGS
NY 220 672

An estate two miles east of **Annan.** Hardrigg Lodge is located on a farm road about half a mile from either the A75 or the B6357. John McMurdo, chamberlain of the Duke of Queensberry at **Drumlanrig,** purchased this estate about 1793, although there is no evidence that he ever lived there, as he preferred to live closer to Dumfries. He assumed the title of Hardriggs as a landed gentleman, and is thus described on the indenture of 25th February 1800 with Dr William Maxwell and John Syme as trustees for the widow and orphans of Burns.

HODDAM
NY 156 730

A castle and estate in the parish of Cummertrees, Annandale. The original castle, a seat of the Bruces at the beginning of the 14th century, stood at Hallguards but was demolished under the terms of a Border treaty. It was later relocated on the west bank of the Annan at the foot of Repentance Hill. Its square, thick-walled beacon-tower standing 25 feet high dated from the 15th century. The Hoddam estate was held from that time by the powerful Herries family. The sixth Lord Herries sold it in 1627 and it underwent various changes of ownership until 1690 when it was sold to John Sharpe whose line ended in four brothers. Their father was Charles Sharpe (1750-1831). Born Charles Kirkpatrick, the grandson of Sir Thomas Kirkpatrick of **Closeburn,** he changed his surname when he inherited Hoddam from his kinsman, Matthew Sharpe in 1769. The following year he married Eleanora, daughter of John Renton of Lamerton, to whom Burns wrote a brief verse epistle in 1787 (C.W. p.280). Although he trained as a lawyer, Charles Sharpe never practised. Instead, he lived the life of a country gentleman of considerable cultural refinement. An excellent violinst, he composed music and wrote poetry. Sharpe was a subscriber to Clarke's Sonatas, a matter mentioned by Burns in a letter to Thomson in February 1796 (C.L. pp.676-7). Burns wrote to Sharpe from Dumfries on 22nd April 1791 one of his most humorous letters which he signed 'Johnie Faa' (the name of a celebrated Irish tinker) and alluded to Sharpe's poetical propensities by saying 'I have the honor to belong to the same Family with you' (C.L. pp.580-1).

General Matthew Sharpe, Liberal MP for the Dumfries burghs (1832-41), enlarged the castle to a design by the architect Robert Burn (who also, incidentally, designed the tomb of Robert Fergusson, commissioned by Burns). Charles Sharpe's third son, Charles Kirkpatrick

Sharpe (1781-1851), sometimes dubbed 'the Scottish Horace Walpole', but best remembered nowadays for his spiteful literary gossip, has left a curious word-portrait of Maria Riddell: 'She was an affected-painted-crooked postiche — with a mouth from ear to ear and turned-up nose — bandy legs — which she however thought fit to display — and a flat bosom, rubbed over with pearl powder, a cornelian cross hung artfully as a contrast, which was bared in the evening to her petticoat tyings. This pickled frog... Burns admired and loved...' This singularly ill-natured description is oddly at variance with the well-known portrait of Maria by Sir Thomas Lawrence and the impression conveyed in Maria's letters and other writings.

HODDAM CASTLE

HOLM OF DALSCAIRTH   NX 931 735
The original name of the estate, subsequently renamed **Goldielea** and **Woodley Park**. Under its original name it was the property of the Crosbie family which played a leading role in Dumfries in the 18th century. John Crosbie, merchant and Provost; died in 1720. His son Andrew was Provost in 1732-4 and 1738-40 and was also a leading merchant in the burgh. Ex-Provost Crosbie was seized by the Jacobite forces in 1745 as one of their hostages, Walter Riddell of **Glenriddell** being the other. His eldest son Andrew suffered a severe setback by the collapse of the Douglas, Heron & Company Bank in 1773 and lost all the fortune he had gained by his eloquent pleadings in court. Regarded as the ablest lawyer in Dumfriesshire in his day, he was the original of Paulus Pleydell in Scott's novel *Guy Mannering*. Andrew Crosbie Junior is said to have been a friend of the poet, and he may therefore be the person referred to in a brief note to Robert Cleghorn, written from **Sanquhar** on 12th December 1792 (C.L. p.277), as 'our friend Crosbie', who was the bearer of a copy of 'Why Should na Poor Folk Mowe' (C.W. p.476).

ISLE   NX 935 832
A farm in Kirkmahoe parish, Nithsdale near the west bank of the **Nith,** 2.5 miles south of **Auldgirth** and about 5 miles north of Dumfries on the A76. It is approached about 300 yards

along a minor road east of the A76. The modern mansion (built about 1880) is known as Isle or Isle Tower, from the 16th century tower now incorporated with it. The farm lies just south of **Ellisland**. As there was no suitable house on the latter when Burns entered his tenancy in 1788 he lodged for some time with the outgoing tenant in a 'very humble domicile, overshadowed by the tower of Isle', once the seat of the Fergussons. The poet's temporary host was David Cullie, a devoted member of the Anti-Burgher Congregation of **Loreburn Church** in Dumfries, and it was in this house that Burns first met the Rev. William Inglis for whom he had such a high regard. Mr Inglis was accustomed to visit Cullie's house to hold the pre-Communion catechism and this was followed by a dinner at which Burns and Jean Armour were frequently among the guests. Jean Armour has left some interesting details of this period:

'Before this time Burns had written the "Holy Fair" and an impression had gone abroad that he was rather a scoffer or a free-thinker. David Cullie and his wife were aware of this; and although they treated him civilly as the incoming tenant, during the five months he resided under their roof, still they felt for him as for one who was by no means on the right path. On one occasion Nance and the bard were sitting in the spence, when the former turned the conversation on her favourite topic, religion. Mr Burns, from whatever motive, sympathised with the matron, and quoted so much Scripture that she was fairly astonished. When she went ben she said to her husband, "Oh! David Cullie, how they have wranged that man; for I think he has mair o the Bible off his tongue than Mr Inglis himsel." The bard enjoyed the compliment...'

Nance Cullie was obliquely referred to in a letter from Burns to Jean dated 12th September 1788 while she was still in Ayrshire but making preparations for the move to Nithsdale. 'I have just now consulted my old Landlady about table-linen', he wrote (C.L. p.478). A month later he informed her 'I have an offer of a house in the very neibourhood with some furniture in it, all of which I shall have the use of for nothing till my own house be got ready... The house is one in which a Mr Newal lived during the summer, who is gone to Dumfries in Winter.— It is a large house, but we will only occupy a room or two of it.' The tenant was David Newall, Dumfries lawyer and at that time factor to the estates of Isle and Steelston.

ISLE TOWER

KELLO WATER

A mountain stream of Sanquhar parish in the northwest of Nithsdale. Rising on the northern slope of Blacklorg Hill (1980 feet), it runs three miles northward along the boundary with Ayrshire and then about six miles eastwards to join the **Nith** 2.5 miles northwest of **Sanquhar.** It is believed that 'Kellyburn Braes' (C.W. p.461) refers to the slopes above Kello Water. An allegedly traditional ballad, similar to this, appears in Cromek's *Remains of Nithsdale and Galloway Song* (1810).

KELLS CHURCH   NX 633 785

Situated in the centre of Kells parish, about half a mile north of New Galloway. A stone in the kirkyard commemorates Adam McWhan who was shot in 1685 for his adherence to the Covenant. Robert Heron (1764-1807), Burns's first biographer, worshipped here as a boy. The Rev. William Gillespie (1776-1825) a minor poet, succeeded his father, the Rev. Dr John Gillespie as minister in 1801. Burns met him in the course of his Galloway Tour of 1793 at **Kenmure Castle** and rode with him by boat down Loch Ken. Burns carried the minister ashore at Boat o Rhone and quipped about being 'priest-ridden'.

KELLS KIRKYARD

KELTON   NX 989 707

A hamlet on the mutual border of Dumfries and Caerlaverock parishes, on the east bank of the **Nith** estuary. The village straddles the B725 three miles south of Dumfries. In Burns's time there was a boatyard at Kelton, where small ships were built and repaired. The brig *Rosamond* was brought here from **Sarkfoot** and held until auctioned off by public roup at the coffee house in Dumfries on 19th April 1792. During the six weeks between the seizure and the sale of the ship, it was repaired at the Kelton boatyard. A note in Burns's hand shows that two carpenters were employed for eleven days and four seamen for nine days at a cost of £8 18s before the brig could be refloated. The sale realised £166 16s 6d. As the total expenses amounted to £45 15s 4d, the profit was therefore £121 1s 2d, part of which would have been divided between the Excise officers who apprehended the ship.

KEMPLETON   NX 682 545
An estate in the east of Girthon parish, north of the minor road between Twynholm and Tongland, on the west bank of the Tarff Water. The proprietor in the late 18th century was William Bushby, son of John Bushby (1703-81) of Dumfries. William Bushby was ruined by the crash of the Douglas, Heron & Company Bank in 1773. Subsequently he went to the East Indies where he made a fortune in circumstances (not untypical of the period) which Burns with pawky humour alluded to in the Second Heron Election Ballad (C.W. p.545):

> And there'll be Kempleton's birkie,
> A boy no sae black at the bane;
> But as to his fine nabob fortune —
> We'll e'en let the subject alane!

Bushby purchased Kempleton on his return to Scotland from the Indies.

KEMYS HALL   NX 973 824
A farm in Kirkmahoe parish, Nithsdale, half a mile north of Kirkton village, on the minor road to **Dalswinton.** In Burns's time it was more commonly spelled Kemmishall. The farm was owned by Robert Riddell of Glenriddell who leased it to William Lorimer after he moved from Morton. He was listed as 'William Lorimer in Kemyshall near Dumfries' in the subscription list compiled by Burns to Anderson's magazine *The Bee* on 1st November 1790 (C.L. p.571). Lorimer had given up the lease by August 1795, to judge from an advertisement in the *Dumfries Weekly Journal* on 24th February 1795 signifying that it was to let for four years from Whitsunday.

KEMYS HALL

Lorimer died at Dumfries on 25th October 1808. These facts prove beyond any shadow of doubt that William Lorimer, the father of 'Chloris', was not the 'Mr Lorimer' referred to by Burns in his letter of June 1791 to Alexander Findlater (C.L. p.540) as previously supposed. For the identity of this Lorimer see under **Cairnmill**. Kemys Hall was only two miles from **Ellisland** so Burns was a frequent visitor. The Lorimers scarcely ever had company at their house without inviting Burns, and they often sent him delicacies from their farm. Whenever he passed their way, on his professional tours, Mrs Lorimer was delighted to give him a cup of tea when he called in.

Lorimer's daughter Jean (1775-1831) was the subject, directly or indirectly, of at least two dozen songs by Burns. Maurice Lindsay avers that Burns's friendship with the Lorimers declined towards the end of his life, but this is not borne out by the letter addressed to 'Mr Wm Lorimer, Farmer' in August 1795, inviting him to dine with him, in the company of John Syme, Dr William Maxwell, Dr James Mundell and Robert Cleghorn. 'I called for you yester-night, both at your own house, and at your favourite lady's — Mrs Hyslop of the Globe — but could not find you,' wrote Burns, concluding, 'Jeany and you are all the people, besides my Edinburgh friends, whom I wish to see; and if you can come I shall take it very kind.' Sad to say, Lorimer suffered from senile dementia in his last years and Jean became a family governess. Late in life, Jean visited her erstwhile husband, the worthless Whelpdale, in the debtors' prison at Carlisle. She died at Newington, Edinburgh.

KENMURE CASTLE   NX 635 764

A country seat in Kells parish, Kirkcudbrightshire, situated above the Kenmure Holms, half a mile above the head of Loch Ken, and about a mile south of New Galloway. It stands on a high, round, isolated mount which was in ancient times surrounded by a fosse. The oldest portion, a roofless, ivy-clad tower, dates from the 13th century, but the main building was constructed in the 17th century. The interior was noted for its winding staircases, secret passages and heirloom collection of Jacobite relics. Originally a stronghold of the Lords of Galloway, Kenmure was acquired in 1297 by Sir Adam Gordon whose sixth descendant was created Earl of Huntly while his tenth in the younger line was created Viscount Kenmure in 1633. The latter family gradually acquired the greater part of the Stewartry. William, sixth Viscount, was executed for his complicity in the Jacobite Rebellion of 1715, but his descendants regained his forfeited estates and titles in 1824. John Lowe (1750-98), author of 'Mary's Dream', was the son of a gardener at Kenmure Castle.

John Gordon (1750-1840) redeemed the family honour by loyal service in the Army (17th foot regiment). From 1780 he was for some time MP for the Stewartry but was forced to sell part of the estates to pay off debts, though he managed to retain Kells and Balmaclellan. Burns stayed with him and his wife for three days at the castle (27th-30th July 1793) during the Galloway Tour. Syme relates that when Mrs Gordon's pet dog Echo died she asked Burns for a suitable epitaph. He agreed, but his lack of enthusiasm for the subject is obvious in the uninspired lines beginning 'In wood and wild, ye warbling throng' (C.W. p.495). Gordon was referred to in the Second Heron Election Ballad (C.W. p.545) as 'Kenmure sae generous', and also named in a stanza of 'John Bushby's Lamentation' (C.W.548). Burns also reworked the old Jacobite ballad whose subject was Kenmure's grandfather — 'O, Kenmure's on and awa, Willie' (C.W. p.451). Captain Adam Gordon, younger brother of Kenmure, served in the 81st Regiment and was the recipient of the verse epistle beginning 'Dost ask, dear Captain, why from Syme' (C.W. p.507).

The Rev. Dr John Gillespie dined with the poet at the Castle and it was in Gordon's barge that they sailed down Loch Ken on 30th July, visiting Airds Hill and going ashore at Boat o Rhone, where the loch narrowed and there was formerly a ferry-crossing.

KIRKBEAN CHURCH   NX 979 593
The parish church of Kirkbean on the west side of the **Nith** estuary, 12 miles south of
Dumfries. It lies on the north side of the **Carsethorn** road, just off the A710. Admiral John
Campbell (1719-90), who sailed round the world with Anson in 1744, Dr Edward Milligan
(1786-1833), the distinguished medical scientist, and John Paul Jones (1747-92), co-founder
of the American Navy, were born and brought up in this parish. The church was built in 1766,
to a design by William Craik of **Arbigland**, but its handsome tower was not added till 1840.
The kirkyard contains the tomb of the Rev. Edward Neilson, minister from 1789 till 1824 and
an intimate friend of Burns who referred to him, in a letter to Dr Moore (C.L. p.259), as 'a
worthy clergyman in my neighbourhood, and a very particular acquaintance of mine.' Neilson
was on his way to France at the time (March 1789) in urgent quest of the Duke of Queensberry,
and Burns took the opportunity to entrust him with the letter to Moore in London. Apparently
the Duke, who had the living of Kirkbean in his gift, had forgotten to sign the Presentation
before he left Scotland for Paris. As the Presbytery could not proceed, the worthy minister
had no alternative but to go after the negligent Duke himself. There was probably more to this
matter, however, because Burns discussed the chicanery of the Presbytery in a letter to Willie
Nicol, on 9th February 1790 (C.L. p.347): .
    'You must have heard how the Rev. Mr. Lawson of Kirkmahoe, seconded by the Rev. Mr.
Kirkpatrick of Dunscore, and the rest of that faction, have accused in formal process, the
unfortunate and Rev. Mr. Heron of Kirkgunzeon, that in ordaining Mr. Nelson *(sic)* to the
cure of souls in Kirkbean, he, the said Heron, feloniously and treasonably bound the said Nelson
to the confession of faith, *so far as it was agreeable to reason and the word of God!'*
    It is obvious, from a letter to Peter Hill in February 1790 (C.L. p.315) that Neilson obtained
books from Edinburgh through the good offices of Burns and Hill.

KIRKCHRIST   NX 673 519
An ancient parish in the south of the Stewartry, now forming the southern district of
Twynholm parish. It remained a separate parish until at least 1605 but probably as late as 1654,
and was certainly united with Twynholm long before 1684. Its church and kirkyard were situated
on the west bank of the River Dee, opposite the town of **Kirkcudbright,** and the kirkyard can
still be seen south of the A755. A building for the 'distillation of malted liquors' was erected
near the kirkyard in the late 18th century and must still have been something of an innovation
when Burns composed 'The Five Carlins' (C.W. pp.364-6) and aptly dubbed Kirkcudbright as:
                ... Brandy Jean, that took her gill,
                In Galloway sae wide.

KIRKCONNEL GRAVEYARD   NY 250 755
An ancient burial ground on a meadow within a fold of Kirtle Water, 2.5 miles northeast
of Kirtlebridge. Kirkconnel parish was joined to Kirkpatrick-Fleming after the Reformation.
It lies on the western side of Springkell estate on the east bank of the river. From Eaglesfield
take the right fork north out of the village and after about half a mile take a left turn on to the
estate road. The track to the graveyard follows the bend of the Kirtle Water, bearing round to
the left about half a mile from the estate road-end. The cemetery contains the mortal remains
of 'Fair Helen of Kirkconnel Lea', the subject of Burns's reworking of an old ballad, under
the title of 'Where Helen Lies' (C.W. p.311). Helen, whose surname was either Bell or Irving,
lived some time in the 16th century. She had two suitors one of whom took a shot at his rival;
but Helen, thrusting herself in front of her lover Adam Fleming, received the fatal wound
instead. Fleming killed his assailant on the spot, but fled the country to avoid the legal process
and enlisted in the Spanish army. Years later, he returned to Kirkconnel and died by Helen's
grave. He was interred alongside her. The less favoured suitor was a Bell of Blacket House. Bell's
Tower, the home of the fair Helen, was demolished in 1734.

KIRKCONNELL HOUSE   NX 979 680
An old mansion, said to be one of the oldest inhabited residences in Scotland, in Troqueer parish, Nithsdale on the west bank of the **Nith,** two miles northeast of **New Abbey** and seven miles south of Dumfries. It is approached along a minor road off the A710, turning off to the right about half a mile north of New Abbey opposite Shambellie Woods. The ancient tower is in a good state of preservation, but most of the mansion dates from the middle of the 18th century, having been rebuilt by James Maxwell after his return from Jacobite exile in France. It was anciently a stronghold of the Kirkconnells whose heiress Janet married a nephew of the first Lord Maxwell about 1430. The Maxwells of Kirkconnell were deeply pious and generous benefactors of the Church. After the Reformation they remained steadfast to the old faith, their sons often being educated at the Scots College in Douai, Flanders. William Maxwell of Kirkconnell took part in the Jacobite Rebellion of 1715. His son James fought for the Young Pretender in 1745-6 but managed to escape to Nantes after Culloden. He returned to Scotland about 1750 and, through the intercession of the Craiks of **Arbigland,** got his estates back in April 1753. The rebuilding of Kirkconnell House, using the brick-making technology learned in France, began soon afterwards.

James Maxwell married Mary Riddell of Swinburne in August 1758 and died in July 1762. In the interim, however, he fathered three sons, the second of whom, born in 1760, was William. He was educated at the Jesuit college at Dinant and trained as a doctor. While completing his studies in Paris, Dr Maxwell espoused the Republican cause and was a member of the National Guard present at the execution of King Louis XVI. It is said that he dipped his handkerchief in the blood of the king — a story without foundation but which stuck to him ever after. In 1794 he left France and returned to Scotland where he settled in Dumfries in general practice. He and Burns were the closest friends, on account of their Jacobin sympathies. Maxwell was also the poet's physician and attended him in his last illness, prescribing the sea-bathing that probably hastened his early death. Burns presented Maxwell with his pistols (now in the Royal Museum of Scotland). The poet's son, born on the day of his funeral, was named Maxwell after the doctor. With Alexander Cunningham and John Syme, William Maxwell became a trustee of the fund established for the poet's widow and orphans. He died in 1834.

No letters from Burns to Maxwell are recorded, but the doctor was mentioned in the poet's correspondence on several occasions. In a letter to Mrs Dunlop in September 1794, for example, Burns describes him as 'A gentleman who also lives in town, & who had studied medicine in the first schools — the Dr. Maxwell whom Burke mentioned in the House of Commons about the affair of the daggers...' (C.L. p.211). Maxwell was alleged to have tried to procure arms for the French Revolutionaries — an incident which endeared him to Burns who got into some hot water himself over a similar incident. The letter goes on to describe how Maxwell cured Jessie Staig, an incident immortalised by the epigram 'Maxwell, if merit here you crave' (C.W. p.519). Maxwell was included with Syme, Burns, McCraken and Mundell in the epigram entitled 'Ye Sons of Sedition' composed by the right-wing Loyal Natives. Maxwell was also that 'particular friend of mine' mentioned in a letter to David Blair of Birmingham (C.L. p.504) who acquired Lord Balmerino's dirk for an anker of Ferintosh and subsequently presented it to Burns.

KIRKCUDBRIGHT   NX 68 50
A town and parish of the Stewartry, the capital of the former county of Kirkcudbrightshire and a royal and parliamentary burgh, standing on the east bank of the River Dee, 30 miles southwest of Dumfries. A burgh of regality from 1330, it received its royal charter in 1455 when it was taken out of the possession of the Douglases by King James II. In 1461 it was a place of refuge for King Henry VI of England after his defeat at Towton during the Wars of the Roses. Near the parish church stands the ruined castle built in 1582 by Sir Thomas Maclellan of

Bombie, the town's chief landmark. The old town was an almost perfect square, 350 yards on each side, with a wall and a tidal moat. The Meikle Yett survived till the late 18th century. Piped water on a gravity feed system was introduced as early as 1763. Kirkcudbright was one of the so-called Dumfries burghs which united to return a member to Parliament, and thus figures in Burns's ballad 'The Five Carlins' (C.W. p.364), personified as 'Brandy Jean'.

The town was almost destroyed in 1507 by the Manx led by the Earl of Derby. In the 'Rough Wooing' of 1547 the citizens successfully beat off an English onslaught. The seventh Lord Maxwell conspired with Philip II of Spain and Kirkcudbright Harbour was to have been a landing-place of the Spanish Armada (1588). The town played a prominent part in the Covenanting struggles. On one of its streets a brawl between Sir Robert Grierson of Lag and Viscount Kenmure (stepfather of one of Lag's victims) would have proved fatal to the former, but for the intervention of Claverhouse. The fleet of William III sheltered in Kirkcudbright Bay on its way to subdue Ireland. The Old Pretender hoped to land at Kirkcudbright in 1715, but the citizens were staunch Hanoverians. The ship's captain, John Paul was briefly imprisoned in the town's tolbooth on a murder charge; during the American War of Independence he took his revenge by raiding the mansion of the Earl of Selkirk at **St Mary's Isle** nearby.

The blind poet and early patron of Burns, Dr Thomas Blacklock, was minister of Kirkcudbright (1761-4). Basil William Douglas-Hamilton, Lord Daer (1763-94), second son of the Earl of Selkirk, was a notable agricultural improver in the district, better remembered for Burns's poem 'On Meeting with Lord Daer' (C.W. p.254). Lord Daer, a champion of parliamentary reform and a member of the Friends of the People, was the first nobleman Burns ever met, but was hardly typical of his class. Broughton House in the High Street was the town house of James Murray of Broughton, referred to in the first Heron Election Ballad (C.W. p.544):

'Wi's uncle's purse and a' that.

The second Ballad, sub-titled 'The Election' (C.W. p.545) actually begins with the lines:

Fy, let us a' to Kirkcudbright,
For there will be bickerin there;
For Murray's light horse are to muster
An O, how the heroes will swear!

A later stanza concludes with the lines:

An there'll be roaring Birtwhistle -
Yet luckily roars in the right!

This was a reference to Alexander Birtwhistle, a leading merchant and Provost of Kirkcudbright at the time of the election. The worthy Provost also appeared as 'Whistlebirk' in 'Election Ballad for Westerha' (C.W. p.367). Burns also referred to the election in letters to Mrs Dunlop and Graham of Fintry. To the latter he wrote (C.L. p.432): 'Kirkcudbright is dubious. Sir James Johnston has the Provost; but Lord Daer, who does the honors of Great Man to the place, makes every effort in his power for the opposite interest. Luckily for Sir James, his lordship though a very good lord, is a very poor politician.'

Broughton House became the home of the celebrated artist Edward A. Hornel (1864-1933) and is now preserved as a library and museum, with one of the largest private collections of Burnsiana in existence, including both the Kilmarnock and first Edinburgh editions, the Dublin edition of 1787 and the first American edition of 1788, as well as a unique version of *The Merry Muses*.

The parish kirkyard contains the graves of several men associated in some way with Burns. A Mr Warwick was an Excise officer in **Annan** and later Kirkcudbright. His daughter claimed, at the Centenary celebrations of 1859, that she had frequently seen Burns in her father's house. Warwick lived in a house called the Green Gate, in more recent times the property of the artist, E.A. Taylor.

Burns lodged in the Heid Inn, now the Selkirk Arms, in the High Street, while travelling on Excise duties. During renovations of this old building layers of wallpaper were removed in the room to the right and rear of the hotel and revealed a beautiful sketch of a church. To the left of the sketch were four lines of poetry with the signature 'R. Burns' in bold clear lettering. A few words, however, were obliterated by the workman's wet brush but the verse reads:

> When January winds were blawin caul'
> ... Kirkcudbright I took my way,
> But mirksome night did me enfauld
> ... till earlyest day.

These lines are evidently a draft for the beginning of 'The Lass that Made the Bed to Me' (C.W. p.583), Burns's reworking of the Restoration ballad 'The Cumberland Lass'.

David Blair was an apprentice to Deacon Gray, a shoemaker in the town. On one occasion when Burns arrived in Kirkcudbright and put up at the Selkirk Arms, his feet were so badly swollen as a result of the wet and fatigue of the journey, that his boots had to be cut off his feet. Blair took the boots from the poet and gave them to Deacon Gray who repaired them.

The Selkirk Arms dates back to 1750 and became fully licensed in 1777. Burns and Syme arrived here about 1pm on 1st August 1793 and stayed overnight. In the late afternoon they dined with John Dalzell and it may have been on this occasion, rather than later the same evening at **St Mary's Isle**, that Burns gave the Selkirk Grace (C.W. p408). A panel carved by Tim Jeffs (in the hotel dining-room) bears the poet's bust and the grace.

MACLELLAN'S CASTLE, KIRKCUDBRIGHT

KIRKENNAN   NX 827 581
A country house in Buittle parish in the Stewartry, just off the A711 two miles south of Buittle Bridge and about three miles south of Dalbeattie and a mile north of Palnackie. It was the birthplace of Alexander Reid (1747-1823), the painter and portrait miniaturist. After training

in London and Paris, Reid settled in Dumfries where he had a studio. A number of paintings and drawings of landscapes and antiquities in Dumfries and the Stewarty are extant. Reid also specialised in those miniature portraits, executed in oils on ivory or card, which were so fashionable in an era before photography. Burns referred to Reid in a letter of May 1795 to George Thomson (C.L. p.674): 'There is an artist of very considerable merit, just now in this town, who has hit the most remarkable likeness of what I am at this moment, that I think was taken of any body...' Burns also referred to this miniature in two letters to Maria Riddell, written in the spring of the same year (C.L. p.609). In the first letter he wrote on the same complimentary lines, adding 'When you are at any time so idle, in town, as to call at Reid's painting-room, & mention to him that I spoke of such a thing to you, he will shew it you.' Later, however, he drastically revised his opinion, and complained that the painter had spoiled the likeness, but from the contents of this letter it is obvious that Burns was badly out of sorts at the time. Reid succeeded to the family seat on the death of his elder brother in 1804 and retired thither. He died unmarried in 1823 and was buried in Buittle kirkyard. The miniature portrait, which shows a left-facing bust of Burns, is now preserved in the National Portrait Gallery. It formed the basis for the effigy of Burns on the medals struck in 1987 to celebrate the bicentenary of Burns being made an honorary burgess of Dumfries. On 18th November 1794 Burns composed the song 'Contented wi Little and Cantie wi Mair' (C.W. p.531). He had some idea of linking the portrait miniature and this song 'in order that the portrait of my face and the picture of my mind may go down the stream of Time together.

KIRKGUNZEON   NX 866 668
A village and parish in the Stewartry, deriving its name from St Winning, the Irish saint who also gave his name to Kilwinning. The village lies on a minor road about half a mile northwest of the A711 ten miles southwest of Dumfries. The parish church, standing at the road junction in the centre of the village, was originally built in the late 12th century, but was rebuilt in 1790 with 160 sittings. The minister at that time was the Rev. James Heron who drew down on his head the ire of his Calvinistic colleagues in the Presbytery of Dumfries for ordaining Edward Nielson of **Kirkbean** — a matter discussed at some length by Burns in a letter to Nicol on 9th February 1790 (C.L. p.347).

KIRKINNER MANSE   NX 423 515
The manse for the combined parishes of Kirkinner and Longcastle, united in 1630, in Wigtownshire. It is situated in the village of Kirkinner, at the junction of the A746 and the minor road running in a southwesterly direction towards Barnbarroch. The minister from 1663 to 1686 was the Rev. Andrew Symson, author of *A Large Description of Galloway*. The present church nearby was not erected until 1828, but boasts a four-holed cross of immense antiquity. The minister of Kirkinner in Burns's time was the Rev. John Graham and a letter written by him from 'Manse of Kirkinner' to Mrs Dunlop on 5th November 1793 was included among those which were in the poet's possesion at the time of his death. A precis of its contents was given in Currie's manuscript list, unfortunately badly mutilated on account of damp: 'Laments the loss of a friend ... memorials of a justly honored friend... Mrs D. for her present of a book — Is g... & of Little's poems —'

KIRKMAHOE
A parish in Nithsdale northeast of Dumfries, the parish church being located in the hamlet of Kirkton, a mile east of the **Nith.** The Lorimer home at **Kemys Hall** lies about a mile north of the village. The parish also includes the estate of **Dalswinton.** Writing to Willie Nicol on 9th February 1790 (C.L. pp.346-7) Burns described the ecclesiastical politicking in the neighbourhood, involving the Rev. Mr Lawson of Kirkmahoe: 'Some of our clergy have slipt

in by stealth now and then; but they have got up a farce of their own' — a reference to clandestine visits by 'men of the cloth' to the theatrical performances in Dumfries.

KIRKMAIDEN

A parish in the southern extremity of the Rhinns of Galloway. As including the southernmost point of Scotland it is mentioned conjointly with John o' Groats House in Caithness to indicate the extremities of the Scottish mainland, in the poem 'On the Late Captain Grose's Peregrinations thro Scotland' (C.W. p.373):

Hear, Land o Cakes, and brither Scots
Frae Maidenkirk to Johnie Groat's...

KIRKPATRICK DURHAM   NX 787 702

A village and parish of the Stewartry. The village is about five miles northeast of **Castle Douglas** and about a mile and a half west of Springholm, by which it is approached via a minor road from the A75. The village was founded in 1785 and neatly laid out as accommodation for the families of workers in the cotton and woollen mills established at that time. These enterprises flourished briefly at the end of the 18th century but collapsed in the slump after the Napoleonic Wars. In its heyday the village was largely frequented for balls and horse-races. It was one of the places regularly surveyed by Burns in his Excise duties before his transfer to Dumfries. An anecdote preserved by Joseph Train concerns Jean Dunn 'a suspected trader' in Kirkpatrick Durham, who saw Burns and Robertson (a fellow Exciseman) approaching her house on the morning of a fair. She slipped out of the back door to evade their scrutiny, leaving in her house only her little daughter and a girl who was looking after her. 'Has there been any brewing for the fair here today?' enquired Burns as he entered the cottage. 'O no, Sir,' replied the servant, 'We hae nae licence for that.' 'That's no true!' chimed the bairn, 'The muckle black kist is fu o the bottles o yill that my mother sat up aa night brewin for the fair.' 'Does that bird speak?' asked Robertson, pointing to one hanging in a cage. 'There is no use for another speaking-bird in this house,' commented Burns, 'while that lassie is to the fore. We are in a hurry just now; but as we return from the fair we'll examine the muckle black kist.' Thus warned, Jean Dunn managed to get her stock of beer out of the house before the Excisemen returned. This story is often quoted to show Burns's distaste for the petty bureaucracy which his profession forced upon him.

KIRKPATRICK FLEMING   NY 276 706

A village and parish of Annandale, on the east bank of the Kirtle Water, seven miles southeast of **Ecclefechan.** The parish church was partially rebuilt about 1778. James Currie was born at the manse on 31st May 1756, his father being the minister. He was educated in Dumfries, where John Syme was one of his school-friends. In 1771 he emigrated to Virginia, settling as a merchant on the James River, but business failure and chronic fever drove him back to Scotland in 1776. Unfortunately, the ship on which he was travelling was attacked by the American revolutionaries and he was impressed into the rebel forces. He purchased his freedom, set sail, and was captured a second time. He again escaped in a open boat. Illness and misfortune dogged him but eventually he reached England in May 1777. He decided to study medicine at Edinburgh. Imprudently, he had a cold bath to cool off after a thirty-mile walk, and contracted the rheumatic fever which eventually killed him. He graduated in 1780 and settled in Liverpool. In 1792 he bought **Dumcrieff** near Moffat, and it may have been about this time that he met Burns briefly in a Dumfries street, being introduced by their mutual friend Syme. A great admirer of Burns's poetry, he was approached by Maria Riddell and the family trustees to prepare a definitive edition of the poet's work, together with his biography. He was singularly ill-fitted for the task. In particular, his character (like Heron) as a reformed reprobate made him take a very hard line on what he imagined were the drunken bouts of a poetic rake. Thus was born the *canard* of Burns's drunkenness, which was magnified and distorted by other biographers in the course of the 19th century.

KIRROUGHTREE   NX 422 662

Otherwise Kerroughtree, Kirouchtree or Kirroughtrie, from the Celtic *Caer Uchtred* — 'Uchtred's fort'. It was in Burns's day a mansion with finely wooded grounds in Minnigaff parish a mile northeast of Newton Stewart. It also gives its name to extensive forests in the north of the parish. It is now a hotel about half a mile north of the A75, from which it is approached by a private road just east of the Creebridge suburb of Newton Stewart.

The estate boasts a number of prehistoric cairns and the hillock known as Parliament Knowe, believed to have been a place of assembly in pre-Roman times. It was the Galloway estate of Patrick Heron of Heron (1736-1803), scion of an old Lincolnshire family who had been one of the principals of the ill-fated Douglas, Heron & Company Bank of Ayr which crashed spectacularly in 1773. Patrick Heron eventually recovered from that event and purchased Kirroughtree after marrying Lady Elizabeth Cochrane, daughter of the Earl of Dundonald. In April 1794 Burns wrote to her (C.L. p.705) to thank her for sending him the melody which she had composed on the banks of **Cree.**

KIRROUGHTREE

Two months later, Burns met Heron at Kirroughtree during his second Galloway Tour, in company with John Syme and David McCulloch of **Ardwall.** As a result of this visit, Burns got Heron and his brother, Major Basil Heron, to subscribe to Johnson's *Musical Museum*(C.L. p.299). In 1795 Patrick Heron stood as Whig candidate in the election for the Stewartry and enlisted Burns's help with his campaign. As a 'placeman', Burns was rather apprehensive about nailing his political colours to the mast, hence the self-justificatory tone of the letter which he wrote to Heron from Dumfries in March 1795 (C.L. pp.715-16). Heron was well-connected and had obviously promised to interest himself in the poet's advancement in the Excise. Burns thanked Heron for the sentiments expressed in a letter which Syme had shown him. Burns stated that he was on the supervisors' list and could therefore expect promotion within two or three years. 'Then, a Friend might be of service to me in getting me into a place of the kingdom which I would like.'

In the meantime, he assisted his friend's cause with the series of three Election Ballads (C.W. pp.543-8) which played some part in the defeat of the Tory candidate, Thomas Gordon of **Balmaghie.** In 1796 Parliament was dissolved but Heron was subsequently re-elected and held his seat until 1802. Burns, though now very ill, again composed an Election Ballad, subtitled 'The Trogger' (C.W. p.549). On this occasion Heron's opponent was Montgomery Stewart, younger son of the Earl of Galloway. Burns did not live to see the successful outcome of this contest. Heron won again in 1802 but was declared invalid in May 1803. He died shortly afterwards on his way home to Scotland.

In the Second Heron Election Ballad (C.W. pp.545-6) Heron himself is referred to:

> An there'll be trusty Kerroughtree,
> Wha's honour was ever his law:
> If the virtues were pack't in a parcel,
> His worth might be sample for a'!

Major Basil Heron was eulogised in the following stanza:

> An can we forget the auld Major,
> Wha'll ne'er be forgot in the Greys?
> Our flatt'ry we'll keep for some other:
> Him only it's justice to praise!

Burns composed the 'Inscription for an Altar of Independence' (C.W. p.557) at Kirroughtree about July 1795.

LAGGAN(PARK)   NX 837 901

A farm in Glencairn parish, Nithsdale about two miles east of Kirkland. on the southern flank of the Keir Hills. It is approached from the B729. Travelling north take the right turn to Skaith and Breckonside but after about half a mile turn left on to the unclassified farm road. This remote hill farm of 340 acres was purchased by Willie Nicol on 26th March 1790 from William Riddell of Comieston, using money inherited by Nicol's wife, a daughter of Cairns of **Torr.** Nicol asked Burns to inspect the farm on his behalf, but the poet was too ill to do so and sent two of his friends instead. He subsequently wrote to his friend about 13th December 1789 giving him a report and recommending the purchase (C.L. p.346). In May 1790 Burns inspected the farm and reported to Nicol on the limestone which he discovered there. 'One thing is certain; the next adjoining farm, which has a name beginning with, "Brecken-side" — I think it is, & which is just a continuation of your field, does, as I am positively assured, contain lime.' Nicol took Burns's advice and bought the farm for about £1700. He regarded the farm as an investment, continuing to work as a schoolmaster in Edinburgh and only spending his holidays at Laggan. Chambers stated that it was nothing more than a 'but and ben' and a ruin by 1859, with a heap of stones referred to as Nicol's Wa'. The farm was also known as Meikle and Little Laggan, and as such it featured in a detailed advertisement in the *Dumfries Weekly Journal* on 28th March 1797, announcing its forthcoming roup at the **George Inn.** Details of the sale were obtainable from Nicol's brother-in-law, William Cairns of Torr. Dr Currie claimed that 'Willie Brew'd a Peck o Maut' was written in connection with a housewarming party at Lagganpark, but this is impossible as (a) Burns himself mentions **Moffat** as the location of this bacchanal, and (b) Nicol did not purchase Lagganpark until March 1790 — five months after 'Willie Brew'd' was written.

LAGGAN   NX 885 847

An estate in **Dunscore** parish, Nithsdale about two miles east of **Dunscore** village on the minor road from Throughgate to Burnhead and bounded on the northern side by the Laggan Burn. This once extensive estate bordered with **Ellisland,** hence the desire of its proprietor John Morine to acquire the latter when Burns relinquished his lease. Patrick Miller was keen to dispose of Ellisland as it was on the wrong side of the **Nith** in relation to the rest of his **Dalswinton** estate. Morine purchased it from Miller for £1,900. Morine disagreed with Burns over the value of some manure left behind, and also insisted that the fences and out-buildings should be left in good order. Burns felt that he was being hardly treated, in view of the work he had put in on clearing what was virtually waste ground. On the day of the removal, several things happened to try the poet's temper, so he sent Adam Armour (his brother-in-law), who had been helping with the flitting, back to Ellisland to smash every pane of glass which carried Burns's handwriting. According to Armour, this piece of deliberate vandalism was punctiliously carried out, Burns paying Jean's young brother six shillings for his services. John Morine was the butt of one of the poet's epigrams (C.W. p.495):

When Morine, deceas'd, to the Devil went down,
'Twas nothing would serve him but Satan's own crown.
'Thy fool's head,' quoth Satan, 'that crown shall wear never:
I grant thou'rt as wicked, but not quite so clever'.

LANGHOLM   NY 36 84
A town and parish of Eskdale. The town stands on the River Esk at the influx of Ewes Water from the north and Wauchope Water from the southwest. The old town stands on the east bank of the Esk and included a principal street with a market place, surrounded by fine houses of white freestone. The new town on the west bank was founded in 1778 and was laid out on a grid pattern in the form of a triangle. A cotton factory erected in 1788 was the beginning of the extensive textile industry in the town. Langholm has several literary connections which have some bearing on Burns. William Julius Mickle was born here in 1735. Best remembered for translating Camoens' great epic *Lusiad* from the original Portuguese, he is sometimes credited with the composition of 'There's nae Luck about the House', although authorship has also been claimed for Jean Adams. Burns quoted lines from this popular song in several of his letters. The interleaved volumes of Johnson's *Musical Museum* which Burns presented to Robert Riddell bear the annotation in the poet's handwriting on the relevant page: 'One of the most beautiful songs in the Scots, written by William Julius Mickle...' Jean Lorimer's worthless husband, Whelpdale, spent his last miserable years in poverty in Langholm.

LAUGHT MAINS   NX 896 944
A farm in Morton parish, Nithsdale, about a mile and a half north of **Closeburn,** on the north bank of Cample Water, and a mile east of the A76.
It was part of the Queensberry estates and was leased by William Stewart when he retired as factor at Closeburn. According to his will, at the time of his death in 1812, Stewart was the tenant of two other farms on the Queensberry estate as well as Laught, was a partner in the Kelhead Limeworks and had a fourth share in the woollen manufactory at Cample (200 yards southeast of Laught), under the name of Stewart, Mathison & Company. Burns attended a wedding at Laught in 1792. During another visit to the Stewart family there, Burns heard that Sandie Spence, the son of a ploughman, was dying. Burns went to the ploughman's cottage and offered up a prayer for the child. Corfardin farm, now part of Laught, was at one time tenanted by James Hogg, the 'Ettrick Shepherd' and an early editor of Burns, but this venture was unsuccessful.

LAURIESTON   NX 683 648
A village in Balmaghie parish, seven miles northwest of **Castle Douglas,** at the junction of the A762 and the B795. Laurieston was the meeting place of the war committee of the Kirkcudbrightshire Covenanters. Burns passed through Laurieston with Syme on his Galloway Tour, taking the minor road west through Laurieston Forest and thence to **Gatehouse.**

LINCLUDEN COLLEGIATE CHURCH   NX 966 779

A ruined religious house in Terregles parish, Nithsdale, on a grassy mound above the west bank of the **Cluden Water** which here falls into the **Nith** about a mile and a half north of Dumfries town centre. It was originally a convent for Black or Benedictine nuns, founded by Uchtred of Galloway in the mid-12th century. Archibald the Grim, Earl of Douglas, expelled the nuns for 'insolence and other irregularities' in the late 14th century and converted it into a collegiate church with a provost and twelve canons. Robert Douglas, the last provost, was allowed to enjoy the benefice 40 years after the Reformation and mass was celebrated here as late as 1585, but thereafter it fell into decay. Subsequently it came into the possession of the Earl of Nithsdale. Early in the 19th century steps were taken to preserve this architectural gem. In Burns's day it was a picturesque ruin and a favourite haunt of the poet during his Dumfries period.

According to Allan Cunningham, it was here that Burns beheld 'The Vision' — a ludicrous notion as that poem was composed before Burns moved to Mossgiel in 1784. Nevertheless, it is known that Burns added several stanzas in 1787 so it is just possible that he visited the collegiate church at the conclusion of his Border Tour that year and derived some inspiration on that occasion. What is more certain, however, is that the second version of 'Ca' the Yowes' (C.W. p.519) owed its origins to this spot. Writing to George Thomson in September 1794 (C.L. p.655) he confessed to being dissatisfied with the original version: 'In a solitary stroll which I took today, I tried my hand on a few pastoral lines, following up the idea of the chorus, which I would preserve...' The third stanza refers to 'Clouden's silent towers' — the ruins of Lincluden. Burns also composed the song 'As I Stood by yon Roofless Tower' (C.W. p.570) to the tune of the bawdy Cumnock Psalms, in tribute to this venerable ruin.

LINCLUDEN HOUSE   NX 963 779

A Tudor mansion, formerly known as Youngfield, a little southwest of the collegiate church, it was destroyed by fire in 1875, but rebuilt the following year to designs by the celebrated architect, David Bryce. It has since disappeared as a result of the development of the Lincluden housing estate. In the late 18th century the mansion was the property of Ebenezer Young whose wife on one occasion had used impolite — if not downright rude — language to Robert Riddell. To please Riddell, Burns composed 'Grim Grizzel' (C.W. pp.429-30):

Grim Grizzel was a mighty Dame
Weel kend on Cluden-side:
Grim Grizzel was a mighty Dame
O meikle fame and pride.

Burns himself claimed that he had written this parody about 1791, adding a quite different story as its origin: 'Passing lately through Dunblane, while I stopped to refresh my horse, the following ludicrous epitaph, which I pickt up from an old tombstone among the ruins of the ancient abbey, struck me particularly, being myself a native (sic) of Dumfriesshire.' The tombstone apostrophised: 'Here lyes with Dethe auld Grizzel Grimme, Lincluden's ugly witche. O Dethe, an what a taste hast thou Cann lye with siche a bitche!'

LOCHARWOODS   NY 045 674

A farm in Ruthwell parish, Nithsdale, lying to the south of the B725 and on the north bank of the Lochar Water about two miles southeast of Bankend. The proprietor in the late 18th century was John Clark (1750-1813) who was Provost of Dumfries in 1777-9. Clark was a close friend of Robert Riddell and in that capacity was the recipient of a copy of Burns's 'Sonnet on the Death of Robert Riddell' (C.W. p.513), enclosed with a brief note on 21st April 1794. Two years later, when he was taking the waters at **Brow**, Burns wrote to Clark (C.L. p.706) asking if he would be kind enough to lend him his gig. 'I have a horse at command, but it threatens to rain, & getting wet is perdition.' Clark was the proud owner of a spring-cart, a very recent innovation at the time, and a vast improvement, in terms of comfort, over the unsprung carriages previously in use.

LOCHENBRECK INN   NX 647 651

A hostelry at the side of the road through Laurieston Forest, about two and a half miles west of **Laurieston**. No trace of this inn now exists, but it probably existed at Lochenbreck Cottage, near Lochenbreck Well. Here Burns and Syme took some much-needed refreshment on their way to **Gatehouse** on their Galloway Tour.

LOCHEND   NX 893 687

An estate and mansion-house seven miles southwest of Dumfries, just off the A711. It is located to the west of Loch Arthur in the parish of Kirkgunzeon, half a mile southwest of Beeswing. It was the seat of the Hyslop family. Charles Hyslop obtained the wadset of Lochend in May 1690 and married Margaret Maxwell of **Terraughty**. His eldest son Charles married Margaret Stewart of Shambellie. Their son John (1710-73) was the father of William Hyslop who became a merchant and vintner in Dumfries. William was born on 12th June 1743 and died on 26th May 1803. He was twice married. His first wife, Mary Mercer, died childless. His second wife was Jean Maxwell, third daughter of John Herries Maxwell of Terraughty, 'the Maxwells vet'ran chief'. William Hyslop was named by Burns in the grace beginning 'Lord, we thank, and Thee alone' (C.W. p.408).

William and Jean Hyslop had five sons and several daughters. The eldest son John was born on 12th August 1770 and died in 1835. In 1795 he married Margaret Geddes and from then until late 1796, if not later, they were landlords of the **Globe Inn** owned by William Senior — the Jock and Meg of the 'Grace before and after Meat' (C.W. p.409). The second son was William Junior (1771-1828). Both he and his father joined the Dumfries Volunteers. With Burns, they signed the letter to Colonel De Peyster complaining against the decision to appeal to the public for a contribution towards their expenses. The *Dumfries Weekly Journal* contained detailed lists of the donations in the period 1795-8, which show that the protesters were overruled. The William Hyslops, father and son, often featured in these very subscription lists, and there were even collections taken up by the farmworkers at Lochend and William Junior's servant-girls in Dumfries. The third son Wellwood (1780-1845) emigrated to Jamaica and became a member of the colonial legislature and a merchant in Kingston. Alexander (born in 1782) went to South America. The youngest son Maxwell (1783-1837) was brutally assaulted by a mob during the meal riots in March 1796 and his wounds were treated by Dr William Maxwell. Later in life he married Mary, the daughter of Wellwood Maxwell of **Barncleugh**, became a merchant in Jamaica and died in Falmouth.

LOCHMABEN   NY 08 82

A town and parish of Annandale and a royal, parliamentary and police burgh. Nestling amid a cluster of lochs ten miles northeast of Dumfries at the junction of the A709 and the B7020, it enjoys a pleasant situation in the vale of the River Annan, with the Kinnel and the Ae nearby. In Burns's day there were no fewer than seven lochs around the town giving it the appearance, according to contemporary accounts, of a Venice rising from the water. The predecessor of the present church (built in 1818-20) was badly damaged by fire in December 1593 when the Johnstones tried to burn out the Maxwells who had taken refuge inside, after their defeat at Dryfe Sands. It was closely associated with the Bruces of Annandale, although the tradition that King Robert Bruce was born there is unsound. It claims to have been a royal burgh since the accession of King Robert, although no charter survives earlier than 1612. Lochmaben played a major role in the turbulent history of the Borders, as illustrated by the old ballad 'The Lochmaben Harper'. Burns mentioned this song to James Johnson (C.L. p.299): 'I fear I shall never recover; & it is a famous old song.'

Lochmaben was one of the Dumfries burghs in terms of parliamentary representation and, as such, featured in the election ballad 'The Five Carlins' (C.W. p.364), appropriately as Marjorie o the Monie Lochs. In a letter to Robert Graham of Fintry dated 9th December 1789 (C.L. pp.431-3), Burns described Lochmaben as 'a city containing upwards of fourscore living souls that cannot discern between their right hand or left — for drunkenness, has at present the balance of power in her hands.— The Honorable Council of that ancient borough are fifteen in number; but alas! their fifteen names indorsing a bill of fifteen pounds, would not discount the said bill in any banking-office.— My Lord Provost who is one of the soundest headed, best hearted, whisky-drinking fellows in the south of Scotland, is devoted to Sir James[Johnstone.]'

In a letter of 9th July 1790 to Mrs Dunlop (C.W. pp. 188-90), Burns gives a vivid description of electioneering, country-style in the 18th century. In particular he described the confrontation between the rival factions at Lochmaben: '... the Duke & Captain Miller's friends led a strong party, among others, upwards of two hundred Colliers from Sanquhar Coal-works & Miners from Wanlock-head; but when they appeared over a hill-top within half a mile of Lochmaben, they found such a superiour host of Annandale warriors drawn out to dispute the Day, that without striking a stroke, they turned their backs & fled with all the precipitation the horrors of blood & murther could inspire.'

LOCHMABEN CHURCH

The provost of Lochmaben at that time was Robert Maxwell who held office from September 1782 till September 1790. He then retired from civic affairs and died in October 1792. In the above letter to Graham, Burns mentioned that he had the honour to be a burgess of Lochmaben, but no record of this has survived in the burgh archives, so it is not known when it was conferred on the poet. That Burns was a frequent visitor to the town is indisputable, and he was obviously on intimate terms with Provost Maxwell. A long letter from Burns to Maxwell is extant, dated 20th December 1789 (C.L. p.548), revealing that the worthy provost shared with Burns an interest in bawdy ballads. Provost Maxwell was mentioned in the 'Election Ballad for Westerha' (C.W. p.367) as 'Maxwell true, o sterling blue'.

The Rev. Andrew Jaffray (1723-95) was latterly minister of Lochmaben and Burns sometimes stayed at the manse while on tours of Excise duty. In the above-mentioned letter Burns concludes by saying, 'If you meet with that worthy old veteran in religion and good fellowship, Mr Jeffry, or any of his amiable Family, I beg you will give them my best compliments.' Jaffray was the father of Jean Jaffray (1773-1850), the original of 'The Blue-eyed Lassie' (C.W. p.333) who was about fifteen years old when this song was written. She married William Renwick, a Liverpool merchant with whom she migrated to New York. A son of George Thomson visited her there in 1822, by which time she was a widow. Thomson recollected: 'She has told me that she often looks back with a melancholy satisfaction on the many evenings she spent in the company of the great bard, in the social circle of her father's fireside, listening to the brilliant sallies of his imagination and to his delightful conversation.'

'Many times', said she, 'have I seen Burns enter my father's dwelling in a cold rainy night, after a long ride over the dreary moors. On such occasions, one of the family would help to disencumber him of his dreadnought and boots, while others brought him a pair of slippers and made him a warm dish of tea. It was during these visits that he felt himself perfectly happy, and opened his whole soul to us, repeated and even sang, many of his admirable songs, and enchanted all who had the good fortune to be present with his manly, luminous observations and artless manners. I never... could fancy that Burns had ever followed the rustic occupation of the plough, because everything he said or did had a gracefulness and charm that was in an extraordinary degree engaging.' Jean's son, Dr James Renwick, became Professor of Natural Philosophy and Chemistry at Columbia University. A daughter married Captain Wilks, USN, the 'over-zealous officer' whose seizure of the *SS Trent*, a British ship travelling between neutral ports in November 1861, and the arrest of the Confederate agents Mason and Slidell, almost sparked off war between Britain and the United States.

The manse of St Magdalene's Church, Lochmaben, is now a private residence, Magdalene House, and is situated on Bruce Street on the main Dumfries-Lockerbie road at the junction with Princes Street.

LOCHRUTTON MANSE   NX 913 736
About a mile east of Lochfoot village in the parish of Lochrutton in the east of the Stewartry. It is situated beside the parish church on an unclassified road, half a mile south of the Old Military Road. The present church was built in 1819 with 300 sittings. The manse is now a private house named Kirkbrae. In the late 18th century it was the residence of the Rev. George Duncan and his wife Anne McMurdo (born 1745), who married in 1770. Anne McMurdo was a first cousin of John McMurdo of **Drumlanrig**. They had several sons including Thomas Tudor Duncan (1776-1858), for 54 years minister of the New Church in Dumfries. George Duncan married at Edinburgh in February 1796 Christian Currie, sister of Dr James Currie of Liverpool, Burns's biographer.

The third son was the Rev. Dr Henry Duncan (1774-1846), one of the most remarkable men of the cloth. James Currie himself was related to the Duncan family and was raised by the Rev. George Duncan after he became orphaned. Later in life he was to repay this kindness by obtaining a position with a Liverpool banking-house for Henry where the latter worked for three years. Later he also provided the money for Henry Duncan's education as a divinity student. In 1799 Henry became minister of **Ruthwell** under which further details of his remarkably varied career will be found.

Burns was a close friend of the Rev. George Duncan, having been introduced to him by John McMurdo, and was a frequent visitor to Lochrutton Manse thereafter. Henry and Thomas were eighteen and sixteen respectively when Burns first visited the manse in 1793. The Rev. George Duncan introduced the poet to his sons and said, 'Look well, boys, at Mr Burns, for you'll never again see so great a genius.' Obeying the paternal counsel, they gazed earnestly at their visitor, till from the survey of his features they were diverted by the power and brilliancy of his conversation, as Charles Rogers (1889) rather quaintly puts it. Henry Duncan later played a prominent part in the campaign to have the **Mausoleum** erected, being joint-secretary and treasurer as well as convener of the special committee. His brother, Dr Thomas Duncan, and his cousin, Major Bryce McMurdo, also served on the Mausoleum Committee.

LOCHRYAN HOUSE   NX 065 688

A plain, substantial mansion with finely-wooded grounds, about a quarter of a mile from the centre of Cairnryan village, Wigtownshire. It was built for Colonel Agnew of Croach at the beginning of the 18th century. The heiress of Lochryan, Dame Eleanora Agnew, married Sir Thomas Wallace of Craigie and their eldest daughter was Frances Anna Wallace (1730-1815). In 1748 Miss Wallace met John Dunlop of Dunlop at a party given by the Blairs at **Dunskey.** He literally swept her off her feet, and the couple eloped. She was seventeen at the time and her suitor was 41! Despite the disparity in their ages, it was a love match that lasted till his death in 1785. Mrs Dunlop bore him seven sons and six daughters. On the death of her mother in 1761 Mrs Dunlop became heiress of Lochryan. When her father died in 1774 the estate of Craigie went to her eldest surviving son, Thomas Wallace who took his maternal grandfather's surname. Owing to 'heavy encumbrances' and mismanagement, however, Craigie had to be sold in 1783.

Although Mrs Dunlop resided mainly at Dunlop House (Ayrshire) and Morham Mains (Haddington), Lochryan remained part of her estates. Some 42 of the 77 extant letters from Burns to Mrs Dunlop were preserved at Lochryan for almost a century after the poet's death, and provided the basis for William Wallace's *Robert Burns and Mrs Dunlop* (1898). Subsequently, the Lochryan MS was purchased by R.B. Adam of Buffalo, NY and is now in the Morgan Library, New York.

LOGAN   NX 813 633

An estate in Buittle parish in the Stewartry, south of the Buittle Burn, midway between **Castle Douglas** and Dalbeattie. It can be approached by an unclassified road running west from the A710 at Netheryett, past Milton of **Buittle.** It was the ancestral home of the Rev. James Muirhead (1742-1805), minister of **Urr,** who claimed to be the chief of the Muirhead family.

According to Alexander Young he was a 'man of considerable humour', but also 'of the *irritable genus*, and nowise disposed to submit to the abuse and sarcastic ballads of Burns, whom he purposed to hunt out of society as a public nuisance.' In the Second Heron Election Ballad (C.W. p.546) he was described ambiguously as 'guid as he's true'. In the Third Ballad (C.W. p.548) he was classed with the minister of Buittle (the Rev. George Maxwell):

> Whase haly priesthood nane could stain,
> For wha could dye the black?

In the Fourth Election Ballad (C.W. p.549) Burns twitted Muirhead on his armorial pretensions. Muirhead repaid Burns by publishing scurrilous verses, which he had printed at Edinburgh. They included a paraphrase of Martial's epigram 'In Vacerram' which ran:

> Vacerra, shabby son of whore,
> Why do thy patrons keep thee poor?
> Bribe-worthy service thou canst boast
> At once their bulwark and their post;
> Thou art a sycophant, a traitor,
> A liar, a calumniator,
> Who conscience, hadst thou that, would'st sell,
> Nay, lave the common shores of hell,
> For whisky; eke, most precious imp,
> Thou art a rhymster, gauger, pimp;
> Whence comes it, then, Vacerra, that
> Thou still art poor as a church-rat?

When Young remonstrated with Muirhead for publishing this disgraceful poem, he asked him how he proved that Vacerra was a gauger like Burns. Muirhead replied, 'Martial calls him *fellator,* which means *sucker,* or a man who drinks from the cask.'

The tenant of Logan at the end of the 18th century was a Mr Grierson whose brother, a Writer to the Signet in Edinburgh, had allegedly been a friend of Burns while living in his native **Glenkens.**

LOGAN HOUSE   NX 096 429

An estate, with a Scots Baronial mansion, in Kirkmaiden parish, southwest Wigtownshire, two miles north of Port Logan. It is approached from the B7065, being the first turning on the right after the fork with the A716.

Logan House was built in the 18th century and was the residence of the McDouall family until 1940. It is famous for its walled gardens which contain many exotic plants and shrubs. Captain (later Colonel) Andrew McDouall represented Wigtownshire in Parliament. In 1783 he met Margaret Kennedy, daughter of Robert Kennedy of Daljarrock, factor to the Earl of Cassilis. She was then seventeen years old and was the younger sister of Mrs Gavin Hamilton. Burns himself met her about a year later and wrote the song 'Young Peggy' (C.W. p.125) in her honour. Subsequently Peggy Kennedy had an affair with Captain McDouall and in 1794 bore him a daughter. She tried to get him to admit that she had been privately married to him, but the gallant Captain denied both the marriage and his paternity. An action was raised in the Court of Session but the plaintiff died in 1795 before the case was concluded. In 1798 the Consistorial Court declared in favour of the marriage and the child's legitimacy. The Court of Session reversed the legitimacy but awarded £3000 damages to the dead woman and made alimentary provision for the child.

Colonel McDouall was notorious as 'a rake of the first order'. Burns clearly had this squalid episode in mind when he composed the Second Heron Election Ballad (C.L. p.546) and included the lines:

> An there'll be Logan's McDoual —
> Sculdudd'ry an he will be there!   gross lewdness

Colonel McDouall was also referred to in the epistle 'from Esopus to Maria' (C.W. p.539):

> The crafty Colonel leaves the tartan'd lines
> For other wars, where he a hero shines;

MAHAAR   NX 015 702

A farm in Kirkcolm parish, Wigtownshire, just north of the point at which the A718 becomes the B738. It was the home of the Niven family after leaving Ayrshire. Margaret Niven of Ballochneil married Samuel Broun, the poet's maternal uncle. Burns stayed at Ballochneil while studying at Hugh Rodger's school in Kirkoswald and shared a bed with his school chum William Niven, later the recipient of the earliest surviving letters written by the poet (C.L. pp.37-40). Hugh Rodger's daughter Jean married John Niven who subsequently moved to Mahaar, and the farm has been in the possession of their descendants ever since. Two of John Niven's daughters, Janet and Jane, provided anecdotal material about Burns to the Rev. Charles Rogers for his *Book of Robert Burns* (Edinburgh, 1889).

MARR BURN   NX 859 986

A stream running eastwards through **Drumlanrig** Woods and entering the Nith just north of the ruined Tibbers Castle. The north bank of the burn just east of the minor road from Drumlanrig Castle a mile away is known to this day as Poet's Corner, and alludes to the fact that it was a favourite spot of Burns during his **Ellisland** period. The beautiful song 'Their Groves o Sweet Myrtle' (C.W. p.550), which Burns composed as a tribute to Jean Armour and sent to George Thomson in April 1795, was written here and alluded to it in the opening stanza:

> Their groves o sweet myrtle let foreign lands reckon
> Where bright-beaming summers exalt the perfume!
> Far dearer to me yon lone glen o green breckan,
> Wi the burn stealing under the lang, yellow broom;

MAVIS GROVE   NX 972 736

A private house, now called Laghall, to the east of the New Abbey Road (A710), a mile south of Dumfries and not far from the **Nith** opposite Kingholm Quay. It was the home of Colonel Arent Schuyler De Peyster (1736-1822). Born in New York of Dutch-Huguenot descent, he was raised in Holland and Britain and in 1755 was commissioned in the 50th Foot which had been raised in Massachusetts in 1748. He later transferred to the 51st Regiment and then the 8th (King's Liverpool), serving no fewer than 47 years with the latter. He campaigned in Germany during the Seven Years War (1756-63), but then served in Canada (1768-85), latterly as Military Administrator in the Great Lakes area, with the rank of colonel. From 1787 till his retirement in 1794, he served in England and Ireland. He had married Rebecca, daughter of Provost David Blair, and was thus related by marriage to John McMurdo of **Drumlanrig** who married her sister Jane. On retiring from active service in 1794 he settled in Dumfries, where he had a town house at 75 Irish Street (in more recent years the British Legion Club, but now derelict) and purchased the small estate of Mavis Grove three miles from the town centre.

When the Dumfries Volunteers were formed in March 1795 he was appointed major-commandant. In that capacity he headed the parade at Burns's funeral. Burns was a frequent visitor at Mavis Grove, having been introduced to Colonel De Peyster, shortly after his arrival in the area, by John McMurdo. In January 1795 De Peyster wrote to Burns enquiring about his health, and the poet responded with the verse epistle 'My honor'd Colonel, deep I feel' (C.W. p.564). When it was proposed to raise funds for the Volunteers by an appeal to the public 25 members of the Volunteers signed a letter of protest. While Burns was not actually named as the author of the letter (C.L. p.720) it has the unmistakeable hallmarks of his style. Colonel De Peyster was something of a poet himself, and in 1813 published a collection of verse under the title *Miscellanies by an Officer*. He enjoyed a vigorous, active life right up to the end, and died in 1822 as the result of an accident at the age of 86. Mrs De Peyster embroidered the colours presented to the Volunteers.

John McMurdo himself moved to Mavis Grove towards the end of his life and members of his family were still in residence there as late as the 1860s. The woods upstream from Mavis Grove are still known as the Colonel's Wood, in memory of De Peyster.

MAVIS GROVE

MAXWELLTOWN   NX 967 761
Until 1929 a separate burgh in Kirkcudbrightshire, but then absorbed by Dumfries and now forming the suburbs on the west bank of the **Nith.** In the late 18th century, however, it was a lawless settlement, beyond the jurisdiction of the Dumfries magistrates. It was known as Bridgend, from its location at the western end of the old bridge, and its delinquency was so well-known that it inspired the popular saying: 'You might trace a rogue all over the kingdom, but were sure to lose him in the Bridgend of Dumfries'. For details of the **Old Bridge House,** now a museum, see under Dumfries. Things only began to improve in 1810 when the village was erected into a burgh of barony and named in honour of Maxwell of **Terraughty,** its superior. It came within the Dumfries Divisions of Excise and, as such, was mentioned by Burns in his long letter of 7th January 1794 (C.L. pp.438-40) recommending the re-organisation of Excise administration. Similarly Burns drew to Provost Staig's attention the fact that the vintners in Bridgend operated at an unfair advantage over the Dumfries brewers, the Richardson brothers.

Even before the burgh of barony was established, the area began to move up the social scale and John Syme, John Lewars, John McMurdo and Colonel De Peyster purchased or leased properties on that side of the river.

MAXWELTON   NX 822 897
A mansion in Glencairn parish, Nithsdale, near the north bank of the Cairn Water. It lies in the triangle formed by the A702 east of Kirkland, the B729 and the minor road linking them. From 1611 till 1966 it was the seat of the Laurie family and was the birthplace of Annie Laurie, a celebrated but rather fickle beauty. She was immortalised in song by her fiance, William Douglas of **Fingland,** but instead of keeping her 'promise true' she married Alexander Fergusson of **Craigdarroch** in July 1709. She long survived her husband and died at **Friars' Carse** on 5th April 1764 in her 82nd year. The song was later reworked and improved by Lady John Scott, but the original version was published by Charles Kirkpatrick Sharpe of **Hoddam** in 1832.

Annie Laurie was the mother of Alexander Fergusson of Craigdarroch and aunt of Sir Robert Laurie, the contestants in the famous contest for the whistle. Sir Robert Laurie represented Dumfriesshire in Parliament from 1774 till his death in 1804 and, as such, enjoyed the privilege of free transmission of letters by post. On two occasions Burns wrote to Robert Riddell (a kinsman of the MP) asking him to procure 'franks' for him. On 16th October 1789 he asked him 'to get your guest, Sir Robert Lowrie (sic) to frank the two inclosed covers for me...' (C.L. p.481). On 27th September 1791 he wrote: ''Dare I trouble you, if you meet with the Member, to get me a Frank...' (C.L. pp.482-3). Interestingly, Burns then gave the date on which the letter was to be franked, as well as the full name and address of the recipient, Colonel Fullarton. This was necessary, as the franking regulations had been considerably tightened up to prevent abuse, and it was now mandatory for the person franking the letter (i.e. signing his name in the bottom left-hand corner of the cover) to write out the name and address of the recipient in his own hand, and superscribe the date of posting across the top.

MOFFAT   NT 08 05
A town and parish in Annandale. The town is on a gentle slope with a High Street 300 yards long and 50 broad. In the *Beauties of Scotland* (1805) this thoroughfare is described as 'wide and spacious, handsomely formed and gravelled... a most agreeable walk to the inhabitants, and to the company that comes for goats' whey or the mineral waters.' The town owed its importance as a centre of the sheep industry to the annual Tup Fair, but in 1633 Miss Rachel Whiteford founded the spa and thereafter the town developed as a fashionable watering place, many fine buildings being erected in the 18th century. The town has historic associations with the Border Wars and also the Covenanters, but its heyday was in the late 18th and early 19th centuries when it was patronised by such celebrities as John Home the playwright, David Hume the philosopher, James

Macpherson the fabricator of *Ossian*, James Boswell the biographer and diarist, Joseph Black the chemist, Dr Blacklock the blind poet and Hugh Blair the divine. The last two, of course, played prominent roles in the life and career of Burns. Home, whose play *Douglas* inspired the comment from one of the audience 'Whaur's yer Wullie Shakespeare noo?' met Macpherson at the bowling green in Moffat and it was the subsequent discussion about Highland poetry that is said to have given Macpherson the idea of producing *Ossian*. The source of this story, incidentally, was Henry Mackenzie, Burns's earliest literary critic.

Burns himself was a frequent visitor to the town and lodged at the Black Bull Inn (founded in 1568 and used by Graham of Claverhouse as his headquarters during the Killing Times). It was here that Burns composed his epigram on Miss Davies (C.W. p.491). She was the youngest daughter of Dr Davies of Tenby, Pembrokeshire and was related to the Riddells of **Friars' Carse.** Her sister married Captain Adam Gordon of **Kenmure.** She was famed for her petite beauty, her wit and charm. She became betrothed to a Captain Delaney who wrote her verses using the poetic name of Stella, but he took off with his regiment and as a result she 'went into a decline'.

BLACK BULL INN, MOFFAT

James Clarke (1761-1825), a native of **Closeburn,** was appointed schoolmaster at Moffat Grammar in 1786 and was also the first librarian of the Subscription Library. About 1790 he married Jane Simpson, a native of Cumbria, and they had three daughters. In 1791 he was charged with cruelty to his pupils by the local authorities in conspiracy with the Earl of Hopetoun, who owned Moffat House (now a hotel) in the town. Burns took Clarke's part in the affair and wrote several letters on his behalf, to Alexander Cunningham (C.L. pp.462-3), the Lord Provost of Edinburgh who was a trustee of the school (C.L. p.584), to Alexander Williamson of Balgray, factor to the Earl of Hopetoun (C.L. p.588) and to the Rev. William Moodie (C.L. p.613). In January and February 1792 he wrote to Clarke himself, originally to boost his friend's morale and latterly to congratulate him on the successful outcome of the affair (C.L. pp.595-6). When the affair was at its blackest, Burns tried to get another position for Clarke, through the good offices of Robert Riddell. Clarke, however, was fully vindicated and remained at Moffat until 1794 when he transferred to Forfar. Later he became rector of the grammar school at Cupar and finally retired to Dollar where he kept a boarding-house.

Dr James Currie, the poet's future biographer, spent the summer of 1784 in Moffat, seeking a cure for consumption. Although he was 'nigh to his end' he made an excellent recovery due to the bracing hill climate. He was again in Moffat in May 1792 when he purchased the nearby estate of **Dumcrieff.**

Moffat was also the birthplace, about 1788, of Helen Hyslop, reputed to have been the illegitimate daughter of Helen Hyslop, a local beauty, and Burns. According to a report in the *Pall Mall Gazette*, shortly after the lady's death at the advanced age of 97 or 98, she had resided in the same little back street in which she had been born. 'Helen is said to have borne a strong resemblance to Burns in her earlier days, and indeed the likeness to the portraits of Burns was traceable to the last in the contour of the face and in the dark, bright eyes... Nor was the likeness confined to physical points; in her mental powers Helen showed a strain of the poetic blood. A few years ago her conversational powers and her quickness of repartee were most amusing and attractive.' She married a man called Armstrong and for thirty years was cook to the Glendinning family at the Buccleuch Arms, **Thornhill.**

MONKLAND FRIENDLY SOCIETY — see DUNSCORE

MOSSKNOWE   NY 281 697

An estate in the parish of **Kirkpatrick Fleming,** Annandale, half a mile south of the village. It is approached by a private road running west from the A74. The original mansion-house was rebuilt in the late 19th century.

The laird of Mossknowe was William Graham (1756-1832), who married Grace Gordon, granddaughter of the Earl of Aboyne. He was the subject of Burns's epigram beginning 'Stop, thief!' Dame Nature call'd to Death' (C.W. p.522) and possibly also the Dumfries epigrams on 'Billy' (C.W. p.533).

MOUNT ANNAN   NY 196 697

A mansion with beautiful grounds in Annan parish, near the east bank of the River Annan and two miles north of the town. It is approached by a private road running west from the B722. The estate was acquired in 1793 by Alexander Dirom who had a distinguished military career. He married Magdalen, daughter of Robert Pasley of Mount Annan (then called Cleughead). Burns first mentioned him in a letter of 13th March 1794 to Mrs Dunlop (C.L. p.209), saying that he had been reading an account of the campaign with Cornwallis at Seringapatam written 'by a Major Dirom who was Adjutant general there; & who has bought an estate & is now settling in this neighbourhood.' Dirom's account made frequent mention of officers who were close relatives of Mrs Dunlop. Through the good offices of Alexander Cunningham in the ensuing year Burns met Dirom, who had then been promoted to colonel. In a letter of May 1795 to George Thomson (C.L. p.674) he wrote: '...on wednesday I go to visit a friend of his| Cunningham's|... I mean a well-known Military & Literary character, Colonel Dirom.' Dirom eventually attained the rank of lieutenant-general and served with distinction in the Napoleonic Wars.

MUIRCLEUGH   NS 885 052

Otherwise known as Mirecleugh, it is a farm in Durisdeer parish, Nithsdale, just east of the A76 about a mile north of Durisdeermill village. The tenant in 1790 was Thomas Johnston whom Burns had apprehended for illicit maltings. Johnston was tried and convicted, and fined £5, but appealed against the fine. Fergusson of **Craigdarroch** and Robert Riddell, in their capacity as magistrates, ordered Collector Mitchell to suspend proceedings till Johnston's appeal could be investigated. Burns, who was exceedingly busy at this period, was clearly annoyed at the intervention of Fergusson and Riddell on Johnston's behalf, and one may detect his exasperation in the letter to Mitchell on this matter (C.L. p.563). Burns prepared a very detailed answer to Johnston's petition, couched in official phraseology. This document (C.L. pp.564-5) is of particular interest as the only example of an Excise report by Burns believed to be extant.

NEW ABBEY   NX 96 66
A village and parish formerly of eastern Kirkcudbrightshire but since 1974 in Nithsdale, on the west side of the **Nith** estuary The village lies at the northern base of **Criffel,** eight miles south of Dumfries. It takes its name from Sweetheart Abbey, founded in 1275 by Devorgilla Baliol who also founded Baliol College, Oxford and the old bridge of Dumfries. The corn mill (recently restored and now open to the public) was built by the Stewarts of Shambellie in the late 18th century. James Gracie, the banker and friend of Burns, was born in the village in 1756.

NEW CAMPLE   NX 886 941
A farm in Closeburn parish, Nithsdale, about a mile and a half north of **Closeburn.** It is situated on the east side of the A76 and extends to the Cample Water. Here, in a 30-foot barn, the adherents of 'Mother' Elspeth Buchan (1738-91) found refuge after they were hounded out of Ayrshire. An account of the Buchanites was given by Burns to his cousin, James Burness, in a letter of 3rd August 1784 (C.L. pp.59-60). This band of religious fanatics had settled in Irvine but in the spring of 1784 the citizens of that town had expelled Mother Buchan and her followers had voluntarily quit the place. 'They are fixed at present in the neighbourhood of Dumfries'. Burns had a more personal interest in this strange sect, for one of its adherents, Jean Gardner, was alleged (by the poet's sister Isabella) to have caught his fancy. She was the daughter of an Irvine butcher, in whose house the preacher Hugh White, one of the leaders of the sect, had lodged.

Joseph Train maintains that Jean Gardner was the 'darling Jean' of Burns's 'Epistle to Davie' (C.W. p.88) but there is no evidence to support this, and most editors have assumed that Jean Armour was meant. Train quoted from a statement made by Andrew Innes, one of the sect: 'When I was sent back from **Thornhill** for Mr Hunter, Jean Gardner came with me from Irvine to Closeburn, and when we were in the neighbourhood of Tarbolton, she seemed to be in fear, and in a rather discomposed condition; when I inquired the cause, she said it was lest Burns, the poet, should see her, for if he did, he would be sure to interrupt her, for they had been on terms of intimacy, but we proceeded on our journey without meeting any obstruction.' The story goes that Burns followed Jean to Buchan Ha', as the barn at New Cample was soon nicknamed, and spent an entire night and the following day vainly trying to persuade her to return with him to Ayrshire. The Buchanites remained at New Cample until March 1787 when they were driven out. They settled at Auchengibbert in the Stewartry, in the uplands between Dumfries and **Castle Douglas.** By that time, however, Jean Gardner had left the sect, having married George Hill and emigrated to America with him. She is believed to have died of fever in Philadelphia about 1793.

NEWTON STEWART   NX 41 65
A town in Peninghame parish, Wigtownshire, on the west bank of the **Cree,** linked by a bridge to its suburb of Creebridge in the parish of Minnigaff. The present bridge, carrying the A75, was erected in 1813 and replaced an earlier structure dating from 1745. The village owed its name originally to William Stewart, third son of the second Earl of Galloway who built some houses here, at a point where the river could be forded, and in 1677 obtained a charter making it a burgh of barony. A haunt of the Solway smugglers and a convenient stage on the coach route to **Portpatrick,** it soon developed into a prosperous little town. About 1778 William Douglas purchased the estate of Castle Stewart and changed the name of the town to Newton Douglas in 1793 — a fact referred

to by Burns in the Second Heron Election Ballad (C.W. p.545):
        An there'll be Douglasses doughty,
        New christening towns far and near.
Douglas made vigorous efforts to promote industry; factories for cotton spinning and weaving,
a carpet factory and a tannery were instituted. But the carpet enterprise failed miserably, the cotton
factory was eventually sold to Lord Garlies who used its site as a quarry, and the amount of handloom
weaving fell drastically in the slump of 1828. The new name soon fell into disuse, and the Post
Office formally re-instated the original name on 5th January 1808.

NITH
        The principal river of Nithsdale, it rises between Enoch and Prickeny hills, nine miles south
of Cumnock, and flows with a south-southeasterly course for 71 miles, terminating in the Solway
Firth fourteen miles south of Dumfries. The *Novius* of the geographer Ptolemy, it flows through
seventeen parishes. From **Sanquhar** to **Auldgirth** the river flows through some of the most beautiful
and varied scenery in Scotland. The banks of the river are rich with associations with the poet,
from **Ellisland** and **Friars' Carse** in Dunscore parish to **Lincluden** and **Burns Walk** in Dumfries.
        Consequently the Nith features in several of the poems and songs. By August 1788, for example,
he had composed 'out of compliment to Mrs Burns' the song 'O, Were I on Parnassus Hill' (C.W.
p.329) containing the line:
        But Nith maun be my Muse's well
This was followed soon after by 'The Banks of Nith' (C.W. p.330):
        The Thames flows proudly to the sea,
        Where royal cities stately stand;
        But sweeter flows the Nith to me,
        Where Cummins ance had high command.
The last line refers to the Comyn family, supporters of King John Baliol and enemies of King Robert
Bruce. In 'The Wounded Hare' Burns speaks of 'winding Nith' (C.W. p.354). In the political ballad
'The Five Carlins' (C.W. pp.364-6) Dumfries, the principal town on the river, was epitomised as
'Maggie by the banks o Nith', while 'The Laddies by the banks o Nith' figured in 'Election Ballad
for Westerha' (C.W. p.367). Willie Nicol's mare Peg Nicholson expired in February 1790 and appears
to have been dumped in the river, if one is to believe the recurring line 'But now she's floating down
the Nith' (C.W. pp.380-1). Undoubtedly the best-known lines alluding to this river, however, occur
in the patriotic song 'Does Haughty Gaul Invasion Threat?' (C.W. p.537): 'The Nith shall run
to Corsincon' (meaning that it would run backwards) and, of course, the song 'Adown Winding
Nith' (C.W. p.497), written as a tribute to Phillis McMurdo.

PARK   NX 907 913
        A hamlet straddling the minor road running northeast of Kirkpatrick in Closeburn parish,
about a mile south of **Closeburn Castle.** It had a limeworks which was the source of the lime used
by Burns and carted by him to **Ellisland.** The quarry was underground, worked on the stoop and
room system, and the mineral was hauled out on an inclined plane assisted by a water-powered
haulage system. The water was brought from Loch Ettrick to Heathery Dam (about three miles
overland) and thence to a great water wheel at Park. This water system also served the smithy and
sawmill at Shotts, just north of Park.

PARTON HOUSE   NX 710 695
        A house in Parton parish in the Stewartry, about a mile southeast of Parton village and just
north of the A713, standing in extensive woods commanding a fine view of the River Dee. The
18th century mansion was burned down in the 19th century but later rebuilt. From the 15th to
the early 19th centuries the estate, sometimes known as Parton Place, was the property of the

Glendonwyn or Glendinning family who played host to Burns and Syme on 27th July 1793 during the first Galloway Tour. Syme wrote to Alexander Cunningham describing their visit: 'In the evening we walked up a bonny know and had as grand a view of alpine scenery as can well be found.'

Miss Glendinning of Parton was engaged to David Blair, later Provost of Dumfries. Her sister married Frederick Maxwell of **Terregles.** In a letter of 5th October 1790 (C.L. p.505) to Alexander Dalziel, Burns discussed the Glendinning family and its tragic connections with the **George Inn, Dumfries.**

PARTON HOUSE

PENPONT   NX 84 94

A village and parish of upper Nithsdale near the left bank of the **Scaur Water,** 15 miles northwest of Dumfries and two miles west of **Thornhill.** At the end of the 18th century the parish had only some 966 inhabitants, of whom only 100 lived in the village, but there were no fewer than seven ale-houses. Penpont was one of the parishes surveyed by Burns (1789-91) and on one ocasion he was assaulted by smugglers outside one of these pubs. A man who failed to come to his aid was subsequently charged.

PORTPATRICK   NW 99 54

A village and coastal parish of Wigtownshire, for centuries the Scottish port for the ferry to Donaghadee in Ireland. The harbour was formerly a mere inlet, but it was considerably improved in 1774 by the construction of a pier, designed by Smeaton and regarded as the finest in Britain at that time. The present harbour was not constructed until 1821. A weekly mail between Ireland and Scotland was commenced in 1662 and a daily mail-coach from Dumfries was inaugurated in 1790. There was a large custom-house, erected to cope with the great increase in trade with Ireland from 1774 onwards. It was also to Ireland what Gretna Green was to England, a place for runaway marriages. Between 1776 and 1826 some 198 gentlemen, 15 officers and 13 noblemen from Ireland were married here.

In his only extant letter to Charles Sharpe (C.L. p.580), written on 22nd April 1791, Burns creates a highly fanciful origin for his pseudonym, Johnie Faa: 'No, no, Sir: I cannot indeed be properly said to belong to any House, or even any Province or Kingdom, as my mother, who for many years was spouse to a marching regiment, gave me into this bad world, aboard the packet-boat, somewhere between Donaghadee & Portpatrick.' John Gillespie, formerly Burns's Excise colleague in upper Nithsdale, was later transferred to Portpatrick and it was thither that Burns sent the letter written about 1791, enclosing a copy of 'Craigieburn Wood' (C.W. p.436). The exact date of composition is unknown but it has been assigned to 1791, as that was the year of Gillespie's transfer. The letter (C.L. p.572) ends, 'Pray why did you go away, my good Sir, & never take leave of your friends at Ellisland?— I assure you Mrs Burns is very much in dudgeon, & says that she won't send you her Compliments untill you make an apology for your abrupt departure.'

A statue of Burns and the daisy, sculpted by James Watt of Stranraer, was erected at the rear of the bowling green and unveiled by Lady Inskip in May 1929. In 1983 it was swept away by a landslide in a storm, but was subsequently repaired and restored by the Burns Howff Club of Dumfries.

REDCASTLE   NX 818 656
An estate in Urr parish in the Stewartry, about a mile southeast of Haugh of Urr. It is approached by a minor road running east from the A710, a mile south of the village. It was the residence of Walter Sloan Lawrie who had served in the British Army during the American War of Independence. Lawrie had the misfortune to be engaged in the battle of Bunker's Hill in the opening campaign of the war. His regiment had shown the most unsteadiness of all in that melee which did no credit to British arms. Ever afterwards poor Lawrie was often pursued by a motley rabble jeering him with cries of 'Bunker's Hill! Bunker's Hill!' In the Third Heron Election Ballad (C.W. p.548) Burns alludes to this inglorious affair:
> And then Redcastle drew his sword
> That ne'er was stain'd wi gore,
> Save on a wand'rer lame and blind,
> To drive him frae his door.

Lawrie was also mean and grasping, unattractive attributes on which Burns touched in the Second Ballad (C.W. p.545):
> But we dinna mention Redcastle,
> The body — e'en let him escape!
> He'd venture the gallows for siller,
> An 'twere na the cost o the rape!

In the Fourth Heron Election Ballad (C.W. p.549) the trogger enumerates:
> Here is Satan's picture, like a bizzard gled
> Pouncing poor Redcastle, sprawlin like a taed.

After the American War, Captain Lawrie retired from active service and settled on his estates which had an assessed value of £2000 per annum and were scattered over six parishes. Though he took his title from Redcastle, he preferred to live at **Woodhall** where he had a fine mansion. He is said to have kept a good table and been a man of very superior character to that given him in Burns's election ballads.

ROCKHALL   NY 056 754
A former mansion, now a hotel, in Mouswald parish, six miles east of Dumfries. At one time it was a residence of the Griersons of Lag. It features in Burns lore purely on the statement of Chambers (1851) that the two undated letters by Burns addressed to a Miss Gordon (C.L. p.723) were actually written on behalf of a farmer who was a tenant there (possibly Rockhall Mains). Chambers examined the letters in 1850, but appears to have overlooked the endorsement, dated

22nd March 1836, stating that Burns had written the letters for a farmer named Johnston who lived at Catlins 'near Dumfries'. The only farm of that name, however, is about three miles northeast of Lockerbie. Authority for the Catlins attribution was John Gibson of Whitehaven who was the owner of the letters in 1850. The letters are undated and could have been composed at any time during the poet's Dumfries period.

ROSEBANK   NX 989 739
A small estate on the southeastern outskirts of Dumfries, situated off the Bankend road east of the Crichton Royal Hospital. It was the residence of Mrs Mundell, the mother of Dr James Mundell, a friend of Burns who was lampooned with him by the Loyal Natives. Mrs Mundell's only daughter married Provost Gabriel Richardson and was the mother of Sir John Richardson, the Arctic explorer. A son Robert (1763-1837) was a noted tobacconist and snuff-dealer in Dumfries. The Mundell family had connections with **Closeburn;** Alexander and Robert Mundell who taught at Wallace Hall Academy at the end of the 18th century were cousins. James Mundell trained as a surgeon and served in the Royal Navy but retired after the American War and settled in Nithsdale. He was appointed a surgeon at the Dumfries and Galloway Infirmary on 1st May 1788. It is possible that Mundell was for some time in general practice in the Closeburn area and was thus the doctor whom Burns would have consulted while he was in temporary accommodation at **Isle.** A short note, believed to have been sent to Mundell, was written from there (C.L. p.485) A second letter, of January 1790, was sent by hand of Janet Nievison, a neighbour of Burns at **Ellisland** whom the poet had sent for treatment. 'You will remember that she is just in the jaws of MATRIMONY, so for heaven's sake, get her hale & sound as soon as possible...' Tantalisingly, this letter is merely addressed to Dr Mundell at Dumfries, so his exact address is not known. It is possible, however, that he was living at Rosebank with his widowed mother. Dr Mundell attended the poet and his family in Dumfries until 1794 when he was superseded by Dr William Maxwell. Burns listed Mundell as one of the subscribers to Anderson's *Bee*, and with Burns he was an early member of the Dumfries Volunteers.

Dr Mundell was part-owner of a cotton mill, to which Burns made passing mention in a letter to Maria Riddell about December 1793 (C.L. p.606): 'There is a species of the Human genus that I call, the Gin-horse Class: what enviable dogs they are! Round, & round they go — Mundell's ox that drives his cotton-mill, their exact prototype...' It is not known where this cotton gin was, but the only one listed in the Dumfries area was the Rerrick cotton-mill at Collin, which was still in operation as late as 1804. Sir John Richardson, claimed that he had learned to ride on the back of Mundell's ox.

RUTHWELL   NY 09 675
A village and coastal parish of southeast Nithsdale. The village lies along a minor road south east of the junction of the B725 and B724 and is about a mile east of **Brow.** It was erected into a burgh of barony in 1509, with the right of holding fairs and markets, but these privileges had lapsed by the 18th century and it was a place of neither trade nor manufacture. Its chief claim to fame lies in the magnificent runic cross inscribed with verses of Caedmon's 'Holy Rood', the oldest fragment of English literature. The cross dates from about 680 and stood by the parish church until 1642 when it was cast down and broken into several pieces. This priceless relic was repaired and restored in 1802 by the Rev. Dr Henry Duncan (1774-1846), who was minister of Ruthwell from 1799 till the Disruption of 1843. The cross formerly stood in the kirkyard but was transferred to the interior of the church in 1887.

Henry Duncan, third son of the Rev. George Duncan of **Lochrutton,** founded the world's first savings bank in the parish in 1810. Many relics associated with him are to be seen in the museum of banking in Ruthwell village. A noted antiquarian, Dr Duncan was also the first person to discover reptilian fossil footprints in the red sandstone from Corncockle Moor. After the Disruption he became minister of the Free Church at Mount Kedar where an obelisk was erected as a memorial to him. His stone statue, on the facade of the Savings Bank in Dumfries, was the first statue erected in a public place in that town. Dr Duncan instituted an Auxiliary Bible Society and a Missionary Society in Dumfries about 1810. In 1809 he founded the *Dumfries Courier* and was also the founder of the *Dumfries Standard* in 1843. A poet and political economist, a novelist and naturalist, an antiquarian and a philosopher, he subordinated all of his many talents to his mission as a minister of the gospel.

As a youth, Henry Duncan had met Burns at his father's manse. His first wife Agnes was the daughter of the Rev. John Craig, his predecessor at Ruthwell. While he was attempting to recover his health at **Brow**, Burns was invited one evening to tea by Mrs Craig, the minister himself being confined to bed owing to ill health. Mrs Craig and her daughter entertained the poet who made an effort to converse in his customary animated manner. Miss Craig, who had a fine literary taste, was a warm admirer of Burns. She was much struck with the debilitated frame and melancholy air of the poet who was all too obviously hastening to the grave, and ever afterwards the look and tone with which he described himself to her mother as 'a poor plucked pigeon'. In the course of the evening the declining summer sun happened to shine in strongly through the window, and Agnes, to save him from supposed annoyance, hastily rose to pull down the blind; but the dying poet prevented her, saying, 'Let the sun shine in upon us, my dear young lady; he has not now long to shine on me.' The manse in which this dramatic incident took place no longer exists. A new manse and vestry were built in 1890 and the former is now the Kirklands Hotel.

Henry Duncan played a leading role in the **Mausoleum** campaign, being joint-secretary and treasurer with William Grierson and convener of the special committee.

RYEDALE COTTAGE   NX 976 755

This house in Troqueer parish is no longer extant, but stood where the car park of the Ryedale Factory of Wolsey Limited, the knitwear company, now stands, overlooking the west bank of the **Nith**. It was the home of John Lewars Senior (1720-89), Supervisor of Excise in Dumfries. He was the father of John Lewars Junior (1769-1826) and Jessie Lewars (1778-1855), both of whom lived in this cottage before moving into the town. It appears that they originally lived in the High Street, after their father's death. On 2nd April 1792, however, their landlord, Samuel Blount, took court action to evict John and Jessie Lewars from their 'high Lodging, cellar and garret lying in the high street of Dumfries'. John Syme, as agent for Dr James Currie then offered the lease of **Stakeford House,** but instead they occupied the house in the Millbrae Vennel opposite **Burns House.** John Lewars Junior was a colleague of Burns in the Dumfries Port Division and was present at the capture of the brig *Rosamond* at **Sarkfoot**. He was the subject of 'The Hue and Cry of John Lewars' (C.W. p.468). In 1799 John married Barbara Howe of Gretna and rented Lauder farm in Caerlaverock parish for a time. Ryedale Cottage, however, seems to have remained in the family's hands, for it was there that John died in October 1826.

Jessie Lewars (1778-1855) married John Thomson, a Dumfries lawyer, in 1799 and had five sons and two daughters. She was the subject of 'Here's a Health to Ane I Loe Dear' (C.W. p.565), the series of four Versicles (C.W. p.566) and the Inscription beginning 'Thine be the volumes, Jessie fair' (C.W. p.567).

RYEDALE HOUSE   NX 976 755

An estate with a mansion in Troqueer parish, Kirkcudbrightshire near the right bank of the **Nith** in the southern vicinity of **Maxwelltown**. In Burns's day this area was open country, but since the beginning of this century it has been developed and is now surrounded by the western suburbs of Dumfries. Nevertheless, the mansion itself still stands, and is occupied by the administrative offices of the Wolsey knitwear company. It was the home of John Syme (1755-1831), son of the laird of **Barncailzie.** In 1791 he obtained the sinecure of Distributor of Stamps in Dumfries and had his office on the ground floor of the house in the Wee Vennel or **Bank Street** where Burns resided in 1791-3. Burns was a frequent visitor at Ryedale and a close friendship developed between the two men. Syme accompanied the poet on his tours of Galloway in the summers of 1793 and 1794 and made a collection of his more acerbic epigrams. Syme visited Burns at **Brow** on 15th July 1796 and at his home in Dumfries a few days later, and was appalled at the rapid deterioration in the poet's condition. After Burns's death, Syme, with Dr William Maxwell, organised the poet's funeral. Later he laboured unceasingly with Alexander Cunningham and William Grierson on behalf of the poet's widow and family. His correspondence with Cunningham on these matters was serialised in the *Burns Chronicle* (1934-42).

Syme was the recipient of a brief verse epistle accompanying a dozen bottles of porter, and a rhyming apology for declining an invitation to dine (C.W. p.560):

> Who is proof to thy personal converse and wit,
> Is proof to all other temptation.

He was copiously mentioned in the verse epistle of 1793 addressed to Captain Gordon of **Kenmure** (C.W. p.507). In the Second Heron Election Ballad (C.W. p.546) his appointment as Distributor of Stamps was alluded to:

> An there'll be Stamp-Office Johnie:
> Tak tent how ye purchase a dram!

The lines derived from the second book of Kings (C.W. p.362) were inscribed by Burns on a goblet which, according to Allan Cunningham, belonged to Syme. The 'Lines Inscribed in a Lady's Pocket Almanac' (C.W. p.492) were actually written by Burns in Syme's copy of the *Della Cruscan British Album*.

Syme has left an interesting description of his friend: 'The poet's expression varied perpetually, according to the idea that predominated in his mind: and it was beautiful to mark how well the play of his lips indicated the sentiment he was about to utter. His eyes and lips, the first remarkable for fire, and the second for flexibility, formed at all times an index to his mind, and as sunshine or shade predominated, you might have told, *a priori*, whether the company was to be favoured with a scintillation of wit, or a sentiment of benevolence, or a burst of fiery indignation... I cordially concur with what Sir Walter Scott says of the poet's eyes. In his animated moments, and particularly when his anger was aroused by instances of tergiversation, meanness, or tyranny, they were actually like coals of living fire.'

ST MARY'S ISLE   NX 675 495

The seat of the Earl of Selkirk, in Kirkcudbright parish, just over a mile from the town, from which it is approached by a long lime-tree avenue. Now a ruin, it stands on a finely-wooded peninsula projecting into the head of Kirkcudbright Bay. In former times it was, indeed, an island at high tide, but land reclamation and cultivation have resulted in it being joined to the mainland. The house occupies the site of a priory, founded about 1129, but the remains of the ecclesiastical buildings were swept away in the late 17th century to create a noble demesne for the first Earl of Selkirk (created 1646). The fourth Earl (1722-99) supported the Government during the Rebellion of 1745-6 and was Lord Lieutenant of the Stewartry. St Mary's Isle was attacked on 22nd April 1778 by John Paul Jones, who planned to take the Earl hostage. His lordship being away at the time, the Americans contented themselves with seizing the Earl's plate. The booty was carried off to France but returned at the instigation of Benjamin Franklin who gave Jones a severe reprimand for an act of piracy. It was not until 1785 that the silverware could be returned, owing to the war, but it was found on arrival that it was in exactly the same condition as it had been when carried off, the tea-leaves still adhering to the bottom of the teapot.

On 1st August 1793 Burns and Syme went from **Gatehouse** to **Kirkcudbright.** That evening, accompanied by John Dalzell of **Barncrosh,** they dined at St Mary's Isle and spent a 'most happy evening' there although Burns had his misgivings. The poet was in his customary temper at the prospect of making for 'the seat of a Lord, yet that Lord was not an aristocrat, at least in his sense of the word.' As the evening progressed, however, Burns gradually softened his attitude. He was asked to recite his poem 'Lord Gregory' (C.W. p.482). Syme later told Dr Currie that 'such was the effect, that a dead silence ensued. It was such a silence as a mind of feeling naturally preserves... The fastidious critic may perhaps say some of these sentiments are of too elevated a kind for such a style of composition... But this is a cold-blooded objection, which will be *said* rather than *felt.*'

During this visit Burns met the Milanese composer Pietro Urbani (1749-1816) who was a house-guest there. Afterwards they travelled back to Dumfries together and Urbani stayed with the Burns family for several days. This was related by Burns to Alexander Cunningham in a letter of November 1793 (C.L. pp.468-9).

The Earl and his country-seat were mentioned in the First Heron Election Ballad, in what Kinsley has described as 'a grudging tribute' (C.W. p.544):

> Tho wit and worth, in either sex,
> Saint Mary's Isle can shaw that,
> Wi Lords and Dukes let Selkirk mix,
> And weel does Selkirk fa' that.

SANQUHAR   NS 78 09

A town and parish of upper Nithsdale, a royal and parliamentary burgh, situated near the north bank of the **Nith,** opposite its confluence with Euchan Water. The A76 runs through the centre of the town, along the High Street. Sanquhar is 26 miles northwest of Dumfries and 32 miles southeast of Ayr. Near the town stand the ruins of Sanquhar Castle, the ancient stronghold of the Crichton family. Sir Robert de Crichton was created Lord Crichton in 1485. His descendant, William first Earl of Dumfries disposed of the lands in 1639 to William Douglas, Viscount Drumlanrig. Even after William, first Duke of Queensberry, built **Drumlanrig** he spent only one night in his new castle and preferred to stay at Sanquhar. The old pile was abandoned by the second Duke. Under the third Duke Sanquhar grew in importance. The post office, instituted in 1763 and still occupying the original building, is now the oldest in the world in continuous use. Woollen manufactures were encouraged, but collapsed on the outbreak of the American War of Independence, as the principal outlet had been in Virginia. Brick and tile manufacture, coal-mining and the manufacture of mining equipment were developed by the late 18th century. The high road through Sanquhar was constructed in 1777 and was frequently traversed by Burns in the summer of 1788 when he was commuting between his new farm at **Ellisland** and Mauchline, and later when he was engaged on Excise riding work in upper Nithsdale. While acting as Supervisor in 1795, for example, Burns left **Thornhill** at 5 a.m. on 23rd February, rode four miles to Enterkinfoot, where he made a call; thence three miles to Slunkford, where he made another call; thence six miles to Sanquhar where he paid twenty official visits; thence two miles to Whitehall where he made two calls; and the return journey to Sanquhar completed his day's work at 7 p.m. Tom Wilson, author of a booklet (1904) adds: 'Is it wonderful that he confined his poetic efforts to jotting down a stanza or two he had composed by the way, and left the task of essaying some great work to the time he hoped to see when he would have the greater responsibility and the more abundant leisure of a collectorship? He would attend, as a matter of course, the three great fairs of Sanquhar — the Feeing Fair at Candlemas, the Wool Fair in July, and the onion Fair at Martinmas.'

When he visited Sanquhar Burns usually put up at the Queensberry Arms, or New Arms as it was then called, no longer extant (a shop now occupying the site at 88 High

Street). Mine hosts in the late 18th century were Mr and Mrs Edward Whigham who were the recipients of two letters (C.L. p.512). Whigham (1750-1823) was Provost of Sanquhar from 30th September 1793 till 29th September 1800 and it seems likely that it was due to him that Burns was made an honorary burgess and freeman on 23rd December 1794. Mrs Whigham was Jane Osborne (1758-1846) and their coaching inn was one of the oldest licensed hostelries in Scotland. Burns met the Whighams on his first jaunt into Nithsdale in 1788 and thereafter was a frequent guest at their inn and described them as 'my particular acquaintances'. It was with the Whighams that Burns was taking a drink on that particular night in January 1789 when the arrival of Mrs Oswald's funeral party ejected him and forced him to ride a further twelve miles to the next inn. As he rode on that bitterly cold and stormy night he composed the ode which, according to Carlyle, 'might have been chanted by the Furies of Aeschylus'. Later he sent copies of the 'Ode Sacred to the Memory of Mrs Oswald of Auchencruive' (C.W. p.342) to Dr John Moore and Mrs Dunlop. The latter mildly reproved Burns: 'Are you not a sad, wicked creature to send a poor old wife straight to the Devil because she gave you a ride on a cold night?'

Edward Whigham apparently shared Burns's interest in the recovery of traditional ballads. Burns presented him with a copy of his Poems which is still preserved in Sanquhar. On the window of the breakfast room of the inn he scratched the lines beginning 'Envy, if thy jaundiced eye' (C.W. p.350). The pane was subsequently removed and is now believed to be in New Zealand.

John Duff of Sanquhar possessed a drinking glass which had allegedly been used in a *second* contest for the Whistle. Burns apparently borrowed the famous ebony whistle after Fergusson of **Craigdarroch** won it in the contest at Friars' Carse, so that he could show it to his friends in Mauchline. Passing through Sanquhar, however, he organised a drinking tournament at the New Inn, barely a few days after the famous contest. On this occasion the contestants were Edward Whigham, John King (a music teacher), Provost William Johnston of **Clackleith**, and Burns himself. The contest was judged by Edward Whigham's son John. Instead of the bottles of claret used originally, the Sanquhar contestants drank whisky toddy, and the punch-bowl used for the event was later cherished by Mrs William Kerr of Sanquhar. It is not recorded who won on this occasion. John King, a native of Beith, set some of Burns's songs to music.

Sanquhar joined with the other Dumfries burghs to return one Member to Parliament, and thus features in 'The Five Carlins' (C.W. pp.364-6) as

    ... Black Joan, frae Crichton Peel,
    O gipsy kith an kin:

A granite monument, erected in 1860, marks the site of the old town cross, to which were affixed the two famous Sanquhar Declarations — by Richard Cameron on 22nd June 1680, and by the Rev. James Renwick on 28th May 1685. The glens and moors in the neighbourhood were the frequent refuge of the persecuted Covenanters. The old parish church, replaced by the present structure in 1824, had a gallery or laird's loft which was approached by an outside stair, known as the Duke's Stair because it had been used by the Dukes of Queensberry when they lived in Sanquhar. There is a hazy tradition in the town that Burns worshipped here and on one occasion was mounting this stair when he overtook an old lady clad in red and made some facetious remark, but the quip itself has long been forgotten. The neighbouring kirkyard contains the graves of several persons associated with Burns. In addition to Edward Whigham, they include William Johnston of Clackleith and John Rigg of **Crawick**. Thomas Barker (1760-1825) of Bridge-end of Crawick was the lessee of the coal mines and is said to have been a crony of Burns, although his daughter Susan inspired another poet, James Hyslop, to compose 'The Cameronian's Dream'. Dr Purdie, who was present with Burns in **Brownhill Inn** when Burns composed

'The Soldier's Return', is buried in the northwest corner of the kirkyard in an unmarked grave. He was in general practice in Sanquhar for upwards of half a century. James Pearson of Littlemark, who died at **Craigdarroch** in April 1865 aged 91, is also said to have been an associate of Burns.

TOWN HALL, SANQUHAR

SARKFOOT   NY 325 664

The mouth of the River Sark where it enters the Solway Firth, half a mile south of Gretna, forming the boundary between Scotland and England. It was mentioned in Burns's bitter anti-Union poem 'Such a Parcel of Rogues in a Nation' (C.W. p.460): 'Now Sark rins over Solway sands'. The course of the river has altered considerably over the centuries, and even within the past thirty years it has altered from time to time. In 1813, however, it was described as a small village with a good harbour admitting vessels of 120 tons burden. This was a favourite haunt of smugglers in the 18th century, mainly operating out of the Isle of Man. Under the terms of the Revestment Act of 1765 the Duke of Atholl (then Lord of Man) sold his rights to the Crown. This abolished the exemption of the island from British Customs and had the desired effect of curbing the smuggling trade with the Solway coast, but did not entirely eliminate it. The Revenue officers (belonging to the Customs and Excise, at that time quite separate services), assisted by detachments of soldiers, patrolled the coast on a constant lookout for smugglers and their vessels. Smugglers would land their illicit cargoes of brandy and tobacco at Sarkfoot. A nearby house called Alisonbank has a series of deep cellars to this day, believed to have been used by the smugglers. From Alisonbank the contraband was taken by pack-mule up a lane, known to this day as Whisky Loaning, up to Gretna and Springfield for onward distribution.

Sarkfoot was at the eastern extremity of the Dumfries Port Division, and thus came within the area covered by Burns, following his promotion in February 1792. Within a month, he was involved with John Lewars and Walter Crawford in the seizure of the brig

Rosamond on 29th February. Various accounts of this incident appeared in the Glasgow and Edinburgh newspapers the following week, but the fullest version was that printed in the Edinburgh *Evening Courant* of 8th March. A highly-coloured and not very accurate account of the seizure was given by Lockhart (1828) which gave Burns undue prominence in the affair, at the expense of his colleagues, and also included a wholly imaginary narrative of the composing of 'The Deil's Awa wi th'Exciseman' (C.W. p.467). To Lockhart also we owe the story that Burns subsequently purchased four carronades from the ship and sent them to the French Convention with a letter requesting that body to accept them as a mark of his admiration and respect. 'The present, and its accompaniment' were intercepted at the custom-house at Dover.

Allan Cunningham (1834) cast doubt on the tale of the carronades, and subsequent biographers were sceptical of the whole incident. Lockhart, son-in-law of Sir Walter Scott, had used manuscripts which had been given to Sir Walter by Joseph Train, Supervisor of Excise at **Castle Douglas.** These documents consisted of (a) the journal of Walter Crawford, riding-officer of Excise, (b) an account of the seizure in the handwriting of Burns himself, and (c) a statement written by John Lewars, detailing the circumstances of Burns having purchased the carronades. Train acquired these documents from Lewars's widow. Sir Walter, unable to find any reference to the carronades in the *Moniteur*, the French official newspaper of the time, applied to the Custom House authorities in London. They, after considerable search, found that the guns had been seized at the port of Dover, as stated by Lewars in his memorandum.

For many years these documents were apparently mislaid at Abbotsford, and this merely added to the scepticism. As recently as 1932, for example, Franklyn Bliss Snyder dismissed the entire *Rosamond* affair as a complete myth. In 1933, however, a mass of miscellaneous papers at Abbotsford was sorted and catalogued by the National Library of Scotland, and two of the documents came to light. Unfortunately the Lewars memorandum has not been found, although a fourth document, in Lewars's handwriting, was discovered and consists of an inventory of the ship and her equipment. The record of the seizure at Dover has apparently been destroyed at some time since 1828. From Crawford's Journal it appears that a landing of smugglers had been expected some time that week. On 27th February news reached Crawford that a landing was in progress. He set out from Dumfries late that night with John Lewars, leaving Burns, Penn and Rankine to follow as quickly as possible. Crawford and Lewars reached Annan at 5 a.m. and immediately set out with a party of Dragoons. They searched Mr McDowall's 'a notorious smuggler' and other premises associated with smuggling, and about noon rode down to the shore.

The ship was waiting the tide to make sail. Crawford and his soldiers tried to board her, but were stopped by the crew which threatened to fire on them. As the Excisemen and soldiers were only armed with pistols, Crawford alone went on board. He found 24 men on board, with fifteen round of shot each. Crawford went ashore and consulted his men. Clearly a larger force was required. Lewars was despatched to Dumfries to bring up another 24 Dragoons, while Crawford went to **Ecclefechan** for reinforcements, with which he patrolled the shore till Lewars returned with the Dumfries force.

About 9 a.m. on 29th February Crawford mustered his forces. He had 23 Dragoons from Dumfries, 13 from Annan and 8 from Ecclefechan — 44 men mounted and fully armed. Meanwhile the *Rosamond* had slipped down the Firth about a mile from where she had been the previous day. The depth of the water and swiftness of the current made it impossible for the troops to get out to the ship on foot or horseback, so Crawford and his men searched the shore for suitable boats. 'But the Country People guessing our design got the start of us and staved every Boat on the Coast before we Could reach them, the vessel in the mean time keeping up a fire of grape shott and musquetry, we resolved as last resource to attempt the passage on foott as the quick sands made the ridding on horseback dangerous or rather impossible.' The troops were divided into three groups — fore, aft and broadside — 'The first party being Commanded by Quarter Master Manly, the Second by myself and the third led by Mr Burns.

'Our orders to the Millitary were to reserve there fire till within eight yards of the vessel, then to pour a volley and board her with sword & Pistol. The vessel keept on firing thou without any damage to us, as from the situation of the fire they could not bring their great guns to bear on us, we in the mean time wading breast high, and in Justice to the party under my Command I must say with great alacrity; by the time we were within one hundred yards of the vessel the Crew gave up the cause, gott over side towards England which shore was for a long long way dry sand. As I still supposed that there were only Country people they were putting ashore and that the Crew were keeping under Cover to make a more vigourous immediate resistance, we marched up as first concerted, but found the vessel compleatly evacuated both of the Crew and every movable on board except as per inventory, the Smugglers as their last instance of vengeance having poured a six-pounder Carronade through her Broadside. She proved to be the Roseomond (sic) of Plymouth, Alexander Patty Master, and about one hundred tons burthen, schooner rigged.'

The second document consisted of two pages on the backs of blank Excise receipt forms, in Burns's handwriting, with the exception of corrections and the prices which were written in by Crawford. This consisted of a list of the expenses incurred in watching the captured vessel and subsequently repairing it at **Kelton**. The expenses included £1 2s for advertising the sale of the ship in the Edinburgh, Dumfries and Whitehaven newspapers. The third surviving document was the ship's inventory, written by John Lewars in the form of a draft advertisement.

Among the 53 items listed were 'Four four Pounders Carronade Guns mounted on carriages with takle and furniture compleat Round Carr double headed & Grape Shot &c. &c. &c.' The guns weighed 33 cwt and were sold at half a crown per hundredweight, making a total of £4 2s 6d. Chambers (1851) stated that Joseph Train had a copy of the sale catalogue annotated in Burns's handwriting, showing that he had purchased the four guns for £3. The discrepancy between the two sums may be explained by the fact that Burns was entitled to a fourth part of the net proceeds of the sale.

Lewars's journal, which allegedly detailed the poet's purchase of the carronades and their despatch to France, has not yet come to light, but the existence of the other documents in the Abbotsford Collection affords strong presumptive proof that it was also handed by Train to Sir Walter.

SCAUR WATER   NS 73 03

A trout stream of Nithsdale, rising within a mile of the meeting of the three counties of Ayr, Kirkcudbright and Dumfries at an altitude of 1600 feet, and flowing 18.375 miles southeastward through the parishes of Penpont, Tynron and Keir. It enters the **Nith** about two miles south of **Thornhill**. In its lower reaches this stream flowed through the lands of Sir Robert Laurie, hence the reference to him in 'The Whistle' (C.W. p.369) as 'the lord of the Cairn and the Scaur'.

SOUTHERNESS   NX 97 54

A hamlet in Kirkbean parish on the Solway Firth, ten miles southeast of Dalbeattie and sixteen miles south of Dumfries. It was built some time after the middle of the 18th century by Oswald of Auchencruive in the expectation of its becoming a mining village and coal depot, but early prospects for that mineral were never fulfilled. Instead it became a sea-bathing retreat. To the south of the village stands the lighthouse, built in 1748 and now the second oldest extant in Scotland. After Oswald's death in 1784 his widow, Mrs Mary Oswald, had the tower heightened. She was the lady whose memory was the subject of Burns's bitter ode (C.W. p.342).

SOUTHWICK HOUSE   NX 930 574

A mansion in Colvend parish in the southeast of the Stewartry, just north of Caulkerbush and eight miles southeast of Dalbeattie on the A710. The proprietor in the late 18th century was Lieutenant-General Dunlop (c.1760-1832), MP for the Stewartry (1813-26) and fifth son of Mrs Dunlop of Dunlop. He was Chairman of the **Mausoleum** Committee when it was established in January 1814.

TERRAUGHTY   NX 935 752

Sometimes spelled Terraughtie, a mansion in Troqueer parish, Nithsdale, 2.5 miles west of Dumfries and lying just south of the A75. In Burns's day it was probably no more than a farmhouse, for the present mansion was not built until 1825. It was a seat of the Maxwells of Breckonside, descended from the second son of the Lord Herries who was the doughty champion of Mary Queen of Scots. His great-grandson John Herries Maxwell (1720-1814), being a younger son, had no patrimony and was therefore apprenticed to a joiner in Dumfries. In that trade, however, he succeeded to such an extent that he was able to purchase the ancestral estate of Terraughty in 1754 from John McGeorge of Cocklick into whose hands it had fallen. Subsequently he added, by purchase, the estate of Portrack in Holywood. By his first wife, Agnes Hannay, he had three sons and six daughters, the third of whom, Jean (born 1750) married William Hyslop of **Lochend,** landlord of the **Globe Inn.** After the death of his first wife John Maxwell married Agnes Maxwell of Munches who succeeded to that estate on the death of her brother in 1793. On the death of William Maxwell of Nithsdale, only son of the last Earl, John Maxwell became heir male to the fourth Earl in 1778.

This explains the reference to him as 'Maxwell's vet'ran chief' in the verse epistle by Burns in honour of his 71st birthday (C.W. p.417) on 7th February 1791. Though Burns foretold that Maxwell would live for another 49 years — 'a tack o seven times seven' — he did not quite achieve that patriarchal span, but died on 25th January 1814, only six years short of his century. In the Second Heron Election Ballad (C.W. p.546) he was referred to as 'Teuch Johnie'. 'The Toadeater' (C.W. p.569) is said to have been delivered by Burns at a dinner-party at Terraughty. John Maxwell of Terraughty was the recipient of the scurrilous verses lampooning Burns by Muirhead, which he burned in disgust. James Bogie, present at the re-interment of Burns and the burial of Jean Armour, was originally a gardener at Terraughty.

TERREGLES HOUSE   NX 932 778

The seat of the Herries family, it was demolished some years ago and no trace is now extant. It stood to the north of the village of Terregles about two miles northwest of Dumfries. Sir John Herries got a grant of 'Travereglis' from King David II in 1359. In 1547 Agnes, Lady Herries, married John Maxwell who became Lord Herries in 1566. He helped Mary Queen of Scots to escape after the Battle of Langside and gave her refuge at Terregles before she crossed into England. In Burns's reworking of the old ballad 'The Rowin 't in her Apron' (C.W. pp.578-9) 'Young Terreagles' was John Maxwell, seventh Lord Herries, who succeeded his cousin as eleventh Lord Maxwell and third Earl of Nithsdale. In 1716, however, all three titles were attainted in the person of the Jacobite fifth Earl who escaped from the Tower of London disguised as a woman. By a deed of

1712, however, the estates were disponed on his son William whose daughter and heiress, Winifred, married William Haggerston Constable of Yorkshire in 1758. Lady Winifred Maxwell Constable (1736-1801) returned to Scotland about 1789 and began rebuilding the ancestral home, an event commemorated by Burns in 'Nithsdale's Welcome Hame' (C.W. p.377).

Burns, a Jacobite in sentiment if not in politics, often visited Lady Maxwell Constable at Terregles. In a letter of 16th December 1789 (C.L. p.546) he referred to his sympathies: '... with your Ladyship I have the honor to be connected by one of the strongest and most endearing ties in the whole Moral World - Common Sufferers in a Cause where even to be unfortunate is glorious, the Cause of Heroic Loyalty.' He then recounted his cherished belief that his ancestors had been 'out' in the 1715 Rebellion - a belief which is not substantiated by the facts. With this letter Burns sent her a copy of his verses to William Tytler of Woodhouselee (C.W. p.276). In the spring of 1791 Lady Winifred sent Burns a snuff-box with a miniature portrait of Mary Queen of Scots set in the lid. Burns was then laid up with a broken arm, but in his reply enclosed his 'Lament of Mary Queen of Scots' (C.W. p.400). The snuff-box eventually passed into the hands of William Nicol Burns who took it to India and damaged the portrait irreparably while leaping aboard a ship.

Frederick Maxwell of Terregles was one of the subscribers recruited by Burns for Dr Anderson's *Bee* in November 1790. He was also mentioned in a letter to Alexander Dalziel (C.L. p.505) as having married a sister of Glendinning (Glendonwyn) of **Parton.**

THORNHILL   NX 87 95
A village in Morton parish, Nithsdale, within half a mile of the left bank of the **Nith**, and at the junction of the A702 with the A76, fourteen miles north of Dumfries. The original hamlet was at Townhead, to the west of the present village. It was erected a burgh of barony in 1662 under the name of New Dalgarno, referred to in 'The Braw Wooer' (C.W. p.556):

> But a' the niest week, as I petted wi care,
> I gaed to the tryste o Dalgarnock.

The present town was laid out at right angles to the cross in 1714 by the Duke of Queensberry, the houses 'so small that they might have been built to stamp a character of insolent pride on his own huge mansion of **Drumlanrig**, which is full in view on the opposite side of the Nith' as Dorothy Wordsworth described it in 1803. After the introduction of the Carlisle-Glasgow mailcoach in July 1788 Thornhill grew in importance as a staging point. The Queensberry Arms Inn was built in 1714 at 99-102 Drumlanrig Street and somewhat later the George Inn was established farther up the street. Burns was a frequent visitor to both hostelries in his official capacity. John Kellock, a bailie of Thornhill, was the landlord of the George Inn. A letter written from 'Bailie Kellock's' (C.L. p.585) was sent to the Rev. Thomas Smith at Auchinleck on 4th July 1791. Mrs Kellock featured in Burns's answers to the petition of Thomas Johnston in September 1790 (C.L. pp.564-5). Mrs Kellock had apparently given evidence on Johnston's behalf. 'As to Mrs Kellock's oath,' wrote Burns, 'It proves nothing.— She did indeed depone to a line being left for me at her house, which said line miscarried.— It was a sealed letter; she could not tell whether it was a Malt Notice or not.'

The United Presbyterian church in Thornhill was erected in 1816, on the site of the seceders' meeting-place, which was also mentioned by Burns. Thomas Johnston and his family were of this sect and during their weekly jaunts to Thornhill to attend worship they were accustomed to transmit the notices and other documents concerned with maltsters and other traders in the parish, to the post office in the village.

GEORGE HOTEL, THORNHILL

Professor Gillespie of St Andrew's recalled how, as a boy of twelve, he had seen Burns at a Thornhill fair in August 1790. In Old Street lived a poor woman, Kate Watson, who on these gala days kept a shebeen. 'I saw the poet enter her door, and anticipated nothing short of an immediate seizure of a certain greybeard and barrel, which to my certain knowledge contained the contraband commodities our bard was in search of. A nod, accompanied by a significant movement of the forefinger, brought Kate to the doorway, and I was near enough to hear the following words distinctly uttered: "Kate, are ye mad? Dinna you know that the supervisor and I will be in upon you in the course of forty minutes? Good-bye t'ye at present". I had access to know that the friendly hint was not neglected. It saved a poor widow from a fine of several pounds for committing a quarterly offence by which the revenue was probably subject to an annual loss of five shillings.'

A woman named Jean Davidson, who kept a small public-house, was suspected of watering her whisky. Burns accordingly called one day unexpectedly and detected the irregularity at once. 'Now, Jean, my woman,' he said, putting his hand on the keg, 'I canna tak this wi me the night as it is ower late to go to Dumfries, but I'll seal it wi the King's seal and lift it in the mornin.' After he had gone to his lodging for the night, Jean sent for a local cooper. Acting on her instructions, he removed three hoops from the barrel, and underneath bored a hole. Through this hole Jean drew off about half of the diluted contents, and poured into it an equal quantity of full-strength whisky. The hole was plugged, the hoops were replaced, and the condemned whisky was made into legal consistency without the King's seal being in any way tampered with. Next morning Burns called to collect the keg. 'One meenit, Mr Burns!' cried Jean, 'Ye micht juist test that whisky to convince me, for I canna see hou I've made sic a mistake.' 'Certainly, Jean.' replied the unsuspecting gauger, 'It means breakin the King's seal, but I can juist mak anither.' The seal was broken, the sample drawn, tested, and lo — it was all right. Burns could not account for it. 'Was there aught wrang wi me last nicht, did ye notice, Jean?' he asked. 'Weel, Mr Burns, it's really no for me to say, but — weel, I juist thocht ye were fully smert wi yer tester.'

Burns had his boots made at Thornhill by Andrew Johnstone, whose shop was at the foot of Old Street where the Buccleuch Hotel now stands. On one occasion Andrew was late in completing an order and told his young friend, Archibald Maxwell, that the boots were three days late. 'Man, Airchie, laddie,' he said, 'I was terrible feart he wad mak poetry about it.'

Archie had his own secondhand reminiscence about the poet: 'Andra aye maintained that he never saw bonnier een in ony heid. They were dark but awfu kindly, an there was something aboot them that lichted up his hale face. He hadna much colour, and his hair was dark and hang ower the side o his face like a pow.' One other item Archie remembered Andrew telling him was that 'Burns was weel made in body, but he was coorse a wee aboot the legs.'

Dr Thomas Boyle Grierson (1818-89), son of William Grierson who played such a memorable part in the **Mausoleum** fund, practised medicine at Thornhill from 1842 till 1887 and created a private museum (1869-72) which contained many relics of the poet, since transferred to the **Robert Burns Centre** in Dumfries.

THORNHILL CROSS – BUCCLEUCH ARMS IN BACKGROUND

TINWALD DOWNS   NY 000 793

An estate with a mansion-house, long since demolished, in Tinwald parish, on the borders of Nithsdale and Annandale. The mansion was demolished many years ago but it was located where the Dumfries Trading Estate now stands, east of the town, between the A709 and the A701. John Bushby Senior (1703-81) moved from the north of England to Dumfries in the mid-18th century and became established as a vintner. His three sons all flourished in the area. Thomas (1740-1807) became Collector of Customs at Kirkcudbright, William Bushby of **Kempleton** was one of the justices who witnessed Burns's induction into the Excise service, and John Junior became a lawyer, banker and businessman. Naturally clever and astute, he had one of the busiest law practices in Dumfries and was factor over **Rockhall** and other estates in the county. He was a partner in the ill-fated Douglas, Heron & Company Bank of Ayr, but successfully weathered the crash. He made two prosperous marriages and purchased the estate of Tinwald Downs.

In 1776 he was appointed Sheriff Clerk of the County, a position which he continued to hold until his death in August 1802. The Dumfries Burns Club own a portrait of John Bushby holding papers entitled 'Contested Elections 1774-1790'. Despite his prominent role in the election of July 1790, however, he was not mentioned by name, nor alluded to, in the 'Election Ballad' of that year (C.W. pp.402-6). The Third Heron Election Ballad was sub-titled 'John Bushby's Lamentation' (C.W. pp.547-8) and not only John but his brother William and his son John Maitland Bushby were included:

> And there I led the Bushby clan:
> My gamesome billie, Will,
> And my son Maitland, wise as brave,
> My footsteps follow'd still.

The ensuing stanza, beginning 'The Douglas and the Heron's name' was a side-swipe at the bank failure of 1773. The 'gamesome billie' was alleged to have absconded with some of the bank's funds and used it to build his 'fine nabob fortune' (C.W. p.545). Maitland Bushby, who succeeded to the estate of Tinwald Downs in 1802, became Sheriff of Wigtownshire at the age of 28, hence the lines in the Second Heron Election Ballad (C.W. p.545):

> An there'll be Wigton's new sheriff -
> Dame Justice fu brawly has sped:
> She's gotten the heart of a Bushby,
> But Lord! what's become o the head?

Burns returned to the same theme in 'From Esopus to Maria' (C.W. p.540):

> The hopeful youth, in Scottish senate bred,
> Who owns a Bushby's heart without the head.

John Bushby himself was savaged in the Second Heron Election Ballad:

> An there'll be black-nebbit Johnie,
> The tongue o the trump to them a':
> Gin he get na Hell for his haddin,
> The Deil gets nae justice ava!

The Fourth Ballad (C.W. p.549) referred to him as 'Black Jock, from the downs o Tinwald'. As if this were not enough, he was also the butt of the mock epitaph (C.W. p.521):

> Here lies John Bushby — honest man,
> Cheat him, Devil — if you can!

Which may explain why John's last resting-place in **St Michael's** kirkyard mentions his father and brother, but omits any reference to himself! Bushby was not upset by these lampoons on himself and his family, though he observed 'that he could not conceive why the poor devil |Burns| had thought proper to run a muck against all those who could best do him a service, and none of whom, as far as he knew, held him an ill will.' Burns was at one time a frequent visitor to Tinwald Downs, but of his own choice did not always join John Bushby at dinner, preferring to dine in the kitchen with the housekeeper, allegedly because he did not see eye to eye with the ladies of the Bushby household. At a dinner party at Tinwald Downs, John Bushby once played a rotten trick on Burns. He passed him a plate of pudding telling him that it was cold when, in fact, it was scalding hot.

Bushby laughed uproariously when the poet burned his mouth, with the result that Burns never spoke to him again. This incident is said to have taken place in 1793.

Perhaps the last word on John Bushby should go to Ramsay of Ochtertyre who wrote, shortly after Bushby's death, that 'He was one of the few men who could lead counties by the nose with the mask of honesty; to him bankruptcy proved the road to wealth and luxury.'

TINWALD DOWNS RACECOURSE   NX 995 791

The level ground about two miles northeast of Dumfries, lying between Mabie Forest and Lochar Water, was the site of the old racecourse. The stream running northwest from Lochar Water to Cullivait north of Locharbriggs is known as Old Course to this day. This area was occupied by the RAF airfield (known as RAF Dumfries or RAF Tinwald Downs) during the Second World War and now forms part of the trading estate. The *Dumfries Journal* of 30th October 1792, summarising the racing season just ended, stated that 'the diversions of the turf through the day afforded the highest satisfaction, not only to those immediately interested, but to thousands of spectators...' The Dumfries and Galloway and the Caledonian Hunts regularly met in Dumfries, with hunting and steeplechasing by day and balls and assemblies by night. On 29th October 1794 Burns wrote to Mrs Dunlop (C.W. p.212): 'We have had the Caledonians here for this bypast fortnight; & of course, we have had a roar of Folly & Dissipation. — Most of our fashionable young men have all that Profligacy & Outrage which have sometimes accompanied Superior Understanding & brilliant Wit — but without those bright talents which might throw a kind of veil over mischievous Folly & unprincipled Wickedness. One of the Corps provoked my ire the other day, which burst out as follows.' There followed the epigram to the Hon. R. Maule of Panmure on his high phaeton (C.W. p.527):

> Thou fool, in the Phaeton towering,
> Art proud when that Phaeton's praised?
> This the pride of a Thief's exhibition
> When higher his pillory's rais'd.

Despite this lampoon, William Ramsay Maule (1771-1852), later Lord Panmure, settled an annuity of £60 on Burns's widow in 1817.

TINWALD HOUSE   NY 017 803

A mansion-house on the western skirt of the hills east of Dumfries, about two miles southeast of Amisfield village. It lies on an unclassified road between Tinwald and Torthorwald, to the northwest of Side Burn and is roughly equidistant from the A701 and the A709. Designed by William Adam and built between 1738 and 1740, it was once a seat of the Marquis of Queensberry, but declined in the late 18th century and became a farmhouse.

In 1794 Maria and Walter Riddell gave up **Woodley Park** and decided to go abroad, but the progress of the French Revolutionary War prevented this. Walter went off to the West Indies to recoup his fortunes, and Maria, after a brief spell in London, returned to Dumfries where she took a short lease of Tinwald House. In a letter to William Smellie at the beginning of 1795, she described her new home as 'a crazy, rambling, worm-eaten, cob-web hunting chateau of the Duke of Queensberry, which God be thanked, I abandon and evacuate with all my household next May; for such a *Hybernaculum* never poor sinner was immured in. There are sufficient loop-holes in the walls to save window-tax, and they are spunges, excellent spunges for imbibing moisture. After a fall of snow or a shower of rain, one might set a moderate sized lugger afloat in the bedchamber; and I have some thoughts of erecting a steam-engine in the parlour to pump out the water, as there is always smoke enough there to set it a-going.'

Burns wrote three letters to Maria Riddell during the time she was at Tinwald House. The first is not actually thus addressed, but is of particular interest as the rather stiff and stilted communication, written in the third person, which was the means of ending the rift between them. Mrs Riddell subsequently moved to **Halleaths.**

TORR   NX 801 527

An estate and mansion in Rerrick parish, in the Stewartry, about a mile north of Auchencairn. Torr Hill and Torr Point jut into Auchencairn Bay. The house lies on the west side of the A711. The laird of Torr in the late 18th century was Edward Cairns whose sister Janet married William Nicol, the poet's travel companion on the Highland Tour of 1787. Tradition has it that Janet's machinations led to Edward Cairns separating from his wife Anne Humphries after she had borne him several children. It was Janet Cairns's dowry that enabled Willie·Nicol to purchase **Lagganpark.** Their brother George was known as 'Kipp' Cairns from his estate at Kippford, and was a well-known humorist. All three members of the Cairns family had their portrait miniatures painted by Alexander Reid of **Kirkennan.** Their father, incidentally, was a Midlands button manufacturer who made a fortune and became Lord Mayor of Birmingham. Apart from being Willie Nicol's brother-in-law, Edward Cairns is alleged to have been a friend of Burns. According to Scott Douglas (1879) a copy of 'The Whistle' (C.W. p.368), written on Excise paper, was sent to him, accompanied by a short verse epistle:

> But one sorry quill, and that worne to the core,
>   No paper — but such as I shew it;
> But such as it is, will the good Laird of Torr
>   Accept, and excuse the poor Poet?

After Willie Nicol's death in 1797, his widow moved back to Torr and occupied a cottage on the estate where she died in 1827 at the age of 84.

TROQUEER HOLM   NX 975 750

An estate and mansion house in Troqueer parish on the west bank of the **Nith,** now a suburb of Dumfries. It was in the estate adjoining **Ryedale,** with a commanding view across the river to the Royal Infirmary. To the west lay the estates of **Terraughty** and **Goldielea.** The estate comprised 32 acres and was purchased by Mary Maxwell, widowed mother of Dr William Maxwell. When her eldest son, James, laird of **Kirkconnell** married in 1794, Mary moved in with William at Troqueer Holm and kept house for him until her death in 1805. William himself continued to reside there until 1808.

It was from here that Dr Maxwell attended Burns in his last illness.

URR

A parish in the south of the Stewartry, containing the town of Dalbeattie, fourteen miles from Dumfries and five miles southeast of **Castle Douglas.**

After leaving **New Cample** the Buchanites resided in this parish for a time at Auchengibbert before finally settling near Crocketford. The parish church is near Haugh of Urr, the present edifice having been erected in 1815 on the site of the original building. The minister of Urr in the late 18th century was the Rev. Dr James Muirhead of **Logan,** whose pretensions as hereditary chief of the Muirhead clan were lampooned by Burns in the Fourth Heron Election Ballad (C.W. p.549):

> Here's armorial bearings frae the manse o Urr:
> The crest, a sour crab-apple rotten· at the core.

WANLOCKHEAD   NS 87 12

A former mining village in the northeast corner of Sanquhar parish in upper Nithsdale, eight miles northeast of the town of Sanquhar. It lies 1350 feet above sea level and is the highest village in the British Isles, at the top of the Mennock Pass by which it is approached along the B797. It is surrounded by the Lowther Hills and was at one time the centre of the Scottish lead-mining industry, although both silver and gold were also extracted. The Wanlockhead mines were in operation as early as 1512. The zenith of the lead-mining industry was from 1792 till 1842; during that half century some 47,420 tons of lead were raised. About 11,000 ounces of silver were extracted annually in that period. The district once known as God's treasure-house in Scotland also yielded gold worth over £100,000 in the reign of King James VI. The largest nugget, weighing 5 oz., is now in the British Museum. A chapel for the miners was erected in 1755 by the mining company at a cost of £70, but it was not until 1848 that the church was built. The library, founded in 1756, is the third oldest subscription library in Scotland, after Innerpeffray (1691) and nearby Leadhills (1741). William Symington and James Taylor, though both born in the village of Leadhills across the county boundary in Lanarkshire, lived and worked in Wanlockhead. Symington constructed the atmospheric steam pump at the Bay Mine, used in 1790-99, and devised the engine used to power the world's first steamboat, in whose design Taylor also played a prominent part, the experiment being funded and supervised by Patrick Miller at Dalswinton. James Taylor was tutor to the Miller family at **Dalswinton**, but his father John was the mine-manager at Wanlockhead.

During the early part of 1788, when he was commuting between Ayrshire and **Ellisland,** Burns met Thomas Sloan, a native of Wanlockhead who had moved to Dumfries. During the winter of 1789-90 Burns, accompanied by Sloan, paid a visit to Wanlockhead. Because of the icy conditions on the road they called at the smithy in order to have the horses' shoes 'frosted' (i.e. sharpened to give a better grip). The blacksmith, however, said that he was too busy to attend to them there and then and told them that they would have to wait their turn. Burns and Sloan put up at Ramage's inn, and from there Burns penned the verse epistle to John Taylor entitled 'Pegasus at Wanlockhead' (C.W. p.344). Sloan wrote a more conventional note as well. Their combined efforts had the desired effect; Taylor immediately spoke to the smith and rectified the matter. Pegasus, of course, was the name of Burns's horse, after the winged steed of Bellerophon.

Sloan was the recipient of at least three extant letters from Burns. He and Burns were to have paid a visit to Robert Riddell, but a lame horse and a broken arm prevented Burns from keeping the appointment, as indicated by the letter tentatively ascribed to April 1791 (C.L. p.576). Sloan was also the addressee of the letter describing the disgusting scenes at the roup of Burns's crops at the end of August 1791. He may also have been the recipient of the invitation to spend New Year's Day 1791 with Burns (C.L. p.724). Little else is known of Sloan except that he seems to have got into business difficulties. Burns was unsuccessful in soliciting the help of John Ballantine and subsequently Sloan moved to Manchester. It is not known whether he actually received a copy of the 1793 edition of the Poems, promised in a letter from **Friars' Carse** on 18th March 1793 (C.L. p.577).

On 30th January 1792 Maria Riddell wrote a letter from Edinburgh, probably to her mother, giving an account of a visit to Wanlockhead prior to her going to Edinburgh. The visit took place on 23rd January, the day after Burns had written a letter of introduction to William Smellie on Maria's behalf (C.L. p.597). Maria's account of the expedition to the leadmines is of considerable interest:

'We set out on Tuesday morning from Friars' Carse, accompanied by our Caledonian bard, the celebrated Burns, on an expedition not very dissimilar, I think, to that of the memorable Don Quixote in the Cave of Montesinos. It was nothing less than to explore the Lead Mines at Wanlockhead, reckoned one of the most curious in Scotland. I do not look upon rising a couple of hours *before the sun* in this dreary month of January, as one of the most trifling proofs of our Knight Errantry. We set off before day break, and arrived in time for breakfast at **Sanquhar.'**

Here a post-chaise was taken for Wanlockhead, and the beauties of the majestic scenery joined to the interesting remarks and fascinating conversation of our friend Burns, not only beguiled the tediousness of the road, but likewise made us forget its danger; for it borders the edge of a profound precipice, at the bottom of which a clear brook guides its rapid course over a pebbly bed intersected with rocks.

'When we had attained (on foot for the most part) the summits of these hills, one of the principal miners conducted us across to the foot of another mountain, where a dark and narrow cavern is carved in the solid rock. This we entered, each of us holding a taper and bidding Adieu for some hours at least to the fair light of day. The roof is so low, that we were obliged to stoop almost double, wading up to the mid leg in clay and water; and the stalactical fluid continually dropping from the rock upon our heads, contributed to wet us completely thro.

'The roof is supported by beams of timber; these our conductor desired us to hold by, as the footpath is extremely narrow; but the beams were so wet and slimy that I found them of little service, and soon cut my gloves to pieces by clinging to the points of the rocks. After we had proceeded about a mile in the cavern, the damp and confined air affected our fellow adventurer Burns so much, that we resolved to turn back, after I had satisfied my curiosity by going down one of the shafts. This you will say was a crazy scheme — assailing the Gnomes in their subterranean abodes! Indeed there has never been before but *one* instance of a *female* hazarding herself thither.'

Disappointingly, Burns himself left no account of this incident.

OLD MINE-WORKINGS, WANLOCKHEAD

WATCARRICK   **NY 247 963**

Farm in Eskdalemuir parish, about a mile south of the village of that name. Take the minor road due south of the village following the west bank of the White Esk. The farm lies half a mile west of this road, on the eastern edge of Castle O'er Forest. It takes its name from Wat Carrick, an ancient district wherein was located the original parish church and burial ground of Eskdalemuir.

The church was discontinued in 1722 and has long since disappeared, but the burial ground remains. Burns was a frequent visitor to Watcarrick and delighted in listening to Elizabeth Burgess playing her spinet. She is said to have been the model for his song 'Bessy and her Spinnin-wheel' (C.W. p.452). Parts of her spinet are preserved among the Burns relics on display at **Ellisland**.

According to Robert Malcolmson, Burns gave a copy of the following lines to John Kennedy, factor to the Earl of Dumfries at Dumfries House, Cumnock. Kennedy gave a copy to the Rev. Yates, Unitarian minister at Liverpool, who favoured John Heughan of Dumfries with a sight of them. Malcolmson took them down from Heughan's recitation about 1830. Heughan was personally known to Burns with whom he had many a merry hour at the **Globe Inn**. The Rev. John Dun, minister of Auchinleck (see The Ayrshire Book of Burns-Lore), was travelling in the Watcarrick area when he fell from his horse and got a soaking in the White Esk. Dun, who published a reply to Burns's 'Address to the Deil', in a volume of sermons (1790), provoked the following response, couched in the sharpest irony and certainly having all the hallmarks of Burns:

> Ye Calvinists o Auchinleck,
> In mournin weeds yourselves bedeck,
> An shew how much ye did respect
>   Your great divine,
> Wha fell, poor saul, and broke his neck,
>   On Esk langsyne.
>
> Had he been deaf, blind, dumb or lame,
> Like mony a priest that I could name,
> Wha's merits nae encomiums claim,
>   You might indeed
> Let dark oblivion blast his fame
>   Since now he's dead.
>
> But sure an aye ye a' can say
> He took good tent for mony a day,
> That nane 'mang Whigs might doit astray
>   To yon hill head;
> He was a nonesuch in his way.
>   But oh! he's dead.
>
> His hame-spun zeal an catechizin,
> His lecturin an sermonisin!
> Set mony an auld wife's heart ableezin;
>   But now I dread
> In spite o fate they'll a' fa' freezin,
>   Since now he's dead.
>
> When frae his horse his carcase fell,
> His saul went -- but I darena tell --
> Ye cannot fail to guess yoursel;
>   For fifty head
> Can swear his Reverence wrote frae Hell,
>   Since he was dead.

WESTERHALL   NY 319 894

An estate and mansion of **Westerkirk** parish about a mile south of Bentpath, in Eskdale district, on the east bank of the River Esk and approached from the B709 by a bridge across the river, leading to a private estate road. Westerhall, five miles west of **Langholm,** is backed by steep hills and embossomed in woodlands. The mansion was badly damaged by fire in February 1873 but was subsequently restored. For five centuries it has been the seat of the Johnstone family, the baronetcy being created in 1700. Sir James Johnstone, fourth baronet (1726-94) retired from the Army with the rank of lieutenant-colonel at the end of the American War and entered Parliament in 1784 as member for the Dumfries burghs. He was up for re-election as Tory candidate in September 1789 but lost to Captain Patrick Miller of **Dalswinton.** Johnstone featured in 'The Five Carlins' (C.W. pp.364-6) as the 'belted Knight, bred of a Border band' and was also named in the 'Election Ballad for Westerha' (C.W. p.367), although Burns was really attacking the Duke of Queensberry, the 'turncoat Whig' who had set up Captain Miller as Johnstone's opponent.

Sir James died unmarried, and was succeeded by his brother William (died 1805). He married Frances Pulteney, heiress of the Earl of Bath, and became one of the richest men in Britain as a result. Burns referred to this immense wealth in the 'Election Ballad' addressed to Robert Graham of Fintry (C.W. p.406): 'Not Pulteney's wealth can Pulteney save'.

WESTERKIRK   NY 312 903

A parish of Eskdale in the northeast corner of Dumfriesshire. The parish church, at the village of Bentpath, stands in the centre of this upland parish. The present church was built in 1881 on the site of an ancient church dating back to the Middle Ages and given in 1321 by King Robert Bruce to the monks of Melrose. The kirkyard contains the handsome mausoleum of the Johnstone family, with its circular colonnade of fluted Doric pillars. Thomas Telford (1757-1834), the father of civil engineering, was the posthumous son of a shepherd in this parish and was brought up with difficulty by his poor widowed mother. After receiving an elementary education in the parish school he was apprenticed at an early age to a builder and worked for several years as a stonemason. A tombstone in his father's memory, still extant, is believed to have been chiselled by him. He afterwards rose to great fame and amassed a huge fortune, some of which he bequeathed to Westerkirk, which explains why it boasted the largest and finest parochial library anywhere in Britain in the 19th century. In his early life Telford contributed poems to various Edinburgh periodicals under the pseudonym of Eskdale Tam. One of these was sent to Burns from Shrewsbury Castle (where he was employed as an architect) about September 1792:

> Nor pass the tentie curious lad
> Who o'er the ingle hangs his heid,
> But begs of neighbours books to read,
> For hence arise
> Thy country's sons who far are spread,
> Baith bold and wise.

No doubt Burns replied to this 'beautiful poem address' (as it is annotated in Currie's list of the letters to Burns), but no letters from Burns to Telford are extant.

WHITHORN   NX 44 40

A town and parish of Wigtownshire, 32 miles southeast of Stranraer. It derives its name from *Candida Casa,* the 'white house' of St Ninian, the first known apostle to Scotland about the middle of the 4th century. Burns never visited the town and never waxed poetic about it either; but it features in the only letter by the poet written in the vernacular. Writing to Willie Nicol from Carlisle towards the end of his Border Tour of 1787 (C.L. pp.342-3), Burns eulogises his spavined jade: 'I could wager her price to a thretty pennies that, for two or three wooks ridin at fifty miles a day, the deil-sticket a five gallopers acqueesh Clyde and Whithorn could cast saut in her tail.'

WILLIE'S MILL
NT 124 059

A house in the vicinity of **Craigieburn,** no longer extant, where Burns met with Allan Masterton and Willie Nicol in the autumn of 1789. It was allegedly the location of the bacchanal celebrated in 'Willie Brew'd a Peck o Maut' (C.W. p.364).

WOODHALL
NX 66 67

An estate in the parish of **Balmaghie,** on the western side of Woodhall Loch about two miles northwest of **Laurieston.** No trace of the mansion now exists, but it was the residence of Walter Sloan Lawrie of **Redcastle,** mentioned in the second and third Heron Election Ballads (C.W. pp545-8). According to Grierson of **Dalgonar,** his grandfather's name was Clautenpluck, but he changed it to Laurieston and latterly to Lawrie. Grierson also mentioned that Lawrie was 'a very little man — a landlady once made a bill reckoning one short of the number in company... she had missed Mr Lawrie, pointing to him — O says she, as for little master, clasping his hand, I do not mind him!' Hence Burns's slighting reference to him in the Second Ballad:

> But we dinna mention Redcastle,
> The body — e'en let him escape!

WOODLEY PARK
NX 931 735

An estate in Troqueer parish, Nithsdale, formerly known as **Holm** and later as **Goldielea,** to which name it reverted after it was briefly occupied by Maria and Walter Riddell (1792-4). It was renamed in honour of Maria whose maiden name was Woodley.

Maria and Walter spent their first three months in Scotland at **Friars' Carse,** before their new home was ready, and it was there, at the home of Robert and Elizabeth Riddell, that Maria first met Burns. By that time, of course, Burns had moved into Dumfries and was not such a frequent visitor at Carse. Walter and Maria lived at Friars' Carse over the winter of 1791-2 so it seems likely that Burns first met them in December 1791. Certainly Maria was sufficiently well-known to him by 22nd January 1792 for him to write a letter to William Smellie (C.L. p.597), introducing Maria as 'a Character that even in your own way, as a Naturalist and a Philosopher, would be an acquisition to your acquaintance... Lest you should think of a lively West-Indian girl of eighteen, as girls of eighteen too often deserve to be thought of, I should take care to remove that prejudice. To be impartial, however, the Lady has one unlucky failing; a failing which you will easily discover, as she seems rather pleased with indulging it; and a failing which you will as easily pardon, as it is a sin that very much besets yourself; where she dislikes, or despises, she is apt to make no more a secret of it — than where she esteems and respects.'

Smellie subsequently published Maria's account of her *Voyages to the Madeira and Leeward and Caribbee Islands.* By February 1792 Burns himself was addressing letters to her beginning 'My Dearest Friend'. From then until June 1796 some 25 extant letters reveal the course of their friendship as it gathered momentum in 1792 and 1793. He composed a poem 'On Mrs Riddell's Birthday' — 4th November 1793 (C.W. p.508).

Then came the unfortunate incident of the 'Rape of the Sabines' at Friars' Carse in December 1793. Robert and Elizabeth Riddell were outraged by the poet's conduct and Maria felt bound by family loyalty to support them and snub Burns. There is an uneasy, jokey element in his letter, written shortly after the event (C.L. p.606), ending 'Farewell, thou first of Friends, & most accomplished of Women; even with all thy little caprices!!!' The following letter, however, swung completely the other way and introduced a note of frigid formality, admitting 'Tis true, Madam, I saw you once since I was at Woodley park; & that once froze the very life-blood of my heart...' In vain he tried to make amends, with the epigram 'On Maria Riddell' (C.W. p.501) which had probably been composed in August 1793, but she spurned this. He retaliated by returning her Commonplace Book: 'I have perused it with much pleasure, & would have continued my criticisms; but as it seems the Critic has forfeited your esteem, his strictures must lose their value...' The song

'Farewell Thou Stream' (C.W. p.486) had been sent to Maria in April 1793. In December, however, he sent a new version of it to Mrs Dunlop, with 'Eliza' substituted for 'Maria', and this was the version subsequently published.

Not content with that, he took a mean revenge, prostituting his muse in the composition of unpleasant and spiteful epigrams, 'Monody on a Lady Famed for her Caprice' (C.W. p.511) and 'Pinned to Mrs Walter Riddell's Carriage' (C.W. p.514). If Maria's 21 year-old heart were really as rotten as he alleged, her later conduct would have been very different. Burns composed a mock epitaph for Walter Riddell (C.W. p.516) and also the ode 'From Esopus to Maria' (C.W. pp.539-41) in which he made slighting references to Maria's own poetic accomplishments. There is no evidence that Burns ever sent her these verses, but he sent copies to some of his friends and one may rest assured that news of them eventually got back to her. In mitigation, however, it should be noted that during January and February 1794 Burns endured one of the worst and most prolonged bouts of depression he ever suffered. Doubtless this was brought on by the rift with the Riddells, but it also helps to explain the vindictiveness of his actions. In a long and very revealing letter to Alexander Cunningham on 25th February 1794 (C.L. pp.469-70) he spoke of 'a deep incurable taint of hypochondria, which poisons my existence' and hinted at events which 'have so irritated me, that my feelings at time could only be envied by a reprobate spirit listening to the sentence that dooms it to perdition.'

The breach lasted until the end of December 1794, when Maria forgave him and sent him a book, which he acknowledged in a very stilted letter, written in the third person. Thereafter the friendship was gradually resumed and Maria proved to be one of the poet's staunchest friends, right to the end of his life — and beyond; for it was to Maria that the responsibility fell for writing the lengthy and perceptive memoir that appeared in the *Dumfries Weekly Journal* and was subsequently published by Dr Currie.

Walter Riddell himself had been in the West Indies in 1793 and missed the 'Rape of the Sabines' incident and its aftermath. He returned to Dumfries in March 1794 and, having been unable to raise the balance of the money due on the purchase of Woodley Park, was forced to sell up. He and his family then moved to **Tinwald House** and later to **Halleaths.**

INDEX

INDEX

INDEX

INDEX

INDEX

INDEX

INDEX

INDEX